Zygmunt Bauman

Zygmunt Bauman

Dialectic of Modernity

PETER BEILHARZ

SAGE Publications
London • Thousand Oaks • New Delhi

First published 2000

SAGE Publications Ltd
6 Bonhill Street
London EC2A 4PU

SAGE Publications Inc
2455 Teller Road
Thousand Oaks, California 91320

SAGE Publications India Pvt Ltd
32, M-Block Market
Greater Kailash – I
New Delhi 110 048

British Library Cataloguing in Publication data

A catalogue record for this book is available
from the British Library

ISBN 0 7619 6734 6
ISBN 0 7619 6735 4 (pbk)   20468881

Library of Congress catalog record available

Typeset by Mayhew Typesetting, Rhayader, Powys
Printed and bound in Great Britain by Athenaeum Press, Gateshead

Contents

Preface

Does sociology have a future? In one perspective, Zygmunt Bauman might be its last man. Well recognized for his major work, *Modernity and the Holocaust* (1989a), Bauman is often also widely imagined as the leading sociological representative of postmodernism. What lies before us? And, how do we make sense of modernity, of its century and of what now opens before us? As sociology enters the millennium, some will have cause to wonder about its prospects. Others, including Zygmunt Bauman, will wonder too but will likely rather persist in believing that we have barely begun this project in earnest at all; critical theory, in this vista, is more like an anticipation than a result, though it is also that. So this is good news, as well. The purpose of this book is to enter into this field by introducing, surveying and interpreting Bauman's work for an audience which, living at a postmodern pace, may know it only fleetingly, or else partially. Of course this is an interpretation in itself, therefore partial in its own way; it reflects my own curiosities as well as his, and says something about the difference of our life paths and the connection of our moment, and our passions and shared commitments as well as our differences.

Why an introduction? Bauman's work is extensive, awesome, different; it denies the systemic nature or relatively clear trajectory which characterizes other bodies of work like, say, those of Habermas or Foucault. Bauman's work is notoriously difficult, by comparison, at least inasmuch as it is slippery and shifting. Those who choose to pursue Bauman's work further are welcome to head to the library or the bookshop; they might find the profiles in my *Bauman Reader* (2000), published simultaneously by Blackwell, to be of some use. In Freud's sense, the present book is more like a prosthesis, a way to handle the work just as culture is a way to handle the world. The present study works as a lengthier conversation with Bauman, conducted through the medium of his books and many of his essays published in English across the past 30 years. There is nothing here on the Polish pre-life of Bauman's sociology. We await a biography of Bauman; Dennis Smith's interpretation of his work will appear in the same year as this book does, and though we two have communicated we have worked independently of one another, as we have worked independently of our subject. From differing perspectives, again, Dennis Smith and I seek to rectify the awkward situation in which the widespread deference to Bauman's ideas has remained unaccompanied by any more elaborate appreciation of his work. To this point, the most extended acknowledgement of Bauman's work has been that registered in Richard Kilminster and Ian Varcoe's 1996 *Festschrift*

– *Culture, Modernity and Revolution: Essays in Honour of Zygmunt Bauman* – and charted by various writers in a special issue of *Theory, Culture and Society* (1998). Hopefully this reception will open into the millennium.

I first made acquaintance with Zygmunt and Janina Bauman in the 1990s, partly through the medium of *Thesis Eleven*. It has become a happy ritual, this annual pilgrimage to Leeds, from whence I inevitably depart light-headed and physically heavier. Ours is necessarily a long distance relationship, yet it has intimacies of its own, and I will always be deeply grateful for the willingness of the Baumans to take me in in this way. It is not always the case that intellectual enthusiasm transfers across onto other levels. For my own part, Bauman's *Memories of Class* (1982) had much influenced my thinking about modernity and labour, published in a book called *Transforming Labor* (1994a) and in its sequel, *Postmodern Socialism* (1994b). I had sent a copy of my 1988 review of *Legislators and Interpreters* (Bauman, 1987) to Leeds; a line of contact opened between us which has developed in the past decade. We discovered shared enthusiasms for labour's utopias; but he was the teacher. Reading Bauman's work coincides with my intellectual formation from the mid-1970s through marxism to somewhere else.

Moving into the 1990s I had begun researching the work of the Australian art historian and cultural theorist Bernard Smith, which resulted in a book entitled *Imagining the Antipodes* (1997). In the process I redis-covered the wonder of engaging directly with the thinking of a single, exemplary writer. This was an intellectual approach I had learned in my doctoral work with Alastair Davidson, who applied it brilliantly in *Antonio Gramsci: Towards an Intellectual Biography* (1977), and which I had then extended critically to the work of Leon Trotsky in *Trotsky, Trotskyism and the Transition to Socialism* (1987). Working on the project of Bernard Smith was a different kind of experience, because I was dealing with a living thinker, and because I wanted to appraise his work positively, to value it anew as a source or tradition to carry forward. This is also my motivation in the present study, for Bauman is good to think with, to follow not as a leader but as an example of how to go about the activity of interpretation and criticism, and this is his invitation to sociology. So this is a sympathetic and expository study, based on the search for spirit rather than letter. As in *Imagining the Antipodes*, I do not offer strict distinctions here between Bauman's thinking and my own. This is, then, a hermeneutic reading, and in this it follows his own work and example.

The structure of this book rests on an attempt conceptually to cluster Bauman's work, in order to open different lines into his labyrinth. The approach is often chronological, especially in its broad sweep, but chronology does not govern the structure of the book. My object here is to establish something of how the works hang together, rather than necessarily to plumb their inner conceptual depths. My purpose is to chase themes, to connect and where possible to identify resonances in classical, modern and postmodern social theory. There are, then, three levels of voice in this book. First, there is Bauman's voice, with mine as its sometime medium. Second, there are presences, echoes and dissonances with contemporaries, such as Castoriadis and Heller, which I attempt to spell out or explain. Third, there are echoes with the classics, not least Marx, Weber and Simmel, to which I allude but do not always elucidate. The attraction of Bauman's work is based on a combination of sociological insight and personal commitment; its approach is not that of the professional, or managerial sociologist. Its classical exemplar is Simmel, not Durkheim.

This is a beginning book, together with Dennis Smith's, a beginning of that moment in which we take some perspective on Bauman's extraordinary achievement, that which hitherto we as readers have followed instalment by instalment. So this book does not seek to establish the inner nature or secret of Bauman's work, as much as to discern its larger contours, its shifts and its continuities, recurring themes or motivating curiosities. There is certainly no single clue to Bauman's work, not even in the idea of ambivalence or in the overarching theme of the critique of order. My sense is that Bauman's work shifts by the pattern of at least three different possible intellectual movements. First, there is a way in which it is continuous, or linear; some themes lead on to others, some books emerge as it were directly out of others, as though the entire project were one long conversation, extended over 30 years, with such varying interlocutors as pass by, cut into parts from the longer cloth. Second, there is a sense in which to plot the path of Bauman's work is to deal with the principle of eternal recurrence or repetition, for the problems which animate us across time recur and recycle. As Bauman says, we do not solve problems in social theory, we become bored with them. But third, there are also moments of effective opening, reorientation or innovation across this story, or at least there are turning points or moments of realization like those born in *Legislators and Interpreters* (1987), after which perspectives change more radically or forcefully, or after the collapse of marxism, one primary source of Bauman's theory and life.

In Bauman's own, conversational self-understanding, his more recent books have figured perhaps as trilogy, or triptych. The first trilogy consists of *Legislators and Interpreters* (1987), *Modernity and the Holocaust* (1989a), and *Modernity and Ambivalence* (1991a). The second includes *Postmodern Ethics* (1993a), *Life in Fragments* (1995) and *Postmodernity and its Discontents* (1997a), and the final trio consists of the shorter, more directly political essays in *Globalization: The Human Consequences* (1998a), *Work, Consumerism and the New Poor* (1998b) and *In Search of Politics* (1999b). From any other perspective, of course, different profiles emerge; so that it seems to me, for example, that the books on the Holocaust and Ambivalence are directly continuous, whereas say *Postmodern Ethics* (1993a) and *Mortality, Immortality and Other Life-Strategies* (1991b) are distinct critical excurses, while what unites the books published after *Life in Fragments* (1995) is the essay form itself, especially with the return to the more specifically political themes as a kind of postmodern reprise of what earlier was carried by marxism. I suppose that this means that my book, like Bauman's work, can also be entered by any door, though I hope that there is also some advantage in following its own narrative structure through. For in that structure some themes, such as power, culture and utopia, also return with the passing of time, and some openness to these possibilities ought be important for Bauman's readers, for it will not do to seek arbitrarily to classify this most avid critic of classification. Arguably this is the key factor explaining the hesitant general reception of, or engagement with, Bauman's thinking: you have to work at it.

My personal delight in constructing this project, as earlier in *Imagining the Antipodes*, has been to come to know an exemplary thinker, exemplary in that precise sense, that one can emulate only by going on one's own way. In Zygmunt Bauman's case, there was also another, Janina, his wife. I cannot say how much I value their example, their work, their way of going about the conduct of ordinary life. I hope that this book might help to acknowledge my debt, as that of others, and to reinforce the process of their recognition.

For years now I have discussed Bauman's ideas with various folks in strange and familiar cities and places, from Tokyo and Montreal to New York and Northcote. My Honours students at La Trobe shared an elective with me in 1997, establishing the canvas. Fuyuki Kurasawa and Vince Marotta helped me with materials and with perspectives on Bauman often different to my own. Chris Rojek at Sage exemplified the editorial ethic of pastoral care. My colleagues on *Thesis Eleven* provide the immediate theoretical matrix which makes my intellectual work possible. This is my eleventh book, and my first book with Sage, publisher of our journal, *Thesis Eleven*; perhaps it is not too much to say that it is a sign of a superb working relationship between us. My thanks to Chris, and all the others at Sage, especially to Jane Evans, my production editor, and to Jill Birch, for fastidious copy-editing. I also discussed the ideas involved with Robert Rojek, John Carroll, Trevor Hogan, David Roberts, Johann Arnason, Michael Crozier, Agnes Heller, Claus Offe, John Clammer, Jeff Alexander, Craig Calhoun, Don Levine, Steve Seidman, Harald Welzer, Bob Tristram, Simone Clark, Frank Jones and Bill Martin. The office staff at La Trobe – Bron, Elaine and Merle – have tolerated my idiosyncrasies for longer than I can remember; I am grateful to them. La Trobe remains a great place to work, even as its morale is eroded by the state shrinkage of Australian universities; its culture persists. The support of Graeme Duncan as Dean is something I shall miss. Parts of this book were drafted in Canberra, where I worked as an Affiliate Fellow in Sociology at the Research School of Social Sciences at the Australian National University, whose support I appreciate. In those recent evenings, as I sat in University House, where Zygmunt and Janina had stayed 30 years earlier, I could not but ponder what might have happened had they remained in Australia, had Zygmunt accepted the chair he was then offered, in 1970. I am glad they moved on to Leeds, for it becomes them, and Bauman's fate in the antipodes would have been different; it remains, still, more difficult to be heard from the edge. But that distance also affords perspective, and it may help to have an outsider's view on this outsider's work. In the antipodes, at least, we might perhaps know a cultural messenger when we see one.

This book is for Zygmunt and Janina, as it is for those I love and depend upon the most: my family, Dor, Nikolai and Rhea. It has been my immaculate good fortune to be stuck in the middle with them; they are more than I deserve, but I am grateful for their love and patience. Finally, it is for my sister, Sue, who has taught me about love in adversity – to persevere, still laughing. The spirit endures.

Peter Beilharz
Melbourne
April 1999

Prologue

The work of Zygmunt Bauman has a curious presence in English-language sociology. In everyone's footnotes, the arguments and larger themes themselves often seem to elude attention. The field covered by Bauman's work is massive, diverse and challenging, shifting from class and culture, through utopia and its difficult bearers, the intellectuals, to the Holocaust and the postmodern, to globalization, tourists and vagabonds. More, Bauman offers his writing in a kind of take-it-or-leave-it sensibility; he will not act as his own interpreter, rather he posits his concerns and moves on. He will not put more value on his own work than to claim it, and he does not like to talk about his life's path.

There are some clues to his biography in the second volume of Janina Bauman's autobiography, *A Dream of Belonging* (1988). There she part fictionalizes Zygmunt as 'Konrad'; Janina still has mixed feelings about this book. She prefers the first volume, *Winter in the Morning* (1986), a book that was obviously a hard act to follow. Alienated from life in Poland after the war, the young Janina had contemplated exile, perhaps in Palestine. While she had been trapped in the Warsaw Ghetto, the two yet unknown to each other, the young Zygmunt had fled east with his family into the extremities of the Soviet Union. The two of them met in Warsaw in 1948. Zygmunt was born in Poznan in 1925. Zygmunt had studied at a Russian university and joined the Polish Army in Russia aged 18. He rose to the rank of captain and was a proud communist, a member of the Polish Workers' Party (J. Bauman, 1988: 45). Zygmunt was, as Janina put it, an honest communist, one who believed that the state would deliver on its claims, or at least, later, should be held to them (1988: 49). Soon he was to become a Major. Janina, too, became a communist. Yet in retrospect it all seemed more plain. As she now wrote, part admonition, part parable:

> My children, my grandchildren beware. There is no fair play in the game of power, no small steps, no meeting halfway with a chance of return. Beware of those who promise you to bear responsibility for your deeds. What they want is your compliance. The responsibility will remain your own. Ignorance is no excuse for complicity. Do not let the powerful catch hold of your finger: they will take the whole arm. And you will not even notice when they engulf the rest of you. (1988: 89)

So Janina and Zygmunt Bauman learned hard together the nature of those abstract philosophical problems of conformism and heteronomy. Janina worked for Polish Film, Zygmunt continued to study philosophy and social sciences at night school. Anti-semitism was again afoot; 1952 marked Stalin's Doctors' Plot, and in 1953 Zygmunt Bauman was sacked on suspicion (1988: 105). Doors were slammed closed; Zygmunt took an alternative path, out through the mind, becoming a junior lecturer in Philosophy and Social Sciences at the University of Warsaw, though his marxism had slipped (1988: 115). He took his doctorate, and spent a year alone in London on a postdoctoral fellowship at the LSE. A door had opened.

Having been driven hither and thither by the forces of world history, the Baumans were developing the English leg they were later fully to stand on. Leeds beckoned, but only after the pain of further marginalization. Zygmunt took a visiting fellowship to Manchester in 1966, reinforcing the suspicion of the state. But another door was opening. They handed in their Party cards, but then came the boot. That visceral anti-semitism which had ended Zygmunt's army life returned, now, to the academy. In March 1968 Zygmunt Bauman became a public victim of the state's hostility, this time for corrupting Polish youth; why else would they bother themselves with the activity of protest (1988: 187)? These professors were not just eggheads, or 'dirty Jews'; worse, they were marxists. They would not take the word of the putatively marxist state at face value. Janina, too, was dismissed as Head of Unit at Polish Film. The children were being harassed. It was time to leave their homeland. They escaped out through Tel Aviv, and visited Canberra then to settle in Leeds, as it then seemed, a dying industrial city in the English Midlands, now to belong to several places, perhaps nowhere. So Janina closes her book, *A Dream of Belonging*, in remembering Poland:

> I left that country in the distant past abandoning all my young hopes and passions. Now I belong nowhere. But perhaps to belong means to love and be loved and this is all that truly matters. (1988: 202)

All of the writing discussed in this book comes from that period, opening in the 1970s, when Zygmunt and Janina Bauman settled in Leeds, where they remain. We begin at this beginning, in 1972, in Chapter 1, with *Between Class and Elite*, connecting it laterally into the 1982 text *Memories of Class* and the just recently published return to these matters of inclusion and deprivation in *Work, Consumerism and the New Poor* (1998b). Chapter 2 begins from another beginning, *Culture as Praxis* (1973a). I connect this to *Towards a Critical Sociology* (1976b) and then into Bauman's 1990 text, *Thinking Sociologically*, before turning to the more recent essays in which Bauman negotiates the postmodern and the field of sociology together. Chapter 3 links up *Socialism: The Active Utopia* (1976a) – the first Bauman text to have a profound effect on me – and two other books on the pros and cons of interpretation and its interpreters – *Hermeneutics and Social Science* (1978) and *Legislators and Interpreters* (1987). The discussion of *Modernity and the Holocaust* (1989a) opens Chapter 4, continuing into

Modernity and Ambivalence (1991a), and the associated problems of modernity and socialism. Chapter 5 covers *Postmodern Ethics* (1993a), *Life in Fragments* (1995), *Freedom* (1988), and *Postmodernity and its Discontents* (1997a). Finally, Chapter 6 draws the themes of *Mortality, Immortality and Other Life Strategies* (1991b) together with the concerns of *Globalization: The Human Consequences* (1998a) and *In Search of Politics* (1999b), where, at the time of writing, Bauman's writing ends, though there will probably be another book, *Liquid Modernity*, out before this one appears. For Bauman's is, as he knows, a journey without end. His is the restless spirit of interpretation and rediscovery, and this is his legacy to us, for here there is so much to discover, whether for the first time or not, about sociology, about the interpreted and the interpreters, about us.

ss and Labour

The idea of class has always connected sociology to socialism. The image of modernity has long been that of the working society, where work, as Marx could have put it, might have been everything but in fact was nothing. The labour movement, in turn, became widely seen not least on the left as the practical bearer of modernity, of modernization as industrialization. Not only the Bolsheviks but also leading Western Marxists such as Antonio Gramsci identified Americanism as a working class and cultural imperative. In the 1960s, labour history was remobilized as history from below. The popular story overlooked by generations of institutional and elitist scholars was rediscovered as social history. This particular turn in historiography and sociology was directly to mirror the extraordinary efflorescence of marxism itself in the 1970s. Before it changed everything, interpretatively speaking, or as it did, marxism also disappeared throughout the period from 1979, burned up by the dread and disintegration from the experiences of Kampuchea and Afghanistan to the fall of the Berlin Wall in 1989. The marxism which was largely obligatory in the radical ranks of the academy throughout the 1970s left its traces, but problems of labour, for example, were very largely replaced by concerns with language or representation. Bauman's achievement during this period was to shift, and to move with the tide, while maintaining the sense that to be human was always to labour. His curiosities about class and culture thus run in tandem from the work of E.P. Thompson to that of Foucault and, later, Baudrillard, and more generally, throughout this period, with Marx, against Marx.

Between Class and Elite

Between Class and Elite was where, in the English language, it all began, in 1972. The original Polish work stretched back to 1960, and to Bauman's earliest traffic in the late 1950s between Poland and the LSE. Bauman's modus operandi is already marked by that combination of modesty and incision which characterizes his later work. He opens by doubting the significance of his own work, even as he introduces us into it. Why should you read this book? the author asks, and answers, that it is interpretative rather than pioneering in nature, or configurational, rather than substantive in form (1972: ix). In a different language, Bauman understands his own curiosity as sociological, rather than historiographical: 'Here I must confess that I intended to arrive at a relatively coherent theory of labour movements, this being an analytical starting point to a more general theory of social movements as a whole' (1972: x). The themes posited here, as elsewhere in Bauman's work recycle and reform. For just as Bauman foregrounds social movements as the generic field of his concern, and labour movements as his particular curiosity, so does he insist on the presence of intellectuals as their interpreters, advocates, critics or theorists. So there are already at least two distinct, if connected levels of analysis in Bauman's hermeneutic: one concerning the movements themselves, the other concerning the intellectual representations of and projections upon these movements which become the bearers of other people's hopes (1972: x).

Bauman names this problem of duality here under the category of messianism. Because intellectuals feel powerless they are compelled to search for a prime mover, an omnipotent, elemental force; they live in hope of the continuous dream of a salutary union of 'the thinking minority and the suffering majority' (Bauman, 1972: x). The vulnerability of marxism or Marx's work itself to this line of criticism is not established in these pages, only anticipated. The victims of Bauman's critique are all those, reformists and revolutionaries alike, who ascribe to the suffering peoples some historical vocation or mission, forcing on them a mirror in which they cannot see themselves. Millenarians might want to cleanse and to purify the world; the others simply want a place in it. The interpretative problem, then, is that studies 'of actual labour movements became exercises in censuring their closeness to or deviations from the assumed ideal' (1972: xi). Of course, as Bauman observes, the projections of radical intellectuals who behave in this way tell us infinitely more about the intellectuals themselves than about the plight of the suffering classes. Yet it would also be a mistake, as Bauman observes, to view the labour movement as a thing in itself, *sans telos*, or at least without higher aspirations. The point, as Bauman puts it, is to try to look at the labour movement as an active, adaptive, and self-regulating system, assimilating its outer environment by seeking to impress upon it hoped-for structural changes while accommodating its own structure to the changing requirements of that assimilation (1972: xii). To make sense of labour movements, we need then to comprehend them spatially and temporally as agents of creation and adaptation: 'To those who feel more at home when dealing with labels instead of phenomena, I must confess that, in my opinion, this understanding of social reality is what Marxism in its activist, uninstitutionalized version is all about' (1972: xii). Thus Bauman indicates his position, committed, yet independent, interested in labour's institutions, but located of necessity and desire outside them.

This kind of recognition of limits is necessary, not least of all, because of the historicity of social movements. So Bauman's optic in making sense of labour is to enquire into where it has come from and how it has come to be, for the culture of labour is also its history. Pre-class histories, in other words, will affect patterns of class formation. Patterns of working class formation in Britain would remain embryonic even while a modern engineering industry came into existence, for contrary to E.P. Thompson's sense in *The Making of the English Working Class* (1962) the industrial revolution created the working class. It may be politically tempting to insist that the working class made the industrial revolution, but this is also to project the categories of class analysis back, anachronistically (Bauman, 1972: 2). Knowledge, including self-knowledge, comes late. Marx's error here was to imagine the creation of a working class as too clean and complete. Workers in the making, however, were dragged screaming into the factories, so that their culture and identities often remained elsewhere. The mass worker came much later. Marx, that son of the steam engine, never fully internalized the significance of the idea of uneven development, or the rationality of the politics of popular refusal of or resistance to modernization. Max Weber, as Bauman observes, got closer to sensing the limits of modernization when in *The Protestant Ethic* he discussed the ways in which sensible peasants and artisans could decide to work less, and not more, for piece-rates, and leave their levels of consumption intact (Bauman, 1972: 3). Marx considered the possibility in the Jamaican case in the *Grundrisse*, but apparently viewed the British experience as modernization all the way.

Contrary to Marx's desire, then, the formative working class was not disciplined into a decisive mass by the development of early capitalism, so much as its ranks were fragmented, alienated, left amorphous (Bauman, 1972: 16). The onslaught of modernity on tradition, on culture and consciousness would never be complete, not then, not now. The consequence of this process of uneven development upon the internal organization of the working class was significant. For within the working class, the mass of available hands, there was an elite whose memory and tradition reached back to the guilds. The so-called labour aristocracy was of local lineage, it was not only a phenomenon resulting from the extension of British productive imperialism into India. This labour elite was already advantaged in its capacity to negotiate with employers and to work the newly emerging system (1972: 21). The guilds were less, as Adam Smith thought of unions, conspiracies against the people than instruments of exclusion of the skilled against the unskilled. Little wonder that the actually existing working class failed to live up to Marx's expectations.

The question of the historical relation between the guilds and the genesis of unions has long been subject of historiographical dispute. As Bauman indicates, one line of interpretation, as in Brentano, seems to think of continuity idealistically or culturally, whereas the other line, initiated by the Webbs, interprets the process of historical development materially and posits a rupture between guilds and unions (Bauman, 1972: 26). Bauman's response is that both interpretations have merit, a fact which only becomes apparent when the working class/elite distinction is reintroduced. The sense of continuity is more apparently applicable to skilled workers, the sense of rupture to mass workers and to industrial unionism. And whether the unions inherited patterns of identity from the guilds or themselves invented them, some morphological continuities between the two organizational forms are in any case undeniable. Both guilds and unions, after all, were institutions which sought to construct cultures of occupation out of the conditions of working life (1972: 28). Yet the guilds sought to make of their people a stratum, not a class, to privilege and protect them rather than to make them into a single coherent force representing the rights of labour against capital. The machinery and mentality of the guilds was based on the distinct stratification of a self-organizing community, and its energies were concentrated on the conservative tasks of maintaining that community's social status (1972: 43). This organizational form and culture could not simply be stretched to fit the emerging facts of factory civilization. It was for reasons such as these that union culture often revived not medieval but rather religious symbols and patterns of collective ritual.

The elite of the skilled, however, remained outside the labour movement in its formative moment. For the labour movement in its earliest years had no organizational structure of the kind we associate with its later ascendancy. It offered no prospects of career advancement, and consequently attracted few outsiders or class traitors on the make (1972: 60). Only closer to the turn of the twentieth century did union organization come increasingly to resemble the organization of capitalism itself. Patterns of mechanization in the mid-nineteenth century saw the emergence of a new stratum of skilled workers, whose particular skills were not interchangeable. This new stratification differed from the old, because it took place within that section of the working population which was created by, and owed its existence to, capitalist industry (1972: 63). Where the old elite was external, or prior to specifically capitalist development, the new elite was its result, and was thus internal to the development of the British working class. This new stratification, according to Bauman, took place within that section of the working population which was created by and was dependent on capitalist industry. This group had no history which preceded capitalism, no collective memory or institutions which went back further than the industrial revolution. The mass worker, in other words, is a new phenomenon; the mass worker is not the craftsman refigured, and it is the emergence of this so-to-say capitalist working class which, into the twentieth century, is to make all the difference.

The social effects of this path of development include the internal differentiation or bifurcation of the working class in terms of material rewards. Bauman's immediate concern here, then, is that puzzle which within orthodox marxism generated the controversy over the so-called labour aristocracy. Only Bauman's concern is not limited to questions of income levels or to the status claims of one group over the other; the larger curiosity is historical in nature, concerned as it is with matters of memory and identity. While the category labour aristocracy as employed by marxists has often been a shadow image of the petty bourgeoisie, the point for Bauman in referring to labour aristocracy is, rather, cultural, addressing as it does the material and neutral consequences of this kind of privilege. To use a different language, the new workers were systemic actors within capitalism in a way that their predecessors were not; the new working class was made in its image. The new workers were social insiders in a way that the older non-conformists were not. The attitudinal resonances to be observed here, rather, are potentially between the new skilled workers and the earlier craftsmen, even if the new workers only yet aspired to increased levels of social esteem, themselves being viewed by their superiors as little better than outsiders (1972: 69–70).

The new working class, in this sense, was yet fully to be made. Only this process would see the modern labour movement become just that, modern, because modernizing, leaving its own model of industrial development alongside that of the capitalists, now in sympathy with it, now in opposition (Bauman, 1972: 70; Touraine, 1987). This in turn meant the adoption of a kind of cultural project of reform and self-reform, construction and reconstruction. Thus the extraordinary historical experience of endless programmes for popular self-improvement, both material and spiritual. Bauman's approach evokes, though it does not name, Max Weber's Protestant Ethic and its staff, Benjamin Franklin, Richard Baxter, or locally, Samuel Smiles. For self-help, thrift, and their institutions, from mechanics' institutes and savings banks to temperance and mutual aid societies all now become significant presences in these local histories. As Bauman puts it, the 'members of the new stratum were in a hurry to discard the garments of their forebears' (1972: 72). At the very same moment, such gestures of pushing away the stigma of humble origins would mean embracing, or inventing status signs and trappings associated earlier with craft.

As Bauman observes in passing, the most powerful significance of the idea of labour aristocracy in this regard is less what it tells us about labour, and more what it indicates about the still dominant symbolic presence of the aristocracy. The captains of industry were still not viewed as public heroes; the connotations of contemporary insights such as Disraeli's *Sybil* indicated that the two nations within England were 'the privileged and the people; the aristocracy remaining both the object of social admiration and political contempt' (Bauman, 1972: 75–6). But it was the aristocratic model, rather than that of modernizing bourgeoisie, which remained the frame of popular as well as entrenched values. The condition of social inclusion for the new skilled stratum was thus social servility. This mobility strategy was therefore based on the logic of assimilation; it rested on trading off subordination against recognition. But this is not a story of inevitable proletarian incorporation, as Bauman makes clear in taking his distance from Roberto Michels' 'iron law of oligarchy' in the latter's *Political Parties*. The process of development involved cannot simply be viewed as a loss, from the stated or invisible critical premise of direct democracy; as Bauman indicates, modern democracy itself depends on elites (1972: 113). As Weber understood, and Marx simply avoided the issue, classes are not actors in themselves, so that the whole texture of *Between Class and Elite* continues to work across that synthesis of Marx and Weber which was a hallmark of postwar Polish sociology. Partly this reflects the practical, scholarly tension between the larger concept, class, and its more manageable, specific section, in the idea of elite; partly it expresses the difference between an unskilled sector, itself alienated from the system, and a sector of skilled workers actively seeking inclusion and mobility within the very same class. Indeed, from a perspective beyond marxism, the aristocrats of labour and the unskilled might well appear to belong in fact to different classes, and not only in terms of their habits, ways of life or levels of consumption. Artisans and labourers could look as distinct as they could similar, depending on the critical perspective brought to bear upon social history. For respectability and poverty remained still worlds apart (1972: 139–40).

The making of the working class was therefore an elongated and contradictory process, where the new production process worked against the older social and cultural superstructures. Only now could the class in itself – Bauman uses Marx's distinction – open the prospect of the transformation to class for itself (1972: 147). The concept of general or national union was one key marker of this process. But the political party, not the trade union, was the appropriate form for a movement which from its beginnings and in its very essence was the institutionalization of class and not of occupational interests (1972: 170). The older ideologies of earlier unionism could readily as not be accommodated into Liberalism. The new unionists were more likely socialists or, more accurately, collectivists. In fact, Bauman argues, every general union was basically more like a formative political party than like a trade union, for its interests and inclinations were general rather than particularistic (1972: 171). Class forms here generate the labour party, partly because they now develop more explicitly popular and national arguments for socialism. This was, however, a particular kind of socialism, linked to collectivist concepts and made manifest as reformism, far from revolutionary socialism (1972: 172). British socialism is therefore the principal antagonist of marxist socialism, though the British scene is also characterized by hybrid combinations of various kinds and proportions. 'British socialism is thus the purest form of a collectivist ideology, springing not from a total rejection of the existing structure but from a willingness to adopt that structure' (1972: 172). This attitude, according to Bauman, is characteristic of a class of which whole sections have, as a consequence of its evolution into a vocal and articulated entity, become rooted in the existing structure before the question of satisfying its own overall interests as a class is raised. A real socialism in its own right, British Socialism is therefore diametrically opposed to the revolutionary and totally unconformist concepts of Marxism (1972: 172). Contrary to the earlier common sense of critics of labourism such as Perry Anderson, however, Bauman's sense was that the middle class reformers of the Fabians and the Social Democratic Federation were not the primary locus of these kinds of ideas. The Independent Labour Party more clearly captured the spontaneous mood of the working class movement (1972: 173), though it, too, took the risk of alienating the margins when it argued for dignity through order, against for example slum dwelling as a wretched way of life (1972: 174). Yet working class socialism was nevertheless excluded from the category of social respectability.

The Fabian Society was different because it was middle class or aristocratic in terms of social origins, and because it did not aspire to perform the role of a political party (1972: 180). It was not of, though it was finally for, Labour. The Fabians and the Labour movement co-emerged before they merged, though the presence of liberalism was never absent from this scenario, right through to the practical victory of Fabianism through the Beveridge Report in 1944 (Bauman, 1972: 181; Beilharz, 1992, ch. 3). All the same, even granted the collusion between Webb and Arthur Henderson on Clause Four of the Labour Party in 1918 and the consolidation of influence into the interwar years, Fabianism could not be said to represent the labour movement except in this formal sense. As I have suggested elsewhere, the Fabian Society in this sense was the prototypical think-tank rather than the immanent product or essence of labour. Fabianism became the de facto ideology of labourism as social policy. Bauman's characterization of labour's ideology itself is that it was more like an ethos; though he does not explicitly make the connection with Durkheim, his view is similar to the latter's sense that socialism (and in the French case, especially communism) was the cry of the oppressed rather than concrete utopias of a sociologically specific kind (Bauman, 1972: 183; and see Durkheim, 1959).

Bauman's own commitment to marxism does not, however, lead him simply to sneer at the Fabians, nor to insist that the revolutionary alternative of Morris or Hyndman could have done better. Labourism, in any case, itself became subsumed to the idea of representation, and to the institution of parliament. The logic of electoralism was built into its programme and its history. This made British Labour distinct from the continental parties from the beginning, for parties like the German SPD had begun as the cultures of alternative society and class. Political Labour in Britain was coextensive with the formal system of parliamentary representation (Bauman, 1972: 186). If there were in this situation to be a choice between socialist claims and trade union interests, then socialism would be first to suffer. Indeed, the ILP focused its attention less on propagating socialism than on detaching the labour movement from the Liberal Party; increasingly its own political logic was to set up an independent ladder of upward mobility (1972: 187). Labourism, in short, sought after a strategy of political integration into capitalism, a long process involving emancipation ultimately from both the trade union movement and the machinery of middle class political structures like the Liberal Party.

The idea of political representation became feasible, now, because many members of the formative class were alienated from its processes of development and its own, natural political leaders. The labour movement thus generated its own elite, initially of autodidactic enthusiasts; those that followed, climbed the ladder which these pioneers had constructed. For as Bauman observes, the agitator and the administrator are distinct types of leader (1972: 201). Agitators are no use in a bureaucratic organization. These were issues identified by Weber in his typology of authority, and traced concretely by Michels in *Political Parties*; they were also the core of the German revisionist dispute between Rosa Luxemburg and Eduard Bernstein, for this was what was at risk when Bernstein had claimed that for socialism the end was nothing, the movement everything. The process of institution building which was itself success, for reformers, was for revolutionaries proof of having sold out. Only reformist practice was everywhere in the west on the ascendant; even the Bolsheviks had to build institutions of their own, and then felt compelled to defend them against enemies real or imaginary, within or without. Everywhere in socialist circles men were arriving in uniforms, or in suits. The dawn of administrative socialism was upon us, and the Fabians were among the prime representatives of this trend in Britain. But as Bauman understands, the Fabians were not with labour at the moment of its political arrival; the Fabian Society was a distinct type of organization, the policy machine of gifted intellectuals rather than primary organizer of numbers in corridors, and this reflected its floating middle-class nature. Labour's political leaders remained, by comparison, evangelical in style, in the manner of Keir Hardie, until Ramsay MacDonald arrived to replace the aura of the agitator with that of the suave administrator. The concrete utopia of socialism as an attainable end meanwhile shifted further and further away (Bauman, 1972: 224). Bauman quotes Hubert Bland's denunciation of MacDonald as a sign of these times: 'It seems that we are to work for socialism, fight for socialism, even die for it, but not, for God's sake, to define it' (1972: 224). Later leaders like Attlee and Gaitskell would have more traditional senses of loyalty, but the hazier aura around the idea of socialism only extended. After the Great War, the Labour Party became one of the two political teams which competed for control of the country, while its elite became a component part of the political elite of capitalist Britain (1972: 228).

This process of political, not economic inclusion was consolidated between 1924 and 1955. Plainly Bauman's sense of this path of development is that it is a long-term historical trend, conservatism following consolidation, rather than, say, short-term cyclical in the manner of business cycles. The consistent combination of Marxian and Weberian themes in his thinking is also apparent. Class is conceptually mobilized here as the larger category, specified in detail through the image of elite; the labour movement achieves some degree of social, or at least economic inclusion, while its leadership becomes politically assimilated upwards. As Bauman is at pains to stress, this is a sociological, rather than strictly historical interpretation; its implication is that these processes are beyond reversibility, if not beyond change. Artisans give way to the skilled, and they in turn to the technically trained, white-collar workers of the post Second World War period. Deskilling erodes the margins historically associated with skill. The consolidation of the welfare state also serves to moderate the effects of these developments, though less, Bauman claims, than is often thought (1972: 235). The welfare state, together with the experience of full employment, may have a levelling effect within the working class, or across its strata, but not across classes. There is, in short, in the postwar period what

Bauman refers to as an increasing standardization of the economic situation of the English working class (1972: 237). If this was a long-term, civilizational process then its achievements to this date were significant, even as they assimilated the nineteenth century's outsiders into the social mainstream. The welfare state, for its part, dysfunctioned in well-observed ways but it also produced the cultural success shown in new senses of security. Decreasing extremes of inequality promote increasing levels of security and civility; this all in marked contrast, in the 1950s, to what was to follow in the 1980s. The point, from the later perspective developed say in *Memories of Class* (1982), is that labour in the postwar period was given social, political and economic recognition. Labour was a legitimate social presence, if not a social actor in the marxian sense; and it is this recognition of legitimacy which has since been eroded, partly because the politics of production has been eroded by the politics of consumption. On the other hand, the politics of exclusion has seen the return of the stranger, this time with a vengeance, just as the traditionally British status claims of birth have been elongated into those of wealth, as the City replaces the country as the place of prestige.

Between Class and Elite thus comes to fruition in the period of corporatism, or social partnership, where the recognition of labour as a social presence is confirmed through the inclusion of its representatives in peak decision-making processes in social as well as economic policy (1972: 272–3). As Bauman observes, with reference to the period work of G.D.H. Cole and C. Wright Mills, trade unionism in consequence becomes more and more a business movement and less and less a democratic fellowship of equals – but how could it be other (1972: 272–8)? Similarly, the Labour Party has become in this period a separate organizational structure, metamorphosing in its class structure at three levels, in the social composition of its elite, in the class composition of its members and voters, and in the mutual relations between policy and the interests of various classes and strata: 'At all three levels the Labour Party has ceased to be a purely working class party. In composition, its elite is today a social mosaic' (1972: 279). Labour's transformation has taken it from a class party to a national party. The labour movement, which was revolutionary in origin, has finally in the 1950s produced what is simply a welfare state in which, as with the middle classes after 1832, a working class elite has been admitted into the ranks of a selective governing group (1972: 301). The trade union hierarchy itself then emerges more clearly as an alternative means of securing social mobility (1972: 304), but it is no less legitimate for that purpose, not least of all in a traditionalistic class culture where life chances are less than meritocratic.

Working class radicalization, in this scenario, is possible rather than probable; Bauman hesitates to predict the future on the basis of the patterns of political sociology thus established. Nevertheless, the general contours in *Between Class and Elite* indicate the accommodation of Labour, whatever the cultural traces of non-conformism which might remain from its formative moment in the nineteenth century. While Bauman does not labour the early marxian theme of alienation in this text, he does work the idea that it is the integration of the working class into capitalist society which changes its nature, making of it a systemic actor rather than the negation of the negation, the denial of everything capitalism stands for. Bauman is at pains to stress that this was only one possible outcome in a bundle of options; but it was the outcome which framed his subsequent work, especially *Memories of Class* (1982).

Memories of Class

'Memory is the after-life of history'. So opens *Memories of Class*, its implications apparent: for while the retrospective time-frame of the 1982 work is coextensive with that of *Between Class and Elite* (1972), it also pushes more firmly into the present and its possibilities, and the eighties are a different presence. The subtitle of the book indicates a stronger sense of the present as history, wedged in between memories of real or imagined pasts and hopes for the future. *Memories of Class – The Prehistory and After-Life of Class –* in this way works a dual axis, or perhaps it even tells two, connected but separable stories, one concerning the historiographical projection of class backward, upon the transition to capitalism, the other detailing the freezing of its mental apparatus into the postwar period. Viewed as two separate stories, the earlier sequence is the sharper, even though it results in working class accommodation into the system of industrial capitalism, for in the formative period there is a higher level of stress and creative tension between the actors and the results of their work. The second, postwar story is rather a story about corporatism, where working class ambitions have been established internally within the system and have even to some extent been successfully achieved. What holds these two stories, or axes, together is the sociological sensibility that class has also been overloaded as a category. That working class movement of which marxists expected everything has in a sense delivered it, by way of meal-tickets to the unequal banquet within.

Bauman's argument about memory seeks, however, to reach deeper than this. For his is an anthropological claim, that we are creatures who remember, and by necessity therefore also misremember, imagine, seek order, generate degrees of chaos or repetition in turn, and so on. We are, then, creatures governed by the after-life of our histories, personal and collective. If modernity's central challenge to us is its demand that we cope with and ourselves generate change, then one key concern is how we think this process. Bauman's argument here is that class society was a kind of unintended consequence of the struggle to preserve semblances of the past, to save tradition or community from modernity or industrialism. Socialism's roots as a practical movement, that is to say, are more fundamentally reactive than progressivist. But of course such a task is by definition impossible, for the older medieval sensibilities and institutions cannot be stretched this far; modernity tears them asunder. Ironically, then, the institutional success of the class politics of labourism in the twentieth century itself in turn embeds us into institutions which now also fall into crisis. The postwar boom delivers, but it also delivers a kind of institutional inertia, which results in dismay and widespread disarray when it, too, falters and stumbles in the 1970s.

Bauman does not make the explicit connection here, but his themes concerning marxism are consistent with those canvassed by Heinz Lubasz in his classic essay on Marx's own shift from liberalism to scientific socialism during the 1840s. As Lubasz shows, Marx's initial problematic was less the proletarian subjection to the laws of surplus-value, and more given to problems of popular suffering, the plight of the paupers, victims of the erosion of habitual rights via the Enclosure Acts, the Wood Laws and so on (Lubasz, 1976; see also Bauman, 1982 : 7). Marxism became along the path of the nineteenth century a theory of the suffering internal slave, the heroic but downtrodden proletarian, to the effective exclusion of the outsider, the pauper. As radical critics from Castoriadis to Baudrillard then claimed, marxism became a mirror of capitalist production. For Bauman – and I think this is true across the extent of his work – the Weberian sensitivity to exclusion outpaces the conventional marxist concern with the figure of the proletarian and his exploitation. Bauman has understood all along that there is one fate worse than exploitation, and it is not being exploited, but being subject to economic and psychological exclusion instead. Outsiders, that is to say, are always likely to head up the queue of potential victims.

A different indicator of Bauman's approach here is the way in which he mobilizes the work not only of E.P. Thompson but also of Michel Foucault in order to problematize the formation of the modern. Both historians, after all, had written about discipline, about the moral economy, about that difficult but vital part of the modern project which depended on making subjects who would work, and who would comply. Prison, workhouse, factory and economy ought in this optic to be aligned rather than detached (Bauman, 1982 : 8). Ontologically speaking, Bauman remains again more open to the Weberian sense that power is multiform and ubiquitous; yet the Foucauldian theme, that subjects can be expected to resist the compulsory modernization of the world, is also evident. The direct conceptual link here is to be located in Bauman's sense that the new power of modernity had through its numerous institutions to chart the entire territory of life: it had to come into direct and permanent contact with the body of the producer. For as Marx observed, but then conceptually elided, labour-power is always embodied, and the consolidation of factory civilization itself is based on force (Bauman, 1982: 11). When confronted with the new order, historical memory now would portray the bliss and tranquillity destroyed by the 'satanic mills'.

If the imaginary of the left was often caught up with the spell of Prometheus, molten steel and the muscular, masculine profile of the heroic proletarian, then the imaginary resources available to the labourers often came closer to romanticism's sense of loss and nostalgia for the green and pleasant land. Yet already from the nineteenth century, the dominant interpretation of labour struggles was economistic, presuming that labour's primary goal in struggle was the 'right to the whole product of labour'. In Bauman's eyes this critique is anachronistic. The point is not that labour did not play capital's game, but rather that it only came to do so on incorporation. The earlier, nineteenth century visions of labour were not constructed in terms of distribution of the social product, so much as they embodied a call to restore the old order (1982: 13). The anachronism of the view which casts labour as a systemic actor within capitalism even before such invitations were potentially issued is that it, too, projects the categories of class analysis back further than they will travel. While class images therefore still shadow labour actors into the 1950s, then, class concepts are simultaneously projected backwards by marxist intellectuals who will sacrifice anything to valorize class analysis itself. Labour historically loses both its relative autonomy and its larger claims to the product, yet labour also gains in this process the mixed blessing of intellectual advocacy at the hands of radicals who identify with the proletariat but do not belong to it.

According to Bauman, then, the formation of workers into a class was more powerfully a response to industrial than to capitalist culture. Yet capitalism is the primary enemy identified for the workers by their self-appointed intellectual representatives. There was, then, a vital third class actor in this story: these were the intellectuals, legislators aspirant later to become the leaders themselves in Eastern Europe. Marxism, in this regard, was the ideology of the intellectuals on the road to class power; but it was not only that. For Bauman, too, was, had been a marxist, carried still marxist memories, or utopias, even as he anticipated the devastating critique which was in 1987 to appear as *Legislators and Interpreters*. For here Bauman described a process in which intellectual critique displaced workers' concerns and sentiments while claiming to represent them. Marx's two-class model, bourgeois against proletarian, became the general prism through which leftist intellectuals interpreted the world, reading out their own interests in the process. As Bauman observed, there had long been a radical sense of unease about this process, beginning with Bakunin and Machajski through to the work of Bruno Rizzi and James Burnham on *The Bureaucratization of the World* and *The Managerial Revolution*, where, as after Weber, it was bureaucrats, technocrats or managers, or even intellectuals who ruled the world and therefore replaced the bourgeoisie as the enemy. Whether in its earlier permutations, as in Harold Lasswell's suggestion that the future lay with the 'permanent revolution of modernizing intellectuals', or in the most recent critiques offered by Konrad and Szelenyi or Alvin Gouldner, those intellectuals so adept in the fine art of social ventriloquism now also were revealed as deeply interested and implicated in power (Bauman, 1982: 24–5). The East European resonances were bound to be strong, whether the critique was Yugoslav, as in Djilas,

Hungarian, with Konrad and Szelenyi, or with Polish resonances, in Bauman's case: for in Soviet-type societies those who owned capital had ceased to rule, yet new rulers were in abundance. But the new theorists were also part of the problem, at the very same moment as they denounced it; for this kind of critique was based on the identification of power with class, so that the two-class model of capitalist society is reproduced and projected back and forward at the expense of any other possible interpretations of the present – or future (Bauman, 1982: 28). All politics here in this view, which Bauman renounces, is economics, which means that there is no such thing as politics any more. For this, to anticipate, is precisely the problem of corporatism, where the only politics admissible is that of competing GNP shares.

Bauman's message, both analytical and social, is that the industrialist mechanism of social reproduction and its mindset are nearing exhaustion. Both as a way to live, and as a way to think, industrialism is in crisis, 'a qualitatively new stage in history which can be passed only with a change in the type of social power as seminal as the one which took place in the times preceding the event of the industrial system' (1982: 33). But it is not yet called postmodern, at least not in 1982; and while Bauman engages with the most significant advocacy of postindustrialism, in the work of Alain Touraine, no major nominal concessions are offered here to postindustrialism either (Bauman, 1982: 31).

Returning to the process of industrialization, Bauman's concern is that the cause of labour dissent be respected, as political rather than economically driven. The civilizing process of the modern project was based on a new imperative to order within urban space, and it was this which elicited resistance. Here the reformers return. In sympathy with Marx's Third Thesis on Feuerbach – who educates the educators? – Bauman reminds that the Enlightenment project drew too easy a distinction between those who could perfect mankind and those who were to serve as objects of enlightenment (Bauman, 1982: 48). In sympathy with Fehér and Heller, Bauman here proposes that there are in effect several logics in modernity, which is not reducible to capitalism. Discipline might run together with the despotism of the factory, but it has other dynamics as well. The zeal of Bentham's urge to reform humanity cannot be explained by a simple appeal to the idea of class interests. Bauman's critical interest, in passing, is as much in Chadwick, or symbolically in Fabianism as it is in the Foucauldian obsession with the Panopticon. But in any case, the focus of *Memories of Class* remains with work relations, and thus with the birth of the factory (1982: 51), though the scope of his analysis is disarming, for Bauman also connects up the factory to the imperial experience of slavery (1982: 3). Within the metropolis, the project of a new moral economy often associated with Weber's idea of the Protestant Ethic also, however, played on images of craft tradition, the job well done for its own sake rather than rattled together (1982: 60). Early factory culture was punitive, rather than efficient, political, in this sense, rather than driven by capitalist economic rationality.

Industrialization was made possible less by the pursuit of a profit ethic than a control ethic (1982: 87). Capitalism, again, could logically therefore only be part of this problem; the larger critical frame implied the problem of modernity, and its own drive to order, that critical impulse which was to hold up so much of Bauman's later work through *Modernity and the Holocaust* (1989a) and *Modernity and Ambivalence* (1991a).

Yet the older themes and memories still return, for author and subject alike. For Bauman must traverse again here the analytical fields of *Between Class and Elite* (1972). How then did labour become a system-actor? Labourism was not simply an extension of the politics of the guilds. Paradoxically, what later came to be considered the working-class movement was born of resistance to enforced labour unification (Bauman, 1982: 88). Yet the dignity of labour remains a constant theme, for labour is that rare commodity which cannot actually be separated from its bearer, and labour is therefore the commodity that speaks back, that says no (1982: 94). Conventional economics loses this insight when it substitutes economic categories for the image of actual groups of people, but so then does marxism (1982: 109). Labour and Capital may be necessary abstract concepts, but it is their sentient, suffering bearers who actually hold the system up; this is something Marx lost sight of, perhaps because he spent too long seeking to decode the abstract culture of capital.

But the sentient, suffering actors have in the meantime, after the long postwar boom, also to be reeducated as consumers, more, now, than as producers; so at this point Bauman's focus shifts to the second axis, or story, away from the development of capitalism towards its postwar reconfiguration. Now consumption looms large as economics, as does corporatism in politics, and both reform culture.

One of Bauman's more recent collections of essays is *Postmodernity and its Discontents* (1997a); now, in *Memories of Class* he twists Freud's book politically, turning to 'Corporatism and its Discontents' (1982: ch. 5). Why the fuss about corporatism? Corporatism became the name associated, as Bauman offers it in acute summary, with the systemic economization of politics. The twentieth century became identified, on this view, as that period when politics was colonized by interest groups, and the older idea that there was a contingent common good negotiable by other means became laughably obsolescent, a throwback to the ancient Greeks. Corporatist arrangements might therefore advantage labour, but only as the peak group representative of its economic constituency. Individual actors within corporatist arrangements might thus gain legitimacy as representatives of producer groups, but never as citizens, and those citizens whose identities lay outside producer groups could never be more than outsiders (Bauman, 1982: 129; Triado, 1984; Beilharz, 1994a). Politics in this scenario would only approximate simulated politics through social contracts mediated via the state. The question of the good society would ever be lost in the politics of the goods society; political issues proper could never transcend questions of distribution. Politics proper might then disappear, as there could be nothing to disagree about, just a representative range of snouts sharing the trough (Bauman, 1982: 139).

The prospect of corporatism thus involves the potential closure of the public sphere, where 'private interests' would now reign supreme. At the same time, the politics of 'personality' stands in for the absent argument about principles (1982: 140). The absence of vigorous political dispute leads to simulated politics, the daytime television skits of Ronald Reagan, later the Bill and Monica Show. Classes become legitimated, but this kind of class politics leads at best to cross-class solidarities between the representatives of producer groups, to the exclusion of the outsiders. Economics replaces politics; distributive issues replace substantive debates about the good society. But even this corporatist outcome is unstable, restricted largely to the postwar period, for it is dependent on the relative abundance of Fordism, where production and consumption develop in tandem, and the producers of automobiles, white goods and so on are also at the same time their consumers. The possibility of corporatist arrangements therefore hangs on the ongoing expectation of economic growth within national, rather than global, economy. Corporatism is thus both simultaneously a standard trend within postwar Fordist regimes and yet inherently unstable, a tendential possibility rather than a necessary concrete trend (1982: 159). Class politics emerges through corporatism as a new possibility, only of a radically displaced kind, where social contracts are pursued in the name of classes as national actors. The right to the whole produce of labour is renegotiated by tripartite means. The very possibility of oppositional politics becomes blurred, because potentially disruptive of these fragile strategies of crisis-management (1982: 161). As Touraine argues, then, labour becomes an agent of order. Politics, in a sense, moves outside the system, which is both its strength and its fatal weakness.

The language of class now outlives its practical application. On Bauman's interpretation, indeed, class is now part of the problem. Both the idea of class politics and the practical political energies expended on the part of the labour movement become invested within the system. Both the real suffering, and the in-principle possibilities of change, lie outside the system, though Bauman avoids the kind of politics-of-refusal advocated earlier by Marcuse and later by Foucault. We cannot simply shift the historic vocation of social change from the proletariat to the outsiders or the marginals, for Bauman; if the world still needs changing, there is no magic conceptual wand which can solve the problem by anointing any single social group as the waiting saviour. The system now has its new victims, who often seem to represent its earlier victims – not the organized ranks of the labour movement, but the new poor, the outsiders themselves, those new victims sacrificed to the momentary victory of corporatist arrangements (1982: 166).

But there remain internal social problems, and not only these problems of exclusion. Throughout Bauman's work there can be detected a residual ambivalence about social engineering. In *Memories of Class*, Bauman identifies the waning will-to-reform as one factor crucial to this new configuration of political economy. The immediate postwar situation was different, because it was based on a cross-class alliance which included the outsiders in its purview, which spoke, indeed as T.H. Marshall did in *Citizenship and Social Class* (1950), of the rights of citizens rather than of the rights of producers. Yet the goal of the labour movement in this context was self-improvement, rather than equality, and the increasing hegemony of the politics of consumption in the postwar boom saw the consolidation of these kinds of indicators of what was to constitute social progress (Bauman, 1982: 168). While the postwar politics of inclusion was not universal, it nevertheless reformed the actors, locking their objectives into those of the state.

The undoing of the postwar pact or historic settlement between labour, capital and the middle classes thus disadvantages anew those whose original plight was to stand outside these locations. Now Bauman's eyes turn elsewhere, outward, away from the implicitly or explicitly British case which is the model for his analysis here, as earlier in *Between Class and Elite* (1972). Like that other great, this time nineteenth-century exile, his focus remains on Britain as the paradigm case of capitalist development. Like Marx, perhaps more so, Bauman connects these problems in turn into the larger conceptual unit of the world system. Having taken a distance from the Marcusean idea of an alliance of outsiders as the potentially revolutionary force against the system, Bauman now identifies the Third World, rather than the inner dynamics of British capitalism, as the major concern. The cunning of history returns with the unfolding consequences of decolonization, which themselves return directly to the heart of the empire, to London, to Toxteth, to Brixton (1982: 172). Here, in a sense, the dynamics of economic growth are simply mislocated, centralized rather than directed to the peripheries. Yet it is also the case, as Bauman observes, that the critique of growth remains a substantially middle class activity (1982: 175). So the critique of capitalist overdevelopment holds all the ambivalence that we, as middle class critics are; we know that this rapacious kind of development cannot occur without drastic effects, but we are also vulnerable, in this situation, to the charge that we want to keep the civilizational proceeds to ourselves: 'The age-old wisdom of the rich, "money does not bring happiness", has always had a hollow ring for the poor' (1982: 178). More, the middle class snobbery which has also affected the left, and Critical Theory in particular, plays on themes of aristocratic radicalism too arrogant any longer to defend. These are the problems facing democratic radicals today. We cannot either give up our criticisms of the way we live, but nor can we decide for others what is in good and bad taste, high or low culture – at least not for others. The temptation of the critics, of course, is also the urge to legislate, which as Bauman knows is at its most poisonous when it is concealed or invisible, presumed as the right of intellectual superiors rather than earned through trust and trial and error.

But criticize we must, for the world we inhabit seems also to decline all around us. While there are always to be found around us examples of the goodness of people and their strivings, the degradations of consumer culture also seem to indicate some kind of decivilizing process underway (1982: 180). Obviously we all need to consume, and only the puritans among us will deny this. When however consumption also consumes us, when commodified pleasures replace all other senses of meaning or obligation, then the very idea of the social and its semantic extension, into socialism, decays before us. If economic growth brings no guarantee of happiness, then its end suggests rather the expansion of resentment. Either way, there seems to be less indication than ever before that modernity can continue to call out civility. The insiders are too busy partying to take in what happens outside, until they get mugged or their car mirrors are ripped off.

Returning to more conventionally sociological register, Bauman quotes Claus Offe, whose work in the critique of political economy of the Keynesian Welfare State he often in this book relies upon. The problem is that 'under State-regulated capitalism, all-out class conflict is no longer the driving force of social change. A horizontal pattern of inequality, that is, disparities between vital areas, is emerging increasingly into the foreground' (Bauman, 1982: 186). Viewed graphically, as sociologists are wont to do, the crude line of division in society is no longer vertical, between two warring camps or classes, but horizontal, between labour and capital inside the system and the excluded, outside and below it. Bauman did not in the writing of this book have Jeremy Seabrook's 1985 classic *Landscapes of Poverty* (1985) available to him, but there are elective affinities between the two critical projects, and by *Legislators and Interpreters* (Bauman, 1987) Seabrook's work became grist to Bauman's mill, not least in the idea that Britain once again had become 'two nations'. Part of the power of Seabrook's work is exactly in its sensitivity to the dimension of both local and global outsiders across the empire, cockneys and Indians in London and in Bombay, cockney Indians in Brixton. There are outsiders, that is to say, both inside and outside the immediate boundaries of the nation-state. Further, this pauperization effect has a structural logic as well as a practical effect. The pauperization of groups or categories of people is a secondary effect of the pauperization of specific areas of public life (1982: 187). Offe's proposal that corporatism redefines patterns of exclusion horizontally rather than vertically then opens the possibility that globalization, or life after corporatism, will punish those outside the renewed boundaries even more ruthlessly than before. As Bauman is later to argue, the victims of corporatism are simply ignored; after corporatism, in globalization they are to be held up as horror stories, cases of failure to be shamed, to be made examples of. The excluded have no voice, their grievances have no specific culprit, nor a concrete adversary. The inevitable result of structural unemployment is the generation of a permanent underclass (1982: 178–88). Beneath this, or beyond it, the problem remains that even redistribution does not deal out dignity.

Memories of Class then works this elongated theme, that while class matters it has been analytically overvalued by those who have projected it back, misleadingly, onto early practices of dissent, and then it has come back to haunt the postwar society which institutionalizes it while relocating the extremities of suffering beyond the labour movement. Memory counts, in this process, because we cannot think without it, yet it disables as well as enables us. Projected back upon different histories, the concept of class colonizes anti-industrial struggles, subsuming them to a marxian narrative at the expense of their specific content. The after-life of class then carries on through the period of corporatism, even when class has ceased to denote struggle or difference or to connote refusal or dignity. As Bauman concludes, though, we can as humans probably do no other, though there always remains hope that we might do better. Memory works by assimilation; we absorb and accommodate new experience into the old, familiar picture of the world even when this involves violation (1982: 192). The accumulation of anomalies over time then sometimes results in the overburdening and collapse of the old ways of thinking. All these things matter because what we define as real has practical consequences. We reproduce concepts and ideas even at the expense of what goes on around us; and yet, we learn, and the old ideas do still enable, do still 'work', even as they disable, for we are creatures of habit, even at our most potentially innovative moments. The point, then, for Bauman, is that concepts have an astonishing capacity for deferring their demise and outlining the reality they once connoted, and this is nowhere more evident than in the case of class (1982: 193). The result is that class, alongside commodity the most critical of marxian concepts, becomes world-denying in the ease with which it self-reproduces. For the conclusion of *Memories of Class* follows, that:

> the historically conditioned tendency to perceive the structure and dynamic tendencies of the late capitalist society through the prism of the struggle between two great classes which confronted each other inside the ascendant capitalist industry clouds rather than clarifies vision. (Bauman, 1982: 193)

The issue is not that the marxists were hesitant to leave their studies, but rather that they like others saw only what they wanted, defended the paradigm or the explanation at the expense of what stood to be explained, and this partly because of the will-to-legislate already in their heads. Industry therefore always looked like capitalism, suffering like exploitation, the victims like proletarians.

The way out? If marxism singed the fingers, then perhaps the problem of interpreting the world would become more immediately urgent than that of changing it; for the coupling of those two verbs also seemed indicative of the problem of the intellectuals on the road to power, 'we' interpret, 'we' change, to know is to understand and to lead. As generations since Marx had also understood, however, socialism could by definition never be legislated; you cannot give autonomy away to others. And it is autonomy, here, which is at risk for Bauman. Returning momentarily to the earlier phase of capitalism-in-the-making, he reminds that

> The formation of class society was the outcome of the submission of the vast masses of expropriated and unemployed poor into a new type of work discipline, which entailed control over their bodies and the denial of their personal autonomy as producers. (1982: 195)

If autonomy is that which is lost, it must in turn be sought again. Politics would then become more political, less economic, again. Politics might again become concerned with the organization of social life, self-management, restitution and preservation of human control over the ways in which human bodily and spiritual potential is developed and deployed (1982: 197).

Can politics reclaim control over economics? Facing the millennium, the prospects are less than cheerful, though the possibility always remains that the dominant social paradigm itself will collapse under the weight of its own anomalies. Humans retain the capacity to learn, however slowly; in this regard Bauman's sympathies touch those of Castoriadis, for whom the human need for autonomy might diminish but will never disappear.

At the same time, the shifts in Bauman's own ways of thinking might here be observed. If marxism was to collapse under the weight of its own hopes, the idea of the alternative possible society would nevertheless remain. While the focus of *Between Class and Elite* would bring the analysis into the middle of the Fordist period, the 1950s, the idea of Fordism as a phase of development would of course only emerge later, as Fordism and the national social policy of Keynesianism began to unravel, though the American story of making the modern was arguably longer (Smith, 1993). Fordism, in short, only really began to emerge in clear contours when talk began of Post Fordism, just as the stronger debate about modernity was also called out by the idea that it had passed, called postmodernity. The crucial conceptual shift in *Memories of Class* is not so directly that signalled by the idea that class analysis itself was inflationary, however. What the postwar period indicated practically, in the west, was the possibility that the older emphasis on production might now give way to the political economy of consumption. Labour's part in this transformation could be seen, in retrospect, in the belated enthusiasm for the policy of distributive justice. The early slogan concerning the 'right to the whole product of labour' referred to the question of who consumes. As labour was fully commodified, workers' struggles became fundamentally consumers' struggles (Calhoun, 1982: 284). If the identity politics of labour in the nineteenth century connected to the politics of production, then midway into the twentieth century the indications were that consumption would now be central to identity. Labour, in turn, was not merely the recipient but also the agent of this process. The brief prospects of postwar corporatism sought then to consolidate the interests of producer groups as consumers of managed shares of GNP. Then the process we now, again after the fact, call globalization changed all that.

Work, Consumerism and the New Poor

In 1998 Bauman was to publish two books returning to and developing these themes. One, on globalization, will be discussed in Chapter 6. The other, *Work, Consumerism and the New Poor* (1998b), involved treading again after the postmodern turn these paths of work and consumption, inclusion and exclusion.

Sociologists in the 1960s seem, in retrospect, to have perhaps run the risk of replacing the earlier obsession with mass society with a new slogan: consumer society. Ideas of postindustrialism were sometimes taken to indicate an end to work, or the arrival of the leisure society. It was as though the Protestant Ethic, which had actually or metaphorically to be beaten into people, could now, amidst potential abundance, be relieved. Such premature enthusiasms for the prospect of a leisure society were to evaporate amidst the rediscovery of scarcity, or at least of the Post Fordist revival of scarcity for some combined with abundance for others. Yet work in the meantime had also become socially enshrined, and this not only because paid work and available consumption levels were often connected. Work had become a norm, a good in itself, in modern times.

Bauman's interim turn into ethics connected all this together powerfully. For the work ethic is also that, a moral insistence or exhortation. And

> whenever you hear people talking about ethics, you may be pretty sure that someone somewhere is dissatisfied with the way some other people behave and would rather have them behaving differently. Hardly ever [did] this advice make more sense than in the case of the work ethic. (1998b: 6)

The need for work – for advancement, motion, progress, development – is necessarily caught up with the extension of systems of needs. Endless work comes together with the open-ended need to consume. As Bauman indicates in *Memories of Class* (1982), and reminds us again here, the Protestant Ethic understood as performance principle was in fact an attempt to resuscitate basically preindustrial or craft work attitudes, under new conditions that rendered them meaningless (1998b: 7). The regime had to be generated; it was one of modernity's greatest challenges. Loosened, perhaps, into postmodern times, it could hardly be cancelled; the new model of desirable behaviour would rather be work hard, play hard. The work ethic is therefore a vital sign of modern aspiration, and not only a tool of would-be capitalist regulation. For symbolically it is connected into what Castoriadis (1987) would call the fantasy of rational mastery. In Bauman's understanding, the work ethic would privilege 'what can be done' over 'what needs to be done'; it would encourage the setting of social goals in terms of the Promethean or Faustian sense that humans would always feel compelled to aspire after that which is technically possible, regardless of its desirability or ethical consequences (1998b: 8). Part of the ruthless modern attack on tradition also took in this strategy, where the idea of limits or limited needs-structures could be ridiculed as old hat. Mere 'traditionalism' was but an obstacle on the road to happiness.

Bauman's own memories of working on the nineteenth century haunt his contemporary narrative. For the astonishing feature of the postmodern story is precisely its replay or replacing of the nineteenth century discourse and practice of pauperism. Disraeli, the 'Two Nations', Carlyle, Gaskell, Ricardo and Mayhew, Bentham and Chadwick, all these voices come back to haunt us, as 'less eligibility' resurfaces and welfare talk, itself born of the culture of *noblesse oblige*, returns now without the compassion which in principle animated its precedents. Today's poorhouse is in the head; its forms of confinement may again be the dubious right to sleep under the overpass rather than in more vigorously policed spaces. Work, in short, or its absence is central to the new industrial mode of regulation. Even in its formative phases, more perhaps in the United States than in continental Europe, however, work was geared into the idea of more, rather than better. Taylorism or scientific management, according to Bauman, worked on developing money incentives rather than work ethics or company loyalties (1998b: 20–1). Work became the price of consumer freedom, opening that long process already alluded to in which consumption stands in for production as a primary source of loyalty. If America led the way in this experience, then it also came to represent the acme of the modern project, which all should follow on pain of extinction.

Whether we learn to love work, as Big Brother, or whether we simply accept it as the precondition of life, its value becomes set in concrete. Work may therefore, despite Weber, not strike us any longer as a superior way of life, but merely as an instrument to earn more money, not to seek the good or the better life but more. The message retreads the memory paths of Bauman's 1982 work:

> What used to be at the start of industrial society a power conflict, a fight for autonomy and freedom, has been gradually yet relentlessly channelled into the struggle for a greater share of the surplus while tacitly accepting the existent power structure and striking its rectification out from the agenda. Increasingly, it was the ability to win a greater share of the surplus that came to be seen as the definitive way to restore that human dignity which was lost when the craftsmen turned into factory hands. (1998b: 21)

Wage differentials, not claims to the nobility of labour, now substituted for the loss. Labour and capital, insiders and outsiders all took up the noonward race. Quality gave way to quantity and to the monetization of everyday life. All, in this sense, became capitalists actual or aspirant; such were the blessings of the image of upward social mobility. In this regard, at least, Weber's expectations were accurate; the legitimacy of capitalism depends crucially on its cultural internalization by rich and poor alike, less now through claims to morality than to the promise of self-advancement. Finally, as Bauman indicates in opening up this optic, it was differences in this sphere which help to explain the struggles between the two dominant versions of modernity in the twentieth century, Communism and Capitalism. Communism, in this sense, was more faithful to modernism as a production culture; consumption was always viewed as secondary, even up to Khrushchev. Capitalism outperformed Communism, *pace* Khrushchev, exactly because it delivered shoes and books as well as tanks and nails. The Soviet Union had hoped to bury capitalism with producer goods like these, not with consumer goods; but consumption won out, as McDonalds in Moscow illustrates (1998b: 22). Yet what this results in, as Bauman puts it, is the long-term replacement of the work ethic by the aesthetic of consumption. Post-Panopticon, consumption becomes the new and dominant form of self-regulation (1998b: 24). Self-choice and the contingent identity in the supermarket or mall replaces citizenship in the workplace or politics in the domestic sphere.

The language of modernity varies, in Bauman's hands, as we will see further later. Often our modernity, our today is for Bauman postmodern, especially in the sense that it is and feels itself to be after the high modernism, say, of the 1950s, when all seemed certain, clear and fixed, and neatly divided between communist and capitalist paradigms. In passing, in this text, Bauman indicates a different and suggestive way of thinking or naming these phases. In the industrial phase of modernity, he suggests here, one fact was beyond all question: that everyone's primary identity be as producer, or provider. In modernity mark two, it follows, that we inhabit the modernity of consumers, where each is a consumer before all else (1998b: 26). As an old marxist, of course, Bauman is well aware that every act of production is also an act of consumption; in what he calls modernity mark two, however, not every act of consumption is also an act of production. Production remains, but consumption rules, both economically and socially. So there now emerges a sort of pre-ordained harmony or resonance between these transient qualities of consumer life and the ambivalence and contingency endemic to contemporary identity-concerns. Identities, just like consumer goods, are mobile, to be appropriated and possessed, but in order to be consumed, to disappear again, in a process that ends only with death (1998b: 29). Modernity, phase one or two, is the epoch of the spirit of restlessness. No stasis, no stable state is possible in economy or in life.

The moral, or rather ethical issue here for Bauman is that consumption society erodes social solidarity. Thus for the first time relatively affluent middle class citizens will approve welfare cuts provided that these go together with tax cuts or personal benefits. Thus the citizen, too, becomes refigured as the consumer, he or she who possesses not solidarity or belonging so much as the means (1998b: 30). The shift in work solidarity is equally profound. Producers can fulfil their vocation only collectively; producers are together even when they act apart. Consumption, by comparison, is anomic, thoroughly individuated. There is no such concrete experience as 'collective consumption'. Consumers are alone even when they act together: 'It is aesthetics, not ethics, that is deployed to integrate the society of consumers, to keep it on course and time and again salvage it from crises' (1998b: 31). Images of the personal sublime replace those of duty to the other. Even the idea of duty itself begins to look silly, tawdry, old hat, a value for 'losers'. This is a long way even from the 1950s, as Bauman tells, because the period idea of full employment implied work both as a right and as a duty. The high modernism embodied in the Keynesian Welfare State may have been both conformist and masculinist, but it was open in principle to the politics of inclusion. Ergo the difficulty we have coming to grips with the idea of the 'working poor', given the historical coupling of the idea of work and that of a decent income (1998b: 37). Poverty, of course, is a social stigma, but working poverty is a quandary which has somehow still to refer to weaknesses in the actors involved rather than in the social arrangements which call out their condition. The new poor of modernity phase two may therefore bear a double stigma; that of not working, compounded by the inability sufficiently to engage in socially approved levels or kinds of consumption. They are what Bauman refers to as flawed consumers (1998b: 38). If our primary duty now is to consume, then the flawed consumer is a kind of blot on the modern landscape. Our task, before God, is to strive for perennial pleasure, eternal happiness, that is, for anything the other side of boredom:

> But to get rid of boredom one needs money; even more than money one needs to stave off the spectre of boredom once for all. . . . Money is the entry permit to places where remedies against boredom are peddled (like shopping malls, amusement parks, or 'health and fitness centres'). (1998b: 39)

Money becomes the passport in modernity, to link into another Bauman motif; for money divides us into tourists and vagabonds, travellers through modernity with the means, or without, those with itineraries and those compelled to move on.

Thrill-seeking connects also into crime and violence. Challenging the forces of law-and-order, in this scenario, may well become the poor man's practical substitute for the affluent consumer's well-tempered anti-boredom adventures (1998b: 39). As Robert Musil (1995) observes, violence is a simple, concrete act in a complex, abstract world; little wonder it attracts. Ours, then, is the dissatisfied society, where as Seabrook observes, the worst confession would be to declare that one was satisfied with one's lot (Bauman, 1998b: 40). Now Bauman returns to the Keynesian Welfare State as a symptom of and response to these developments. Probably all of us living through the heyday of the postwar period were inclined to view the welfare state as part of the problem rather than the solution (Beilharz, Considine and Watts, 1992). Bauman, too, might reasonably be expected to have more than a passing sneer at its results. The state has committed as many heinous crimes as capital, by any account; yet the modern state has also historically been tied to the idea of citizenship and the kinds of material provision which might promote it. In fact, Bauman's appraisal of the welfare state is more positive than might be anticipated, in part, perhaps, because he seems as interested in potential as in results. The idea of the welfare state, as Bauman observes, was typically positive rather than minimalist in design; it held out the hope of something more than mere survival. Its aims, historically, were more like survival in dignity, as understood in a given society at a given time (Bauman, 1998b: 45). More generally, and in sympathy with the work of Claus Offe, Bauman views the Keynesian Welfare State as politically significant because it opens the in-principle possibility that work and income can be uncoupled (1998b: 45). Yet more than Offe imagined in the period of his most creative work in this regard, in the 1980s the welfare state is also reversible, and it has in fact been reversed in most settings known to us, as citizens have been economized, restructured in the later 1980s as consumers or clients. Even the leading institutions of the welfare state – health care systems, universities, public transport facilities – now are based on inclusion and exclusion via the cash nexus. So far away do we now seem from these senses of inclusion and dignity, even when based on inequality, that now even Beveridge's vision of the good society becomes attractive again (1998b: 47). Plainly Bauman prefers universalism to targeting in social policy, for all the reasons advocates like Richard Titmuss made plain. Even if we tire of Durkheim, the most routine of sociologists, we are stuck with his residual sense that community will be constructed or it will not be at all. Solidarity is not somehow naturally given, by class or by gender or by ethnic origins; it is something we must work at. Since Thatcher, and now with Blair, however, ethics, the need of the other, is increasingly subsumed to a certain economy of interest. Means-testing divides rather than integrates; even the principle of social inclusion has now been abandoned as a fiscal luxury.

This is not, however, merely a tawdry political story about the failure of the parliamentary will-to-reform. Neoliberalism is rather the result than the cause of this process of decline in social solidarity. The first question to be answered when we confront this seachange is why neoliberalism was so well received. The rise of neoconservative elites is not the cause, or the explanation, but itself requires an explanation. The focus ought then shift to the contradictions of the Keynesian Welfare State itself. For the welfare state's commitment to full employment opened and extended its formal role in the ongoing process of the 'recommodification of labour' (1998b: 52). In tandem with the long boom, the welfare state project indirectly supported consumerism itself, undermining the prospect of citizenship in the process. Socializing the reproduction costs of labour was also to consumerize them in effect. The end of this story, however, results not in the reproduction of labour but in its expulsion. How wrong Marx was, to imagine even hypothetically that all potential labour-power would be commodified, even subject to the moderating effects of the reserve army of unemployed. Logically, Marx's labour theory of value in *Capital* could never be replaced by the technological inputs to value-creation in, say, the *Grundrisse*. Marx could not imagine the possibility of capitalism without labour, or at least without labour as we came to know it, massified and organized or organizable. The 'recommodification of labour strategy' pursued by the welfare state on behalf of capitalism could only survive as long as profitable production depended on the increasing contribution and available volume of labour (Bauman, 1998b: 53–4).

The Marx of *The Communist Manifesto*, as many commentators left and right have recently observed in the meantime, did indeed offer the acute version of the anticipated scenario we now know as globalization. Capitalism comes now to work through ships with 'flags of convenience', knowing no home, ignoring the fate of geographically fixed workers. This seems, as Bauman puts it, to be the logic of late modern capitalist production: having manoeuvred itself into the use of consumer desires as the major mobilizing, integrating force of postmodernity, capital tends in the long run to 'price labour out of work'. As Joseph Schumpeter was later to term this process out of Marx, creative destruction was to become the hallmark of capitalist progress. The error of sociologists, marxists included, was as ever to imagine the present phase, whatever it is, as stable rather than transient. So the reserve army still exists, only now it is global in reach, while welfare provisions, such as they are, remain local (Bauman, 1998b: 54). The denationalization of economies makes the welfare state redundant, then, as capital can now afford to be indifferent towards the socialization or recommodification of labour. As a result a major problem emerges for social democracy. For capital can be persuaded to stay, say, in Britain or in Australia, only on the condition that governments oversee the reduction of local labour costs. The old 1960s fears concerning 'capital flight' in the face of governments with reforming intentions become a standard expectation of everyday political life. Post Fordist, on Bauman's account, means also postwelfarist; the image of the high-wage, high-consumption relatively closed national economy is now made to look like a Keynesian fantasy, like digging holes and filling them in again. Now the proletarians dig only their own graves, through overwork and superexploitation.

Bauman does not emphatically mobilize the language of class here, but the problem he describes could also be explained in terms of the collapse of the postwar class alliances which held up social democratic experience around the western world. The middle class in the 1950s benefited materially from the welfare state, perhaps even disproportionately so; but they also contributed, and universalism in social policy opened the in-principle possibility that denizens of different class backgrounds might encounter each other as citizens. Now, today, the middle class is not only allowed but is encouraged to take all available opting-out clauses. The 'median voter' has apparently grown in confidence, even in this new age of uncertainty, and seems to be satisfied that he and his family (some things remaining equal, or rather unequal) can cope with the challenges of life without contributing to the costs of the state-maintained safety-net. Or else, perhaps, the new mood is not so much reflective of a newfound self-confidence as it is a sober reflection of the fact that the alternatives to self-reliance are increasingly unattractive. Money in the pocket appeals, after all, these days, more than abstract claims to state or public provision where the latter conjures up images of queues, delays and something less than 'value for money'. Bauman quotes Serge Halimi to emphasize his claim, that increasingly in the public perception 'programmes for the poor are poor programmes' (1998b: 57). The popularity of welfare protection having evaporated, the middle classes agree to its abolition.

The logic of consumerism thus finds its way also into the heart of the welfare state and its institutions. The formal mechanisms called 'choice' insinuate themselves here as well. To depend upon welfare is to have no say in the matter, again to be a flawed or deficient consumer, even if the 'choice' itself is empty or meaningless: 'The no-choice situation – taking what one is given and solely because nothing else is on offer, having no voice in the selection – is accordingly the anti-value of the consumer society' (1998b: 58). Markets therefore claim to facilitate difference, whereas welfare identifies the sameness of its citizens as the operative basis of its activities. Even if the state-offered services were of much better quality than they are, they would still be burdened with the fundamental flaw of being outside the scope of the allegedly free consumer choice.

But as Bauman has already indicated, to rehearse all these kinds of analyses and criticisms is still to leave unanswered the riddle, how did this come to be? How is it that citizen now means consumer? One possible explanation Bauman offers, which opens rather than closes the issue, has to do with the pursuit of dignity, and the backfiring or unintended consequences of the affirmative action mentality which underlies much ordinary welfare strategy. Affirmative action thinking, according to Bauman, not only riles whites in America but also those numerous African-Americans who want to 'arrive' or 'make it' by themselves. Social dignity, on this account, is not something perceived as a gift so much as a reward for conscious effort, personal talent or diligent work. Ironically, however, the confidence which the originally subaltern get to make it on their own itself results in part from welfare's aspirations to citizenship. To put it differently, the aspiration of the welfare state is exactly to level the so-called playing field a little. Thanks to positive discrimination, in short, a newly-self-confident black middle class has been born (1998b: 61), this after rather than because of Roosevelt or the New Deal. Affirmative action also then breeds its own gravediggers; and so in social policy, as in life, it goes. As Bauman summarizes, the

Welfare State came nowhere near the fulfilment of its founding fathers' dreams of exterminating once and for all poverty, humiliation and despondency; yet it did produce a large enough generation of well-educated, healthy, self-assured, self-reliant, self-confident people, jealous of their freshly acquired independence to cut the ground from beneath the popular support for the idea that it is a duty of those who have succeeded to help along those who go on failing. It is to the ears of this generation, empowered by the Welfare State – the 'self-made' men who would not be self-made if not for the material assistance or reassuring impact of a ready-to-help community – that the arguments about the disempowering impact of collective insurance and social wages are most telling. (1998b: 61)

The consequent problem, of course, is that we know that the effects of this process will be dire in the long term; so far, we have only been witness to the possibilities and the beginnings of decay and decadence. The deconstruction of the welfare state will result in problems which would make us regret these processes, if only the 'we' who reaped the whirlwind was the same generation as the we who authorized or submitted to it.

The underclass will haunt us again, those of us who escape its clutches; the poor will always be with us, only in ways both too reminiscent of the nineteenth century and too pressingly present and real. The older pauperism could be justified sneeringly by its superiors as the plight of the ne'er do wells. At that time, as Bauman says, labour was effectively the sole source of wealth; to produce more, and to involve more labour in the process of production meant very much the same thing (1998b: 63). In this setting, the work ethic meant something; it offered the in-principle prospect of social harmony or at least inclusion: 'The idea of work as the route leading simultaneously towards a wealthy nation and out of individual poverty rang true' (1998b: 63). Nowadays economic growth and job growth are no longer unproblematically correlated, but rather are at cross-purposes; technological progress is measured by the replacement or elimination of labour (1998b: 65). What this means, in short, is that capital can no longer 'afford' a working class; the new century, the new millennium opens the possibility of capitalism after labour, or at least after the labour movement. 'Working class', as the category of subordinate or subaltern actors, now gives way to 'underclass', underground, outside society, outside hierarchy (1998b: 66; see also Beilharz, 1994b). This class Marx did recognize, as quickly as he was to dismiss it as the lumpenproletariat, the 'dangerous class', the class in rags. Yet the idea of 'underclass' will not really do, for Bauman, as like many other concepts it offers a classificatory response to a moral or ethical as well as sociological problem. The idea of 'underclass', of course, has a history of its own, growing out of the Cold War and the subordinate status of African-Americans; so there are already reasons why perhaps the category should be handled with care, or will not travel.

'Underclass' indicates obsolescence, for its victims are disposable, and this may well be all they have in common. Like weeds, the underclass take up resources but fail to contribute. They are useless at best, dangerous at worst (Bauman, 1998b: 66). As a danger, they become useful, however, in terms of the potential for moral panic; these are the socially useful bad examples, those who have taken the human paths to be avoided. The idea of 'underclass' nevertheless serves a political as well as a normative or classificatory purpose; beggars, addicts or teenage single mothers are thrown together as a category in this as an exhortation for the decent public; 'thou shalt not'. The meaning of underclass, then, is politically driven and transient. For as Bauman observes, 'underclass' in its earliest usage, by Myrdal in 1963, referred to victims of exclusion through economic processes, not to social failures as scarecrows. These outsiders, in the meantime, have been demonized, othered, reconstructed as enemies. The victims now are habitually blamed, as though they have chosen exclusion. The mobilization of the underclass phenomenon thus normalizes the problem of poverty at the same time as it marginalizes it (Bauman, 1998b: 71). We can forget, or overlook the masses of the poor because of our obsession with these particular demons, drug-crazed and rapacious. The 'merely' poor simply disappear from sight. Bauman's summary is as powerful as it is painful:

> in the beginning, the work ethic was a highly effective means to fill up the factories hungry for more labour. With labour turning fast into an obstacle to higher productivity, work ethic still has a role to play – but this time as an effective means to wash clean all the hands and consciences inside 'the accepted boundaries of society' of the guilt of abandoning a large number of their fellow-citizens to permanent redundancy. Purity of hands and consciences is reached by the twin measure of the moral condemnation of the poor and the moral absolution of the rest. (1998b: 72)

The poor, then, fail finally to act as citizens because they fail as consumers. Inasmuch as identity is consumed, purchased, exclusion from consumption involves the denial of mainstream forms of recognition. The enemies of society are no longer those rabid revolutionaries but the outsiders, those inner demons who are deprived of the right to consume sufficiently and who are then stigmatized for their apparent choice of this refusal. Not revolutionaries, but the criminal classes are now our greatest fear. And none of this can be sidelined as incidental: for linking poverty to criminality helps to banish the poor from the realms of ordinary moral obligation (1998b: 77). Law stands in for morality where ethics is weak, or else absent. This process of generating the poor as counter example, itself generalizing, also has a more general social trend attached to it. Bauman links it to this larger trend of 'adiaphorization', that process whereby ethical opprobrium is separated out from morally repugnant acts (1998b: 80). All around us, but perhaps nowhere as obviously as on television or video-games, we encounter the naturalization of violence and suffering, examples of which until recently would have drawn responses of horror, then sympathy. The rules of 'anything goes' indicate that ultimately, everything is permissible. Adiaphorization thus leads towards the increased presence of nihilism, where we neither approve nor disapprove, say, of representations of human cruelty, but are merely indifferent to them. *Pulp Fiction* becomes just another movie, just a further distraction. Virtual death on film, real death on the television news, it all blurs as we grab for the remote or order pizza.

Moral impulse can never be shifted completely; and here Bauman's suggestion is that we moderns, or postmoderns, both ritualize and commercialize moral response to deprivation, repackaging it through periodic 'carnivals of charity' like Live-Aid. Morality becomes a media morality-play. We offer our momentary remorse, and then get back to the real world of consumption. In order to do this with clear conscience, however, we citizen-consumers must perforce deny our sociality, our dependence, as well as our morality. So it is that 'dependency', too, becomes a dirty word, even though dependency of the other on me is but a mirror image of my own responsibility (1998b: 80). The patterns of order we choose thus translate into our norms, displacing the others. Norm also involves normalizing, and the abnormal. Yet this all smells of crises, not of success. For as Castoriadis puts it, and Bauman concurs with his judgement, the crisis of the western world consists in that it stopped putting itself in question. We can revive the sense of question, for example, by discussing again Claus Offe's suggestion that we need to uncouple work and income or dignity and money (Bauman, 1998b: 95). This means to open, again, those horizons called utopia, not in naïve hope but because our world has changed, and may by that virtue change again.

Life After Class

Class was the great hope of the marxism which carried on from Marx's nineteenth-century legacy through Kautsky to Lukacs and later, to Althusser. The failure of the working class to live up to the vocation which marxism had ascribed to it led to disillusion and to the collapse of the western left. From the outside, the story must look rather hilarious, if not tragic; marxists had expected everything of a class they had adopted, and which then lapsed in turn into nothingness, or else they nursed their residual fantasies for later, when that class failed to live up to the task they ascribed it. Bauman's own path through this labyrinth was different, because even while his earlier work is more marxist and optimistic in tenor, he avoided both the over-investment and the subsequent disillusion with class. As Bauman would later argue, more fully, for example, in *Modernity and Ambivalence* (1991a), the very idea of classification runs the risk that it tells more about the classifiers than the classified. To classify may be necessary, but it is also to objectify, which then leads to dismay when the world fails to live out the expectations which we at an earlier moment have put upon it.

Class, in Bauman's writing, works both as a category and as a name for those bundles of experience that are associated with particular roles or places in the division of labour or the order of domination. His is not, therefore, a frame of interpretation within which we encounter the 'end of class'. What we follow through Bauman's writing on class is rather an expansion of the category of suffering or exploitation from class, in the closer sense, to domination or especially exclusion as the work progresses. Class remains a powerful way to think about the suffering and the validation of the working population in the twentieth century, when politics and culture change, when their representatives become systemic actors and consumptive identity begins to displace production as the apparent centre of life. The point, then, is not that class no longer counts, rather that as a category it fails to illuminate social critique in the way it did earlier. And how could it be other? For if marxism, too, is a product of history, it cannot finally claim by any dialectical tricks to escape the judgements of history itself. Nor, to the contrary of external or cynical critiques, however, can we reasonably expect the impetus of marxism or socialism simply to disappear like water into the arid sands of life after history. As Bauman will make more apparent in later work, sociologists cannot afford to let others do their thinking for them. The essential challenge for all social critics remains Kant's imperative: dare to think for yourself! We can never make peace with dogma, even though, in an existential or ordinary practical sense we of course will. The intellectual challenge raised, then, by Bauman, in these works as elsewhere, is to be ethically consistent at the same time as we strive to be curious or open to the world. Neither, then, can Bauman properly have followers, for he is demanding that each of us also go our own way. At the same time, however, this paradox may help to explain why so few of us seem able to follow his example; we know he is onto something, but the challenge seems simply too big a task in a world which otherwise asks so little.

2   Culture and Sociology

How do we know how to go on practically? And, how can we understand these mundane yet vital dimensions of our lives theoretically? What can we hope for? Two key themes which run across Bauman's work are those of culture and socialism. Perhaps, in a certain way, they are one; for the concern with social reproduction over time is also connected to the fact of, and the need for change. More, as the century has unfolded socialism has returned again to the culture from which it emerged, its claims to an independent existence as a politics exhausted by the travails of communism and the erosion of social democracy. For socialism was also, in a sense, a way of life, and perhaps that is what it is again today, as it was in the nineteenth century, an ensemble of sensibilities which could help actors seek out their own paths of self-development through cooperation. Of course culture and socialism are not the same, not then and certainly not now. Yet in Bauman's formation the two seem inevitably to turn on each other, even if socialism finally is more contingent, dissolving into culture as culture expands categorically into postmodern times.

Culture as Praxis

Between Class and Elite is the first indicator in the English language of Bauman's lifelong curiosity about socialism. Published in 1972, its intellectual genesis goes back into the 1950s. By 1973 Bauman had published another book, *Culture as Praxis*, which opened quite distinct lines of investigation. Culture and praxis – both words are ambiguous, or at least, open to dual meanings, both larger and smaller. Culture in the larger anthropological sense refers to whole ways of life, all their rituals, habits, institutions and artefacts; in the closer, traditional sense, it refers to high culture, culture as innovation or preservation. Ditto praxis: in the larger sense praxis refers merely to practice, to activity in general, to culture as human activity rather than as structure or result; in the closer sense, again, it refers to the particularly marxian sense, beckoning Aristotle, where to act is to change or wilfully to transform the world. Only here, in Bauman's work, the tension is maintained; his concern is not only with culture and praxis as socialism, but also with the conceptual stretch suggested by the ambivalence within and across the themes.

So how should we proceed into this labyrinth? As conversation does, when we offer some definitions as a way into the discussion. Bauman begins by addressing this very ambiguity in the concept of culture. Culture is an essentially contested category, only we use it as though we actually agree on its meaning. Even before we really agree on any kind of basic working definition, however, we discover that there is the stink of a corpse in the cargo. Without our necessary prior consent, the word culture takes on some kind of direct opposition to the idea of nature. Before we agree, the idea of culture as exercised by those who have used it before is smuggled in, in associated notions of civilization and progress (Bauman, 1973a: 3). Bauman proposes that we slow down the chase by identifying three separate universes of discourse within which the idea of culture has been incorporated. This diversity suggests the richness of the field of interpretation; the point is to make sense of these differing discursive usages of culture, rather than to settle on one or another.

The first field of usage indicates that culture is a hierarchical concept, where some have culture and others lack it. Culture in this usage is a possession, whether inherited or acquired; it needs maintenance, else nature and wilderness are reasserted. Culture needs cultivation. This way of thinking, of course, is value-saturated (1973a: 6–8). The second field indicates that culture is a differential concept, one that is used to establish or to claim difference between peoples, times and places. Bauman gives here the example of Herodotus who, when discussing other peoples encountered on his visits to various foreign lands, routinely uses phrases such as 'They do not' and 'contrary to us' (1973a: 17). This usage of the idea of culture may be implicitly hierarchical, in that it silently values the known, 'our' culture, over theirs, over the others. But it can also be used as an open, serial system of classification that is more arbitrary in effect, more like Borges' *Chinese Encyclopedia* or the comically chaotic *Encyclopedia* of the Philosophes than the *Encyclopaedia Britannica A–Z*, all bases ordered and covered.

If the first usage is narcissistic or self-referential, then, the second is more anthropological or at least ethnographic. In the second, difference is observed or posited rather than immediately valued. Paradoxically, then, the second field of discourse can either suggest radical difference or cultural relativism, or else that all peoples do the same things, only differently. The third usage, in Bauman's suggestion, is the generic concept of culture (1973a: 38). The generic concept feeds on the overlooked and unsaid parts of the differential concept: only where that discourse values difference, the generic emphasis focuses on the allegedly essential unity beneath the manifest differences. Here the reality of culture is viewed as its unity. Bauman associates one variation of the argument with the work of Clifford Geertz, where all humans are compelled to work through the same life path or process; the argument is equally compatible, in another form, with the structuralism of Lévi-Strauss, where all difference is emitted cross-culturally from brain patterns that are universal and uniform. Culture, however, involves for Bauman a great deal more than structure, symbol or language: 'Structure . . . is a less probable state than disorder' (1973a: 54). Structure is a hope more than a pattern or achievement. Structuring occurs, but more as an activity of varying impact and durability than as a firm result: 'The continuous and unending structuring activity constitutes the core of human praxis, the human mode of being in the world' (1973a: 56). Praxis, or being-in-the-world, relies on two essential instruments – tools and language. Culture is the perpetual effort to overcome the tension between creativity or freedom and dependence (1973a: 57).

Structuralism is therefore interesting to Bauman, if less than exhaustive in its interpretative potential. Its general weakness lies in a definitional substitution or semantic slide from culture to structure, or else to language. But this is not the only available elision. Others use culture in its Germanic sense, as though it were *Geist* or spirit (1973a: 113). Thus Durkheim in effect defines culture as society, as idea lived out through ritual. This kind of argument is both too materialist and too idealist for Bauman; too materialist, in that culture is reduced to ritual, too idealist, in that we all somehow become the servants of society, morality, or of society as God. Culture as praxis occurs rather between these stultifying or dizzying alternatives:

> Since cultural ordering is performed through the activity of signifying – splitting phenomena into classes through marking them – semiotics, the general theory of signs, provides the focus for the study of the general methodology of cultural praxis. The act of signifying is the act of the production of meaning. (1973a: 119)

Human praxis or activity therefore consists in turning chaos into order, or substituting one order for another. Structuralism mirrors this curiosity, except that it seeks out the generative rules which monitor the process, which is either to ask for the impossible or else, worse, to find it and to insist that all else must follow these rules of the master. What remains of significance here, however, is less the systems of classification which include and assimilate difference than what Roland Barthes, the most supple of structuralists, calls the 'rules of exclusion' (Bauman, 1973a: 122). The practice of ordering, that is to say, is also contingent and problematical. Bauman insists here that the role of rules of exclusion is crucial, indeed fundamental, for it preconditions the applicability of all other rules. Ordering involves transmuting what is fundamentally a continuous, shape-less stream of perception into a set of discrete entities, which we then hypostasize (1973a: 123). The other is taboo. The boundaries are thrown up and must be policed in order to assume group cohesion. 'We' and 'they' routinely allows for no third party or alternative ground: hence ambi-valence is squeezed out and into one category or the other (1973a: 126). This is also to indicate that the hierarchical concept of culture rules; the Herodotus, or differential view could deal with difference without necessary stigma, for the others could be more or less like us without being bar-barians. Only this latter view is, for Bauman, less readily available to us, for it is too heavily subversive of the firmer distinctions which we use to hold up our own image of the world (1973a: 127). 'We' and 'they' tend to be constructed as antonyms, rather than as graduated degrees of meaning. Our sacred depends on their taboo, our certainty on their chaos. 'Marginal men' work here as anomalies, reinforcing the two essential categories rather than validating a third between or across them (1973a: 128). Marginals are everything and nothing: they are in consequence alternately hated, or else granted superhuman powers, as devils, or dirt.

Bauman turns to precedent in order further to probe the issue of marginality. His authorities here are Georg Simmel and Roberto Michels, the latter best known to English-language readers as the primary sociologist of political parties, though this was not his only talent. Both Simmel and Michels are fascinated by the insider-outsider, i.e. the stranger, who comes and stays, not he who is transient, the foreigner or alien. The perverse oddity of the stranger is exactly this dual status, which immediately suggests a third term, but which cannot be legitimately recognized as such given the power of the dominant mental dualism. For Michels, the potency and danger of the stranger was exactly that he represented the Unknown. Paradoxically, the uncertainty impressed upon the figure of the stranger also imperilled the certainty of the host society; uncertainty spreads, like a plague, from the bearer to the host culture. The figure of the stranger violates the order he enters; the host society awaits its chance for revenge. Strangers are precisely people who say things like 'They do not' and 'contrary to us', and they speak too loudly for the comfort of the guardians, even when they say nothing at all; even their visual presence can be disturbing. They move, in an early modernity where tradition is still capable of conferring stability; so that order now becomes a social imperative (1973a: 135). The figure of the Jew, in particular, thus represents chaos.

Now Bauman employs Sartre's notion of the slimy or 'le visqueux' and Mary Douglas' work on purity and danger to amplify the point. Dirt is dirt by social agreement rather than by physiological necessity; dirt is matter out of place, just as the stranger is a perennial candidate for scapegoat, always potentially the subject out of place (Bauman, 1973a: 137–9). When the praxis of the group or community is destabilized, its capacity to tolerate difference decreases. Thus, for example, racism is not caused by economic crisis, but it is often called out by the heightened psychological insecurity associated with crisis. On the other extreme, human creativity is at its best when freedom expands, when actors are free of the immediate necessity to secure the means of survival (1973a: 171). The culture of critique may thus be at its most expansive at that very same moment of relative abundance in which citizens have no need of it. For Bauman wants culture to have a political dimension, or purpose. The voice is more marxian in inflexion than much else that we are offered in the 1980s:

> Culture is the only facet of the human condition and of life in which knowledge of the human reality and the human interest in self-perfection and fulfilment merge into one. . . . Culture is, therefore, the natural enemy of alienation. It constantly questions the self-appointed wisdom, serenity and authority of the Real. (1973a: 176)

Coming towards the end of the book, it is as if Bauman is adding a fourth, alternative definition of culture as critique, rather than as hierarchy, difference or genera. The alternative field of discourse suggested in the idea of culture as critique is that of the 1960s critical theory associated with Marcuse and the early Habermas, where it is positivism in social science which is the major enemy, and marxism lies somewhere between philosophy and science, as critique but also as a political critique or a practical philosophy searching for a transformative praxis. But there is also something else going on here, for Bauman's work may run in tandem with critical theory but it is not the project of an intellectual who believes that all is lost because the theory failed to meet its addressee, the revolutionary proletariat, on proper time. Bauman takes sides rather with Camus, agreeing that struggle or revolt is not an intellectual invention but a human experience and action. Existential nihilism has no place here, for Bauman; alienation cannot be our fate. Human practice is all that we can know; if only we could know it (1973a: 178).

Culture as Praxis is the only one of Bauman's earlier English language books so far to have a second life. Its second edition was published in 1999. Bauman takes advantage of the moment to reflect upon its content and significance (modesty forbids too much curiosity in the latter aspect). So why might we be interested in such matters as culture and praxis today? Bauman comments, laconically, that we never solve any problems, we only get bored by them. On the other hand, in these present, postmodern times, everybody is into recycling. So what endures? As Bauman recognizes, books date partly because their interlocutors do; Bauman's early works argue with or depend upon various authorities whose names are now unknown to us, though some endure; Mary Douglas and Sartre recur much later in Bauman's postmodern concern with the stranger. In between times, of course, there was an extraordinary English boom in cultural studies. By the 1980s culture meant everything to everyone in and around the academy. *Culture as Praxis* was written BSH – before Stuart Hall, before the Birmingham School.

Reconsidering his work nearly 30 years on, recognizing the risk that we invent or discover things in retrospect that may not exactly have been there in the first place, Bauman identifies one central feature of his book to be its claim about the core ambivalence of the concept of culture (1999a: xiv). To concentrate the issue, at least one major tension arises within the concept of culture, as one discourse generates the idea of culture as creation, invention, self-critique and self-transcendence, while another discourse posits culture as instrument of routinization and reproduction, as a tool of social order. These differences correspond to culture in the special sense, and culture in the expansive or ordinary sense. What, then, has changed? Looking back, Bauman's sense is that culture is now seen as much as an agent of disorder as it is the tool of order, a factor of ageing and adolescence as much as of timelessness (1999a: x).

Where the critical focus of *Culture as Praxis* was largely on the stranger, or the problem of exclusion or marginality, one theme that looms larger in the Introduction to the second edition is assimilation. The path of Bauman's work in the interval leads him to focus on both as aspects of domination: cultures seem to need either to swallow others up or else to expel them. Culture in the meantime has been internally pluralized, or multicultured; the necessity of traditional *Einheit*, unity or oneness has been eroded, at least in some quarters of civil society, though as Bauman argues more recently, it has also been tribalized in the process. Theoretically speaking, Bauman now identifies Lévi-Strauss as the *animateur* of his book, especially in the sense that culture is a structure of choices. Lévi-Strauss' impact, for Bauman, was less directly structuralist than it was subversive of the hard science of structuralism. In Bauman's reception of his work, Lévi-Strauss turns structure from a cage into a catapult (Bauman, 1999a: xxvi–xxvii). This was arguably a Lévi-Strauss unavailable to younger readers, like those of my own generation, for whom Lévi-Strauss was read through the lens of the French communist philosopher Louis Althusser, a thinker that Bauman assiduously ignores, with the deafening contempt of silence. What should we learn from Althusser? About this Bauman says nothing, because he believes that there is nothing to learn, and here, as elsewhere, the sympathies with other East European Renaissance marxists such as Agnes Heller are evident. In explicit sympathy, here, with Castoriadis, Bauman argues rather that the theoretical distinction central to structuralism between diachrony and synchrony simply dissolves under scrutiny, as it cannot capture the way in which society, language and culture persist through change (1999a: xxviii).

Intellectuals, in this scenario, insist on the necessity of their own social role as educators by insisting on the ignorance of those to be educated. Their voices become annexed to the modern project of nation-building, for while races seem given, nations have to be built. Civil society is weakened rather than strengthened in the process (1999a: xxxvi). Communitarianism now emerges as ersatz nationalism, the local version of nation-building. We should, with Touraine, solidarize with the slogan multiculturalism rather than support the idea of multicommunitarianism, a thousand little islands of local separatism with no traffic between them. Culture as multiculture encourages traffic; culture as community suggests closure and hostility (1999a: xlii).

Bauman now introduces Stuart Hall into the discussion, for if the fact of multiculturalism shifts the meaning of culture, so has Hall's work radicalized the usage of the term after *Culture as Praxis*. As Hall has argued, identity claims vary between naturalistic and discursive or (new) traditionalistic and modern or postmodern. Culture today is mobile, processual and open-ended. This is not the same as saying, as is fashionable, that culture is hybrid, for culture is not neatly packaged out in some imaginary beginning in the first place. In this sense, the technical idea of multiculturalism is also nonsensical, for culture is multiple by definition (Bauman, 1999a: xliv). At the same time the hermeneutic challenge persists, to seek the fusion of horizons while maintaining their distinction, so that the interpreter's own universe of meaning does not disappear. If modern hermeneutics was too much defined by the universe of the interpreter, then postmodern hermeneutics needs to avoid suspending that position altogether or losing it in the imaginary horizon of the other. Earlier, the risk was that meaning would be lost in translation; today, the possibility is rather that translation collapses into tokenistic assimilation into the other. We are, or should all be translators now, as plurality of cultures becomes cultural pluralism (1999a: xlvii, li).

Towards a Critical Sociology

If the work of Lévi-Strauss was the provocation which helped to draw out *Culture as Praxis* (1973a), where culture, like structure, was an activity, *Towards a Critical Sociology* (1976b), 'An Essay on Commonsense and Emancipation', seemed closer to the concerns of East European marxist humanism. Perhaps one difference between Bauman and, say, Heller, remained that while Heller often thinks sociologically, her vocation is that of the philosopher. While Bauman shares the Hungarian allergy to orthodox marxism, Dialectical Materialism and Laws of History, however, there remains throughout his work a conventionally sociological curiosity about social structure. The inflection of Bauman's work is therefore sympathetic to phenomenology, and this returns later in *Postmodern Ethics* (1993a), his work is also animated by the sense that there is something beyond the subject or the intersubjective which is the proper object of sociological analysis. Sociology's vocation is to look both inside and out.

Towards a Critical Sociology again evokes for period readers the sensibilities of the field of Critical Theory; but this is only true in the topographical sense. Bauman opens this study with a discussion of the idea of 'second nature', for it was second nature that announced the arrival of sociology. Nature is the name we give to the excess, to that which resists our desire to change the world: 'nature' is a byproduct of human practice (1976b: 2). Nature is constraint, to our own need for freedom. Nature is that which is beyond human control, but which we nevertheless seek to submit to our will. Society is to humans a 'second nature', as unchallengeable and beyond their control as non-human nature is, or becomes (1976b: 10). Only mainstream sociology, as in Durkheim, in turn naturalizes society, gives it a determining character of the same kind as nature-in-itself. 'Second nature' is somehow placed outside of us, as actors, which in one sense at least is to miss the point, for as Bauman will argue later, with reference to totalitarian regimes and the western hegemony of consumer culture, second nature is really also part of us, becoming a second order level of habit and mentality which is as contingent as collective choice might be. Second nature does not permeate every fibre of our beings, though it seems to us that it may as well do, as we observe the phenomenology of everyday life in these settings.

What is second nature? Within the history of the discipline of sociology it is 'the social', that category we cannot dispense with and yet which entraps us at every move, for it becomes a kind of dominant disciplinary ideology or culture or ether, logically shifting or sliding the analysis away from practices to this ghostly level of choreography. Between God, or Nature, and us, there is always this third level of 'second nature' which works against our increasing intimacy with the world of subjects that we, also, inhabit. The argument which naturalizes second nature itself is not only traditionalistic, as only the modernist discipline of sociology can be, but also in a particular sense theological. The major culprit in Bauman's unfolding narrative is Comte. For the implication in classical sociology is that human activity is best explained not by immanent analysis but by referring elsewhere, to the social heavens as it were. And this self-deception will become the bane of sociology after the Second World War, where as in the 'dominant ideology thesis' critics will happily blame some abstract capitalistic or individualistic ethos for how it is that the world works, denying the actual actors themselves either nous or intelligence. In this way, the idea of 'second nature' becomes doubly distracting, for it directs our curiosity away from closer accounts of what actually occurs in everyday life, and it at the same time projects second nature away from us, as a level above us, rather than viewing it as a culture which we selectively borrow and only ever partially internalize.

Intellectuals, in this early formative moment of the history of sociology, would be the Priests of the Religion of Humanity, interpreters and legislators all at once; the rest of us would merely follow. For the third level of 'society' would serve to tame the savage beast in men (1976b: 13). Where Comte began, Durkheim took over: 'It was left to Durkheim to deify society' (Bauman, 1976b: 14). God now was society in disguise, as society was God; law and morality were henceforth sacred, and at the very same time were nothing more than conventional and arbitrary. The emphasis is significant: instead of secularizing God, Durkheim deifies society, for he is as fearful of the practical consequences of modernity as he is enthusiastic for its blueprinted prospects through the further cultivation of the division of labour. Postmodern sociology, or a sociology of postmodernity, to anticipate, will in this regard rest on the attempt to get beyond Durkheim's reified metaphysic of the 'social'.

Ideas, or values, are central for Durkheim, as in the 'conscience collective'; and conformism is the goal to be achieved. Durkheim's sociology in this sense at least is further away from us than some would like to think; its imaginary horizons are closer to Gustav Le Bon's fin-de-siècle anxiety about the crowd than to Parsons' image of the well-oiled social system. Conformism, in any case, can lead in various different directions, from good civic mid-Western behaviour to judicious goosestepping through Nazi Berlin; and in either case, its reach can be skin-deep as well as deeply heartfelt. Pathetically enough, the shared distinction of the image of the good society in Durkheim and Parsons is that the social order is sufficiently civilized to call on nothing more than 'soft coercion', a vista which sure beats the prospect of Nazi and Stalinist horrors, but fails to inspire by any other criteria (1976b: 24). For 'Durksonianism', then, as for Hobbes, society is the cure for the wolf in man. Not so, says Goffman, however, for whom society can run wild (as in McCarthyism) exactly when overwhelmed by the zeal of its own moralizing mission (Bauman, 1976b: 24). Masking, on this account, does not make us wicked, but allows us to go on. Even when we kneel before the flag or our fearless leaders, this kind of activity tells us nothing analytically except that we learn how to go on. Compliance does not mean that we love Big Brother, any more than readiness to shop means that we are deeply committed to commodification.

Sociology, however, understood here as the science or critique of unfreedom, finds it easier to explain domination by reference to anything other than the actors – ideas, values, religion, culture, structure, patriarchy, whatever (1976b: 35). Our occupational hazard in sociology is that it is our task to make sense out of common sense, to construct order or to discern pattern out of the chaos of everyday life; and once we do so, we habitually substitute the construction for the problems with which we ostensibly began. Common sense indeed reinforces the view that our lives are closed, because socially determined. Sociology can therefore serve very well if our curiosity is pitched on the level of the question, 'how does society persist?', but it offers to tell us rather less as to the lives of humans themselves, not least in their stubborn struggles to be free (1976b: 42). Officially, sociology is the critique of common sense, all common sense of course except that which we call sociology (1976b: 43).

Bauman turns now to Husserl. Against the empiricism of the things in themselves, we need per Husserl to relocate the subject as itself a valid subject matter of knowledge. To focus again on subjectivity, and intersubjectivity, is also to reconsider intentionality (Bauman, 1976b: 47). Here the 'inside' counts, and not only the sociological 'outside'. Meaning is not objective, but subjective, or rather intersubjective. Existence is primary, but for Bauman this is no ontological puzzle. For existentialists, in opposition to Durksonianism, the herd-society of totalitarianism or consumer society does not gain mastery over the self unless invited to do so, even if more by default than by deliberate surrender (1976b: 55). To be enslaved by society is a matter of decision, or rather non-decision. Existentialist philosophy seems therefore to offer an outright and most radical critique of sociology, while meeting sociology on its own apparent ground. Existentialism, however, also suffers from the residual tendency to reify society, even while it values agency. Within existentialism the actor often seems to be alone; the third term disappears. It is Alfred Schutz who with his emphasis on members rather than subjects identifies the line which leads out of this impasse. Here sociability and individuality are thrown together: it is the sharing of the same structural rules of world perception which assumes the uniqueness of each experience and each individual world of meaning (1976b: 60).

Mead and Dewey are other stimulants to Bauman's thinking in *Towards a Critical Sociology* (1976b: 63–7). The object of sociology here is process, rather than stasis or structure; self and society are irreducible and yet mutually constitutive. Yet this is a minority voice within sociology, at least inasmuch as it stands against positivism; and here it is positivism, as rationalism, rather than Enlightenment or modernity, which Bauman identifies as the cause of the trouble (1976b: 72). This is about as close as Bauman comes to sympathy for Habermas' early critique of modernity as technical reason: emancipatory critique has to be applied to the cult of reason in positivism. To use the terms applied here, Bauman becomes progressively less interested in Habermas the closer Habermas comes to the Durksonian labyrinth. Marx, rather than Habermas, emerges at this point to carry the argument forward. Marx's critique of political economy seeks from the first to denaturalize its object. Here 'second nature' becomes historical; second nature is created, rather than essentialized. Political economy becomes sociology, which in turn becomes history (Bauman, 1976b: 82). Marxism counts here as a critical sociology, as historicism; this is the influence of the early Marx, the *Paris Manuscripts* and *The German Ideology*, *The Poverty of Philosophy* through, tentatively, to the *Grundrisse*. Capitalism, on Marx's view, emerges and sustains itself culturally and materially precisely as second nature, projected upon its bearers so powerfully that we can no longer readily distinguish between first and second nature. Indeed, the champions of the regime announce loudly that capitalism is nature, that greed and avarice are natural, and therefore both good for us and eternal. Sadly enough, as Bauman will have cause to observe on later occasions, the utopian followers of Marx then merely relocated the problem by arguing as though communism or socialism, once achieved, would or could remain permanent as the riddle of second nature solved.

At this point of his work, Bauman closes *Towards A Critical Sociology* again in the company of Habermas, a thinker who hereafter tends to disappear from his project. This was the Habermas of *Theory and Practice*, arguably the most stimulating of his work alongside *The Structural Transformation of the Public Sphere* (1962). Here Habermas sees Enlightenment both, already, as a failure and yet as maintaining a field of tensions between the competing claims and power of practical, technical and emancipatory reason. The idea of emancipation itself evaporates, not only from Habermas' work but also from Bauman's, perhaps with the difference that Bauman made the idea of emancipation dependent, anyway, on the unbreakable dialectic between freedom and domination. Habermas' concerns came rather to be with labour and communicative action, and the scope of his work expanded dramatically, from reconstructing critical theory to recasting the social sciences. Bauman's path was to lead even further away from these kinds of claims to systematicity or comprehensive theory-building. His commitment to critical sociology was to remain, even if its meaning was to shift and to vary, not just with postmodern times, but also depending on what day it was. For Bauman is nothing if not ambivalent about this child of Enlightenment that we call the sociological project itself.

Thinking Sociologically

Bauman still defends sociology today, even if only as we would often defend democracy or equality, or hitherto socialism as the idea which we cannot fulfil but which orientates our action and gives us hope, even against hope. For, of course, it is we who let sociology down, not the other way around – sociology itself does nothing, possesses no great riches, and so on. Bauman's defence of sociology itself gives the lie to any absolutist claims that we inhabit postmodern, resolutely non-modern times. Amidst a some-times apparently widespread sense that sociology either is extinct or else should be, the modern in Bauman continues to argue that sociology potentially enables. So in 1990 he published a text, *Thinking Sociologically*. It is one of the finest introductory sociology texts I know, for it does not condescend to its readers, or presume that they are necessarily young and fresh, only that they are readers of an introductory text, which therefore needs to work laterally, sufficient to be accessible while also working at levels of sophistication enough to provoke and excite. Definitions open the book. Sociology might be viewed as a tradition, or else as a culture, an activity into which newcomers are welcomed (or sometimes not). But these definitions would also be indicative of common sense, descriptive approaches to the task at hand. These approaches would take us to the object called sociology, but not into its content or labyrinth. The question then arises, what is distinctly sociological about these curiosities or activities and practices, other than that we name them in the same way? And what, then, is to be the basis upon which we discriminate between sociology, politics, anthropology, history, economics? Do these divisions not reflect divisions in the way that the world works? More common sense, even if it is professorial, the wisdom of the gatekeepers.

Where did we ever get the idea that human actions divide into a certain number of distinct types in the first place (1990: 4)? The systems of classification precede us, they are conventionalized, second-natured, and we are inducted into them as discrete professional cultures or language-games. In fact, these distinctions violate not only common sense but also good sense; we do not experience the social world as parcellized in this way, and this regardless of whether we are well-schooled or not. The boundaries all bleed and seep across into one another. One does not live now in politics, now in economics; one does not move from sociology to anthropology when travelling from England to Brazil, or from sociology to history when one grows a year older. In academic life, as elsewhere, it is the division of labour that is projected onto the mental map of the human world that we carry in our minds and then deploy in our deeds (1990: 5). The distinctions between disciplines, then, are not entirely arbitrary or accidental, but they are political and artificial. Disciplines are prostheses which we humans often mistake for the object of curiosity, as is our wont. We tell stories about our worlds through intellectual grids which very often tell us more about the grids than about the other, and we become bitterly defensive of these worldviews because of the academic premium on certainty, or being correct. But grids, or ways of seeing, we nevertheless need, if only we can recognize their actual contingency as against their inflationary effects.

Sociology cannot therefore be defined as everything, for in that case it would be nothing, it would have no distinguishing features at all. So Bauman offers us a first definition:

> What sets sociology apart and gives it its distinctive character is the habit of viewing human actions as *elements of wider figurations*: that is, of a non-random assembly of actors locked together in a web of *mutual dependency*,

dependency being a state in which the probability that the action will be undertaken and the chance of its success change in relation to what other actors are, or do, or may do. (1990: 7). So dependence, and its old friend, freedom, loom large in the elementary definition of sociology. Sociology, therefore, is a way of thinking about the world. Now comes another old associate, common sense. As we have seen in *Towards A Critical Sociology* (1976b), common sense is a staple of sociology, which can neither afford to ignore it nor take it for granted. Common sense is second nature, and in one way, it is exactly second nature which is the core concern of a critical sociology.

Bauman offers four possible ways of distinguishing the sociological sensibility from the logic of common sense. First, sociology, unlike common sense, makes an effort to subordinate itself to the rules of responsible speech. What does Bauman mean by this? We are all social animals, therefore we are all specialists or natural authorities on matters social. Prejudice or mere opinion thus often masquerades as sociology, and not only at the hands of non-specialists; sociologists in general suffer from a terrible tendency to generalize the particular, a tendency we need to recognize and to work against. Second, sociology claims to draw on a larger field of evidence in order to arrive at its judgement; no research, no right to speak when it comes to properly sociological (but not ethical, or political) matters. A third difference between sociology and common sense pertains to the way in which we seek to make sense of human reality. Sociology stands in opposition to the overly personalized worldview. It shifts, rather, from figurations (networks of dependencies) to actors and actions, seeking to make sense of the human condition through analysis of the manifold webs of human interdependency. Fourthly, and in some ways most significantly, sociology seeks to defamiliarize the familiar. Routine, habit and repetition all conspire together to generate familiarity, certainty, fixity. Thus:

> Familiarity is the staunchest enemy of inquisitiveness and criticism – and thus also of innovation and the courage to change. In an encounter with that familiar world ruled by habits and reciprocally reasserting beliefs, sociology acts as a meddlesome and often irritating stranger. (Bauman, 1990: 15)

Critical sociology is in this sense alien; little wonder it was viewed by its anti-semitic enemies as the Jewish discipline, modernist, mobile, cosmopolitan, dangerous; or that its aura is often caught up with and sometimes mistaken for that of socialism. Critical sociology is dirty-handed, both in the practical and the symbolic senses.

Throughout this discourse Bauman defines sociology by default as critical sociology. There is another sociology, or perhaps there are two more: there is the mainstream sociology which apologizes for modernism, and offers to help knock off its rough edges (Durksonianism), and there is the conservative, sometimes aristocratic or nostalgic sociology which we could trace back to de Tocqueville and forward, say, to some themes in the work of Robert Nisbet and John Carroll. Would these other sociologies conform to Bauman's four attributes? In different ways, the answer to this question is yes. Conservatives, for example, would simply render them otherwise; responsibility is paramount; one must know whereof one speaks; one ought seek out intelligibility, and still seek to defamiliarize, even though the points of comparison may be with the world we are alleged to have lost rather than with the goals we have yet to achieve (the latter, because they are always beyond us). As Bauman argues in *Towards a Critical Sociology* (1976b), it is mainstream sociology which can be expected to default, perhaps especially on the fourth criterion, for Durksonianism seeks implicitly or explicitly to familiarize the present rather than to defamiliarize the familiar. The radical observation is rather in sympathy with Castoriadis, that we have not always lived this way, which leaves the possibilities open rather than closed.

Sociology, for Bauman, then, is political or more directly, radical, for it moves around concerns such as freedom, dependence, solidarity, contingency. In this regard sociology indeed is dangerous, if only it lives up even to the most modest of its dreams, for to be critical is precisely to be open to arguments for change, in whatever direction (1990: 17). Bauman has set the trap: dare to think! dare to be critical! Now he employs a series of examples, both at the same time thematic and experiential, in order to open the field of sociology to its visitors. The first theme is freedom and dependence. Mutually constitutive, this couplet condenses much of the entire field of Bauman's work, revisiting themes elaborated earlier in *Freedom* (1988) and elsewhere, in *Memories of Class* (1982) and *Legislators and Interpreters* (1987). For freedom is configured with dependency, in ways that generate both slavery and domination or mutuality and cooperation. Here we see Bauman the pedagogue as hermeneut, for all that is of significance to us leads somewhere else, perhaps unexpected. Freedom thus leads into dependence; all our curiosities are but ways into the labyrinth of interpretation. So finally we can say that sociologically speaking the ratio between freedom and dependence is an indicator of the relative position a person or group occupies in society. What we call privilege appears, under closer scrutiny, as a higher degree of freedom at the expense of a lesser degree of freedom (1990: 36).

Bauman's style in this book is friendly, almost avuncular. He combines familiar or ordinary images or experiences with glimpses of the arguments that inform them, Freud, often especially Elias, Mead. The next interval, on Us and Them, follows the same strategy, example and insight, Schutz and Bateson. Us and Them raises questions of proximity, inclusion and exclusion, insiders and outsiders, reciprocity and hostility. Which leads, of course, to the Stranger. The stranger is not nobody, but somebody who does not belong. Hence Goffman returns, as the theorist of civil inattention, pretending that one does not look and does not see the other, a highly developed habit especially in urban spaces where one goes to be seen but not to see (Bauman, 1990: 67). Avoid the eyes! Avoidance of eye contact is the clearest modern prohibition, at least in the street, if not in the café. Enter Simmel, together with his stunning insight that urban life and abstract thinking grow together (Bauman, 1990: 68). The others, here, are truly othered; they become little more than the backdrop to our closed personal paths through the dense traffic of everyday life. Physical proximity persists, indeed heightens, but moral or ethical proximity is eroded. The great risk of modern society, then, is that civil inattention leads to moral indifference. Here strangers may not be enemies, but they may not appear at all; they risk falling between the categories we use to divide up the world, and slipping into nothingness (1990: 70).

How then do we interact? Through bonds of community, replete with the aura of tradition and comfort, or through organizational affiliation, by choice or circumstance. Communities consist of persons, organizations of roles. Both forms generate particular problems to do with conformism. Communities can submerge the individual within their bonds; organizations, by comparison, always run the risk that there is nobody home, for the administrative position is prior to its bearer. Here Bauman's discussant on total institutions is Goffman, rather than Foucault, where total institutions like prisons or asylums are enforced or compulsory, coercive communities (1990: 86), and the parallel by extension is the image of the totalitarian society as a mono-organizational institution, a form where there is no space available for anything other than the party-state and its apparatus. But in less closed situations than these, how do we go on? Now Bauman introduces gift and exchange as alternative forms of currency, both sociological staples and prime needs in everyday life, where love or friendship, and money, remain so elemental, whether we fancy ourselves as modern or postmodern.

Power and choice, self-preservation and the priority of moral duty lead to the themes of Nature and Culture. Agri-culture is not the only fruit; there is also homini-culture, the training of human individuals, imparting to them knowledge of the cultural code, so that they can read the social signs as well as learn to select and display them (1990: 151). As in Barthes' *Elements of Semiology*, the traffic light ceases to be a technical or technological object and becomes part of a whole system of signs and symbols, with moral and cultural effects built in, indicating a whole universe of possible meanings. Through culture humans strive, again, towards order; for culture is a proselytizing or missionary activity: it seeks to convert, and it spurns heresy. When several cultural designs coexist the possibility of mutual tolerance or pluralism emerges, but it lives in tension with the larger impact of the quest for order (Bauman, 1990: 160). State and nation, in turn, are implicated in culture and order. States work through pastoral power, power exercised 'in the best interests' of the subjects who need to be protected against their own morbid inclinations (1990: 167). The nation, in comparison, is an imagined community, which effectively becomes real through the conduct of war. Nation-states claim legitimacy partly through claims to nature or primordial belonging through myths of origin (1990: 171–3).

The idea of the nation-state coincides with the arrival of modernity. But the very success of modernity in its search for artificial order is the cause of its deepest, most worrying ailments: the incredible results of an over-developed division of labour where the pursuit of social rationality generates generalized irrationality, all of which comes back to haunt us, as second nature. Each of us becomes as specialized as our sphere of the system or private life necessitates; we all become professional idiots, even just in dealing with domestic technology (1990: 197). The skill levels we need just to cope with everyday life never stand still, but keep changing. We are consumers of expertise, mortified that we might miss out, look stupid by coming last in the technological race; nothing old will ever do for very long, heaven forfend that you might use a little book and pencil rather than an electronic diary. All these gadgets in turn add up to 'identitykit' lives (1990: 205). It is not, contra Huey P. Lewis, in fact hip to be square, unless this involves buying new means of identity; for styles might be desperately recycled, but the fashion goods we purchase as commodities must be new. The right to revolt, however, remains an individual rather than a tribal affair (1990: 213).

So much for life – what of sociology? Bauman concludes *Thinking Sociologically* with the suggestion that there is an internal alternative. We can choose to follow Durkheim, with his insistence that social science really is scientific, and therefore at once both different and superior to its liberal arts competitors. But this brings us back to where we began, with the problem whether sociology has its own distinct object of knowledge or whether, rather, it is somehow queen of the human sciences, taking in all that it surveys. An alternative would be to follow Weber, where natural science is anything but the model for our activity. In this way of thinking, human reality is different, unique, because it is subjective in various differing ways. Perhaps, then, we still face the same choice as that posited in *Towards a Critical Sociology* (1976b), between science and hermeneutics, Durksonianism and critique, even if these days there may be more critics crossing the lines, seeking to use Durkheim for interpretative, anthropological purposes in cultural sociology. Bauman identifies a third practical strategy, but it is not that of American cultural sociology. Rather, it is the reformist, progressive school of social science associated historically with the Chicago School. Less philosophical than pragmatic, and pragmatist, this variant follows some Durkheimian sympathies in that it seeks to analyse and redeem those social pathologies which modernity throws up and does not automatically or 'naturally' resolve or reform (1990: 224). The risk here is that sociology becomes managerial, is assimilated into the social system whose critique is its other purpose; that sociology disappears into the state.

Richard Rorty gets the last word in *Thinking Sociologically*: 'if we take care of freedom, truth and goodness will take care of themselves' (1990: 232). If Rorty here unwittingly carries the torch for the cause of critical sociology, with Elias as its undercurrent and Durkheim providing the main and predominant alternative variant of sociology (whether as science par excellence or as diagnosis of social pathology and its remedy), one other leonine head has disappeared in the process. Where's Charlie? Marx, with whom *Towards A Critical Sociology* (1976b) closed, has disappeared from these critical horizons, in letter, if not in spirit. For marxism's fate across these years is to return to the critical culture from whence it came. And this particular claim of Rorty's is not that far from a Marx for the 1990s (Beilharz, 1994b). We still follow Marx, even when we do not name him. Marx disappears into Bauman's work like labour into the product.

In actuality, all three strategies or futures for sociology coexist, even if some overpower the others; there is a kind of alliance between the first and the third, Durkheim and the state, which practically marginalizes the second, hermeneutics or critique. Probably this helps explain why it is that Bauman takes a more critical stand on American than on British sociology. The purpose of sociology is to add ambivalence. American sociology is the great success story, even still today; yet its victory is discernibly also its failure, for it has been achieved through the reform–managerial synthesis at the expense of critique. Bauman's view of British sociology seems to be that, at least since the 1960s, its critical and cultural credentials, whether local or continental, better balance out the limits of the local tradition of social administration. This also seems to explain Bauman's higher-than-common levels of critical enthusiasm for the project of Anthony Giddens, though now even Giddens seems to align sociology with the prospect of state power through New Labour in Britain, rather than its critique. Bauman's views on Giddens are scattered throughout his writings, though there are two sources which warrant inclusion here.

Bauman draws Giddens' work and the field of hermeneutics together in his contribution to Held and Thompson's *Festschrift* for Giddens (Bauman, 1989b). Perhaps it is the fate of ageing sociologists all to become reformers rather than radicals. Certainly Giddens' earlier work, like Habermas', was closer to hermeneutics than to the idea of the system. Bauman is full of praise for a Giddens who named hermeneutics as the path sociology should take, the sole alternative to the hilarities of collective amnesia and the Columbus complex (1989b: 35). Here he parallels Giddens' structuration theory with Elias' idea of figuration, the point in both cases being that structure is carried out, it does not float above the players like a *langue* or the system of language in structuralism, but has to be enacted to become apparent. The game, whether say of politics or football, is comprehensible only in its activity (Bauman, 1989b: 39). Simultaneously, however, our need for understanding cannot be satisfied by the game-caller or the after-match interview with the participants. Figuration seems to capture the problem better than structuration, which both reproduces it semantically and gives away the open secret, that this is a nominative solution to a conceptual, or rather a practical problem (1989b: 49). Sociology, on the basis of this judgement, remains too much caught within the nineteenth century. Its central task, indicated by Bauman in discussion of Giddens, is to revise the theory of society rather than the idea of social action (1989b: 55). Perhaps it is this which predisposes Bauman to the larger idea of the postmodern.

Giddens' sociology consists of an interpretative and analytical beginning, in books like *Capitalism and Modern Social Theory*, and *The Class Structure of the Advanced Societies*, which leads into an overextended attempt at synthesis, marked along the way by significant but more regional studies of issues such as the nation-state and violence, passing in turn to political and personal essays about intimacy, private life, and the emergence of New Labour in Britain as a political force potentially responsive to these changes. Bauman responds to some of more recent essays in a review of the anxiously titled book by Giddens called *In Defence of Sociology*.

Unlike, say, Habermas, whose sociological work remains ambitious and systematic at the same time as he acts out the role of the public intellectual in Germany, Giddens seems to have shifted from one role to the next. In the 1990s, he has become the intellectual advocate of Blairism, or the New Labour Third Way in Britain; his books have become shorter, more popular in style and political in orientation. As Bauman notes, Giddens is both the prime-mover and the secretary of British Sociology; via the Polity Press, he continues its European imprint, and in his own essays he monitors the results of the process. Bauman's sense here, as earlier, is that it is mainstream American sociology which is generating the crisis; probably the Americans would disagree, at least in public. Of course there have been various controversies over the question of American academic imperialism, and whether or not sociology might return 'home' to the New Europe after the fall of the Berlin Wall. Only sociology, at least since the Chicago School, has been as recognizably American as it is European, making the distinction less than easy to observe, let alone police. Bauman's worry about American sociology here is that its only obvious imperative seems to be 'business as usual'. Managerialism rules (Bauman, 1997b).

One possible line of interpretation here would be that, as American sociology's failure lies in its very success, so European sociology has maintained a more dispersed emphasis across its romantic and critical streams. Durksonianism has dominated the American scene. Critical theory has not been a major strength in American sociology, though its own internal tensions may well belie this; after all, American sociology also begins with Tocqueville and contains critical thinkers like Richard Sennett and Craig Calhoun along the way. Giddens and Bauman seem to be suggesting here that Americanism sinks together with modernism or with the sociology of modernity. Sociology would be less well connected into, say, the British establishment historically, and would therefore be less likely to share its mentality, whereas American social engineering and sociology were mutually constitutive; with the end of one, it is less than clear what we might expect of the other. In other words, the fate of American sociology has been tied to the figure of the academic as legislator. Only Giddens, too, now offers advice to the Prince. This New Labour Prince speaks a postmodern language, of a third, local, personal way somewhere between capitalism and socialism. If Bauman remains in this sense the sociologist of modernity, then perhaps it is Giddens who really represents postmodern sociology.

A Postmodern Sociology?

By the mid-1990s, the work of Zygmunt Bauman was identified more than any other in its reception as postmodern sociology. Giddens, in turn, played some good part in the promotion of this image, as for example in his cover endorsement of *Life in Fragments*: 'Bauman, for me, has become *the* theorist of postmodernity. With exceptional brilliance and originality, he has developed a position with which everyone now has to reckon'. Bauman thus appears as *the* postmodern sociologist, the sociological equivalent of Lyotard or Baudrillard or Jameson or Foucault (the English language reception of ideas routinely obscuring the distinction not only between postmodernism and postmodernity but also between the postmodern, structuralism and poststructuralism). Yet as we have seen, Bauman remains stubbornly defensive of the sociological vocation, itself often identified by its modernist baggage, statism and reformism, as the very discipline of modernity itself. What would it mean to speak of, or practice, a postmodern sociology? Bauman discusses this issue extensively in the essays gathered together in the collection called *Intimations of Postmodernity* (1992). Bauman establishes the field by defining postmodernity as a state of mind (1992: vii). The postmodern state of mind is the radical victory of modern – critical, restless, unsatisfied, insatiable – culture over the modern society it aimed to improve through throwing it wide open to its own potential (1992: viii). Reason has disenchanted the world; the point is to re-enchant it, and this is one aspect of the enthusiasm we encounter for the postmodern.

The idea of the postmodern travels into sociology from art, for some, more specifically, from architecture. Modernism, the synthetic international style that runs after the fact from Bauhaus to postwar New York, is always contested internally by the avant-garde, surrealism and Dada, where art is anti-art (or anti-art is art, or not art). Modernism in art travelled together with the apparent victory of modernism in postwar American society – growth, progress, abundance, certainty about the world and our place in it. The solution to all outstanding problems as might present themselves was simple – more. As Simmel had anticipated, the surge of modernity brought with it the growth of abstraction, and so abstract art and universal, stripped functional style in architecture came to rule. Until the restless flux of modernism began to upset this style, which itself became institutionalized and therefore open to criticism and change. In art and in architecture collage was revived; postmodern architects bathed in the promiscuity of mixing styles that hitherto were kept clinically, or classically, apart. All the bits were starting to move around, or so it seemed; and so, as Bauman expresses it, postmodern sociology appears as a mimetic representation of the postmodern condition. If culture or its representation or perception changes . . . then sociology will change too (1992: 42).

It is not the world that has changed, however, so much as our attitude towards it. Perhaps, then, sociology should also follow the example of collage, or pastiche; perhaps the possibility of eclecticism is already built into the principle of pluralism. But if the postmodern is an attitude, rather than a period or a type of society like capitalist democracy or totalitarianism, then modernity nevertheless remains, and sociology with it. This latter is one dominant response on the part of sociologists to the arrival of the postmodern; to sneer, to walk away, or simply to insist that the old analytical tools still work, for the nature of the problem is unchanged by such new Columbus discoveries (1992: 43). Some such scepticism is well-grounded, both because what sociology has achieved is also worth valuing, however critically, but again because we have had such radical breaks trumpeted out before; one such false alarm was called postindustrialism. Indeed, sociology as a discipline is not only defined by its modernism, and its immersion in the present, but also by its traditionalism, manifest in its commitment to a recently invented canon, and by its futurism, evident in its tendency to anticipate that what lies ahead is rather closer than it later turns out to be.

As Bauman observes, sociology is also the discipline perhaps most obsessed with its own crisis, contingency and possible extinction. The crisis of society, real or imaginary, also presents itself as the crisis of sociology; sociology is always in crisis, too close to the house of power or else too far away, lost in navel-gazing irrelevance. At the same time, sociology in its more confident mood presents itself as the cure for social crisis, offering the solution to modernity's riddles solved. In this, however, sociology risks missing the sense that the nature of problems or crises involved have shifted; the logic of habit and inertia suggest that we are always ready to fight the last intellectual battle, not the present one. Sociology is like the drunk who looks for his lost keys under the only available street light. What if the world has actually changed? This is the possibility which Bauman is prepared tentatively to entertain:

> The suggestion I propose to consider is the following: in present-day society, consumer conduct (consumer freedom geared to the consumer market) moves steadily into the position of, simultaneously, the cognitive and moral focus of

life, the integrative bond of the society, and the focus of systemic management. (1992: 49)

Little wonder that Marx is of less direct use to us here, for what Bauman is prepared to contemplate is the possibility that culture is organized increasingly around consumption rather than production; that production, from being the locus of popular life in the twentieth century, is symbolically displaced by consumption as the primary source of meaning in everyday life. But Marx persists, as well: for with consumption firmly established as the locus of, and the playground for individual freedom, the future of capitalism looks more secure than ever (1992: 51). The good citizen is refigured less as the good producer than as the good consumer. Post-modernity, then, is not a complete new social form or system so much as it might be an aspect of a fully-fledged, viable social system which has come to replace the 'classical' modern, capitalist society and therefore needs to be theorized according to its own logic (1992: 52).

What kind of sociology would be adequate to this task? The difference of emphasis which Bauman introduces now is that we face a choice between a postmodern sociology and a sociology of postmodernity. The first, rather than being an oxymoron or a redressed modernist sociology, would take the postmodern itself for granted, as the explanation rather than as what needs to be explained. The second – a sociology of postmodernity – is Bauman's own preference, as it posits the postmodern as the puzzle, that which needs to be explained. Obviously an unmodified modern or modern-ist sociology will not be up to this task; yet the implication of Bauman's preference is that the tradition of sociology is continuous, exactly as its object, society, transforms (1992: 65). Bauman's response to the choice, postmodern sociology or sociology of postmodernity, is then a transitional strategy, for it privileges neither the old sociology nor the newly discovered postmodern to the exclusion of the other. The challenge is neither to dig in nor to give way to 'anything goes', but to work in the field between, which leaves us in principle both still located in our traditions and yet open to the possibility of the new, this latter not least, as Bauman hints, because the coincidence of globalization and the postmodern simultaneously under-mines both the nation-state and the modular social systems theory of sociology which corresponds to it (1992: 65). Bauman does not labour the last point, but it hangs heavy. As Touraine has argued, the residual nega-tive effects of sociology's origins include its obsession with system, structure and stasis rather than with change (Touraine, 1992). The modernism of sociology is at its most evident in this identification of society with system and nation-state, this modular prejudice which presumes the nation-state/society to be self-contained, and adds in the world-system or regions as an afterthought, as the sum or subsection of the national parts. This view is hopeless, and not only because it adds in imperialism or cross-cultural traffic after the fact, as a result rather than a primary reality of modernity. For if patterns of consumption as well as production take on a globalized character, just as locality is reasserted, then the central terms of reference of the old modernist sociology are jeopardized.

This is the new context in which the condition of mainstream American sociology appears to Bauman to be most problematical. For American sociology was born in the mid-west in the heyday of the twin processes of urbanization and industrialization, massive immigration and new starts (1992: 76). These problems persist, in the so-called third world, in Mexico and Brazil as well as in Chicago, and as immigration expands as one of the natural narratives of modernity. The American propensity, however, is often to imagine the entire world as though it were the United States, perhaps with the odd nodding recognition of Canada and Mexico. None of this will pass muster any longer, given the extraordinary permeability of national borders, not least of all in North America, for labour and consumption if not for reciprocal intellectual traffic. But it is not the case that Bauman is smug or certain about the postmodern. Indeed, in another essay, 'Is There a Postmodern Sociology?', Bauman plays with the idea that the term postmodern is redundant (1992: 93). Postmodern argument can be playful in the distracting sense, where the intellectual becomes the clown, and the notion of performance replaces that of ethics or politics, analysis or critique. Certainly the debate about the postmodern has generated a surplus of stylized intellectual combat, challenging all, participants and observers, to take sides and kick the heads of their enemies. On the ground, in the streets of cities along the American continent, the problems of life still look modern. Even though the word 'postmodern' now appears in popular media, in the press and sit-coms, it is, as Bauman acknowledges, primarily the novel experience of just one, but crucial social category of contemporary society: the intellectuals (1992: 94). The postmodern is a semantic confession that intellectuals can no longer behave as though they were the legislators of the modern world. We do not set the aesthetic rules of taste, we do not know better than others how to save the world, we can translate or explain, but the world does not follow our rational edicts or insistences. To be postmodern, in this way, is to rediscover self-doubt, to contemplate again the necessity of limits to the developmental manias of modernity.

If Bauman's cautionary note is strong, his conclusion is framed by the sense of possibility rather than the obligatory self-flagellation of the guilty intellectual.

> To sum up: if the radical manifestos proclaiming the end of sociology and social philosophy 'as we know them' seem unfounded, equally unconvincing is the pretence that nothing of importance has happened and that there is nothing to stop 'business as usual'. (1992: 105)

While it is in no way doomed, sociology must adjust itself to new conditions in order to self-reproduce, and to grow. These issues are revisited, finally, in the essay 'A Sociological Theory of Postmodernity'. The title itself suggests a settling clarity of terms: postmodernity needs to be taken seriously, but as the cultural problem rather than the conceptual solution. Postmodernity here is the spirit of modernity looking back, in order to see forward. Postmodernity may be interpreted as a fully developed modernity taking full measure of the anticipated consequences of its historical work (1992: 187). Postmodernity is modernity conscious of itself. It is this very difference which calls out a sociology of the postmodern condition, though as Bauman insists earlier, this is not a matter of judging the postmodern by modernist sociological criteria. The postmodern has distinctive features of its own, which modernist sociology cannot capture, not least because of its own traditionalism. Images like stability, society as the organism, the telos of progress can no longer be presumed. The image of society as system or mechanism, similarly, is disabling. Perhaps even the idea of society has to go, tainted as it is by all of the above connotations. For if 'society' implies fixity, then it may well be sociality or the interdependence of freedom and heteronomy which is actually our concern (1992: 100). Structure, in any case, is now less important than agency, habitat or *habitus*, the way in which we go on in institutions across all senses of the idea, from the dyad or group to the organization or movements of civil society.

Under the postmodern condition, according to Bauman, the habitat is a complex system rather than a mechanical system. Two parts of significant distinction emerge: habitat is unpredictable, and is not controlled by statistically significant factors. This is why the older sociological metaphors of organic or mechanical structure will no longer work. Sociology was built on the image of the human body, and then the machine; the corresponding image of system and isolable subsystem no longer bite (1992: 192). It follows that, contrary to Durkheim's sociology, there can be no 'social brain' or controlling centre. Actors and agencies depend on each other, but there is no clear overall pattern of dependence or coordination. Patterns of constraint, consequently, are also less predictable. Indeterminacy rules. The ways of life which were relatively stable in high modernism – full employment, Keynesianism, nuclear family, male breadwinner – are also displaced: 'The existential modality of the agents is therefore one of insufficient determination, inconclusiveness, motility and rootlessness' (1992: 193). Patterns of identity formation and maintenance are less predictable or stable. The more or less fixed idea of a life-project is displaced by the process of self-constitution. The old romantic idea of making and remaking the self becomes part of ordinary life, mediated by the consumption of fashion and style. Both individuals and institutions become more volatile. From this it follows, further, that body-cultivation becomes a way of reforming or reassembling the self. Even this restlessness must be institutionalized, or organizationally underpinned. Second nature becomes something like the will-to-self-transformation, and this takes cultural as well as individual forms (1992: 195).

While all this has a kind of Hollywood flavour, Bauman also wants to indicate its openings, and not only its closures. One effect of these changes, according to Bauman, is that politics is reborn in the realm of personal lifestyle or habitus. This is a process which coincides with the reduction of state responsibility for politics or policy. Markets are thus strengthened, but so, potentially, are the fibres of civil society, for actors can take on the challenge to remake themselves in various different ways; the heavy hand of mindless conformism does not always reign. Politics might at least potentially shift from claims to redistribution to arguments concerning freedom, or human rights (1992: 197). Arguments to citizenship or solidarity may be reconfigured in this way, but they do not disappear; to believe that they could is to identify politics with its modernist forms. Politics may develop in at least four different possible ways. Tribal politics is one possible path; in Bauman's understanding, this is potentially retrogressive, as tribalism coincides with some forms of retroactive communitarianism, though tribalism of course can also take on more playful forms, as in the Italian cultural radicals of the 1970s, the Metropolitan Indians. Another possibility is the politics of desire. Again, the politics of desire can lead to encouraging autonomy through the reconstitution of sexual identity, but it can also lead to the aestheticization of the body-image at the expense of the suffering of actually existing bodies. A third possibility is the politics of fear, an associated effect of Beck's 'risk society', where fear say of pollution or contamination immobilizes civil society and ultimately expands the authority of the newly emerging ranks of risk-experts. Fourth, there still remains a possible politics of desired certainty, or the manipulation of trust through simulated politics. Here politics becomes impression management, and the private lives of public figures become the most significant measure of their good character in office (1992: 200).

The problem is not, then, that postmodernity swallows up politics – modernity already made a solid start at that – so much as it is that the expressions of politics change. At the same time as these uncertainties appear, Bauman's sense is that the challenges of a postmodern ethics confront us anew: amidst all this choice, we are forced to learn how to deal with choice and with responsibility for the other. We can still walk away from choice, turn our heads or the TV channel, but it is arguably more difficult to do this than before, because we know that individual responsibility counts and that large-scale organizations are incapable of responsibility. So what does this mean for a postmodern sociology? Bauman's point is that we can no longer imagine that we inhabit the world described by rule–governed diagrams of society in terms of inputs and outputs or four-box schemes. The challenge of self-reflexivity can no longer be defined mechanically or functionally by my role in the system. There is still a system, it still holds together, but it allows some of us some room to move, as it puts upon us the responsibility to follow the rules either dutifully, or creatively.

Exit, Pursued by a Bear

Change is, or ought to be, the founding curiosity of sociology; only sociology, like its bearers, is fragile, habitual, given to repetition and to reinventing the wheel. How could it be other? For sociology, too, is a cultural form. Two major facts govern Bauman's sociological trajectory, and the path of his life. One is the dominance and eventual disappearance of socialism as a culture, or counterculture of modernity. The other is the apparent transformation of culture itself as the cult of Reason is exposed, not least in the aftermath of the Holocaust, and as modernism comes unstuck as an intellectual attitude or cultural form in the 1970s. Modernity, however, is like the sun that fails ever fully to set upon us, so that sociology, too, maintains its potential vocation as the critique of modernity: but it needs to earn it, not just claim it. The prospect of a postmodern sociology lies before us, this as an activity, not just as a promise. Do we then change, or remain the same? Bauman's wager is that we remain anthropologically prepossessed with universal problems – sex, love, death, responsibility, maintenance of the self, care for others, putting food on the table, sweeping up after. But the forms of these activities change, and so does second nature. This is as close as we may get to a sociological basis for hope; and this may be why it is that Bauman has staked such a claim on the idea of the postmodern in sociology, and remains open to the possibility of a post-modern sociology. For to contemplate these possibilities is to open the chance that we might push away the dead weight of modernity, or at least of the dark side of modernity, as the historic period which has delivered us into a century of horrors from Gallipoli to Auschwitz and Hiroshima and on to Kosovo. History, as Marx said, progresses by its bad side. As Bauman says somewhere, the average Pole believes nothing good can come of the past. If Bauman dwells upon the depths of the dark side of modernity, this is because he wants us to believe that we might still step closer to the bright side of postmodernity. For postmodernity is not only the cultural self-consciousness of modernity, for Bauman; it is the promise of modernity, after the threat.

3   Intellectuals and Utopians

Sociology, the textbooks tell us, depends on self-reflexivity; for sociologists seem to have a characteristic knack of knowing what is wrong in what other people do, but never ourselves. Zygmunt Bauman's sociology is persistently self-reflexive; his view is that we, too, are part of the problem, indeed that we as intellectuals or legislators aspirant have been a big part of the problem of modernity. Our attraction to the modern possibility of change sometimes leads us to value change over everything else; yet we cannot deny, either, that the world needs changing, even if it is less immediately clear than ever exactly whose responsibility this task is. Thinking, acting, interpreting, dreaming, these are nevertheless some of our major activities. Seeking out the balance seems to be the most impossible of challenges, yet it is also the most interminable.

Socialism: The Active Utopia

Utopia is a ubiquitous presence in the lives of moderns. We love it, we hate it; we know that the world needs change, yet we resist or detest the changes sponsored by others, which often seem to make the world less inhabitable than it was before. In the twentieth century the story intensifies, for now we encounter utopia in power, in the Soviet experiment and then under fascism. Utopia, dystopia, Orwell's *1984*, Huxley's *Brave New World*, alternative models of living from Shakers to hippies, dreams to go forwards or back, utopia seems almost to enclose the modern experience, encompassing both the desire for self-creation and the horrors of rational mastery.

Attitudes towards utopia are also likely to shift historically, and conjuncturally; these are not simply matters of personal taste. The practical and theoretical western enthusiasm of the 1960s for utopia indicates the relative abundance of that moment; we had the luxury of realizing then that social arrangements did not mirror economic potentials. Utopianism, however, can also be romantic or modernizing, as the themes of *Memories of Class* (1982) suggest. Some utopias are born in the blackest of moments, though we should also contemplate the fact that there are, in a sense, no utopias after Auschwitz; or at least, utopia then becomes contemplative again rather than active.

Zygmunt Bauman's vision of utopia was positive when, in 1976, he published *Socialism: The Active Utopia* (1976a). This was a good moment in his life; settled in Leeds, after years of disappointment and harassment, he dedicated the book to their twins, 'To Irena and Lydia – my twin utopias'. Actually-existing socialism, or its concrete representatives, may have expelled the Baumans from Poland, but in spirit with that period of Marx-Renaissance, Zygmunt Bauman opened his book with a characteristic claim: 'Socialism descended upon nineteenth-century Europe as utopia' (1976a: 9). Reality was to be measured against the ideal, against utopia; it was the latter, the project of socialism, which remained both defensible and desirable. But more, utopia is real; it is part of us, that part which remains uneasy at the sense of the achievement or arrival of our great civilizations. If normality generates conformity, then utopianism is vital even in its most fantastic or ridiculous guises. Societies like ours, based on the hegemony of instrumental reason, need mental space to discuss ends, and hopes. Utopias are significant, for Bauman, in four generic ways. First, utopias relativize the present. They offer us criteria other than immanent measures in order to take stock of where we are, and where we are heading. They open horizons of comparison, but unlike history, they also evoke future possibilities, and not only past achievements, more or less imaginary (1976a: 13). Yet, second, utopias are also significant because they are aspects of culture in which possible extrapolations of the present may be explored. Utopias are driven by hope, but they can also be concrete; they express the possible hopes of an age, and they say something about its capacities (1976a: 15). Third, utopias are useful because they pluralize; they generate dissensus rather than false harmony, even though individual utopian projects might themselves enthuse for false harmony or stasis. Utopias split the shared reality we inhabit into a series of competing projects for the future and assessments of the present. This is why one person's utopia is another's dystopia. Utopias are political, in the best sense of the word, in that they express distinct and competing images of the good society, images whose expression often coincides with the activity of distinct social groups (1976a: 15). Fourth, utopias do in fact exert enormous influence on the actual course of historical events. Utopias have an 'activating presence'; yesterday's utopia – as in the idea of guaranteed income – may be on today's social policy agenda.

As Bauman summarizes, utopia is an image of a future and better world, which is not at all inevitable so much as it is desirable; which is critical of that which exists, and in this sense is beyond practical realization; and which relies politically on the possibility of collective action (1976a: 17). Not all utopias, then, are socialist, but socialism has been the most prominent member of the family. Of course, the figure of utopia is also classical, arcing back at least to Plato; but modern utopias are different, and this is where socialism comes into its prominence. For socialism has always been caught up with the sense of change which we identify as modern, and this whether positively, as futuristic, or negatively, as romantic in tenor (1976a: 18–19). Bacon, not Plato, is the driving face of its earlier vision; the distinction in Bauman's mind is similar to that in Durkheim's lectures on socialism, where communism looks back, to simplicity, and socialism is a modern, future-orientated and modernizing force (Durkheim, 1959). The commune seeks stasis; socialism, by comparison, is complicit in the very restlessness of modernity itself. Socialism mirrors capitalism, and this is one of its weaknesses as well as its strengths – it seeks out perfectibility rather than perfection (1976a: 19). Thus the complicity of socialism in social engineering, and ultimately in Jacobinism. Jacobinism is based conceptually on the image of the weak individual who needs only to be led by Those Who Know (1976a: 21). Jacobinism is a kind of utopianism based on contempt for the impassive, the ordinary, for the present, the impure, the unwashed (1976a: 22). Marx short-circuited this logic of contempt and leadership only by introducing the impossible, the idea that capitalism automatically generates its own fatal economic contradictions, or else, its own proletarian gravediggers. This false marxian solution to the problem of political organization in turn opens the door for the Bolsheviks, or the New Prince as the missing link to fuse the gap between the proletariat and history (1976a: 24).

Now Bauman confronts a theme which is to anticipate the path of his life's work into the 1990s: the problem of order. As he announces, with stark clarity, 'It is only recently that we have begun to realize the extent to which modern thought is prompted by the cravings of order' (1976a: 28). While it is less than controversial to observe that the utopian impulse often historically takes architectural form, Bauman's concern here is rather to probe into the motivation involved. For architecture is co-terminous with the thoroughly modern, scientific, social engineering attitude. Utopianism is based on the quest for order (1976a: 29). With the advent of modernity, order shifts from the realm of 'nature' to that of *techne*; this is a fact both 'real' and 'utopian' in its dimensions, for modernity is the field of social self-constitution. The anthropological and ethical issue here is whether we, as moderns, are prepared to live with the mess, or whether we are to become obsessed with the idea of cleaning it up, once-and-for-all (1976a: 30). As Bauman notes, the central utopian socialists, including Saint-Simon, Marx and Bellamy all remained deeply ambivalent on this score. Their work combined in different ways the lust for change and progress together with the very different, residual sense of loss of the past. Perhaps this is why Marx and Bellamy remained caught between Durkheim's imagined options, trapped between communism and socialism, stretched across the desire for simplicity and the thrust towards dynamism.

The emphasis in Bauman's argument, however, is on the distinction between the industrializing socialist intellectuals like Marx and the alternative currents which valued nostalgic dreams about the precapitalist world we had lost (1976a: 31). As Bauman acknowledges,

> Even the most ardent preachers of the new industrial world must have drawn their definition of order, as a safe and predictable situation founded on the regularity and recurrence of human conduct, from the living memory of the past, since it was never demonstrated by the system currently in existence. (1976a: 31)

Utopias, then, will not neatly be classified as exclusively oriented to the past
or to the future; progress and nostalgia, hope and memory will always be
caught up together. The real dividing line runs between the preachers of
greater complexity and admirers of simplicity, where simplicity conjures up
the image of return.

If the presence of Durkheim is often apparent behind arguments in
sociology, so does the ghost of Ferdinand Tönnies shadow many of its
concerns. Bauman acknowledges this directly when he aligns the value
of simplicity with the image of *Gemeinschaft* (1976a: 31). *Gemeinschaft* or
traditional community works as the usually unstated image by which much
of contemporary sociology still will measure the present; modern sociology,
that is to say, has at its heart a deeply traditionalistic core. Marx, too, was a
follower of Tönnies without ever knowing it; for what else could the
critique of alienation imply than a return to simplicity? For Marx was not
only the son of the steam engine; and Tönnies, who historically followed
him, was also a socialist and a utopian.

Socialism has been, and to some extent still is for Bauman in 1976, the
modern utopia. Or else, and here he quotes Tom Bottomore, socialism is
the counterculture of capitalism, both within and without it. Yet if socialism has been historically important, its significance as utopia is more
powerfully as the not yet. If it is realized, as state power, then it will die; at
the other extreme, utopia which rests always somewhere beyond would
seem merely illusory (1976a: 36–7). Yet it is modernity which ultimately
frames socialism, and not capitalism alone; it is modernity, and not just
capitalism, which is the problem, and in a certain perverse sense it will
therefore be modernity (or later, the post modern), which will be the
solution; not socialism. For socialism is also caught up with, continuous
with liberalism and not only capitalism (1976a: 42). More precisely,

> The socialist utopia could present itself as a genuine substitute for the bourgeois
> way of dealing with the issues of modernity, or as a further stage into which the
> previous stages smoothly and imperceptibly merge. (1976a: 48)

But the family resemblances across the different socialisms are weak, and
dispersed, as in Wittgenstein's sense; they resemble each other, but only in
mirroring a different feature. Bauman now addresses Durkheim's use of the
specific category socialism to denote the idea of state-directed economy.
But this, too, is a specific rather than generic image of socialism, and it
privileges images of the desirable over the actually achieved (1976a: 50).
Socialism is made a programme, more than a critical spirit, which is to
presume that the utopia can be realized concretely, like a builder's plan.
This is to substitute an accountant's conception of socialism for its ideal
of freedom, or equality. For socialism has these two goals, freedom and
equality, both of which have been trampled on by its enthusiasts (1976a:
53). But it is also marxism, as an ideology, which opens this slide into
economism and grey industrialism. For it is in the hands of its marxist

spokesmen that socialism is centred upon and thus reduced to economy, or 'necessity'; whereas early marxism, and alternative streams of socialism actually sought to problematize economy itself, not to harness but to transform it. The workers' utopia thus in a certain sense became a bourgeois utopia (1976a: 58).

Bauman earlier in his text, as we have noted, clears his throat on Gramsci's idea of the New Prince, the party to end all parties. Certainly the historical trajectory of Gramsci's own thought is away from council communism and towards the new party; likely under fascism and in Mussolini's prison he could think no other. At this point of his discussion, however, Bauman returns to Gramsci, for whatever the contradictions of the Sardinian's thought his legacy to the Marx-renaissance was among the richest, and Bauman had been contemplating this since the early 1960s, well before the English-speaking new left discovered Gramsci. Further, just as Gramsci was less ideologically available to the thinkers of the Budapest School, who recoiled at mere mention of the New Prince, so was Lukács more part of the problem for Bauman than of its solution.

Why Gramsci? Ideology, culture, civil society were keywords in the reception of his marxism, offering an alternative link to the Bolshevik Party between the socialist idea and its subjects, an argument at once more sophisticated and more democratic in its timbre. Where economy ruled, for the orthodox marxists, for Gramsci humans did, even if in manners mediated variously through habit, custom and belief or common sense. Gramsci stood almost alone in viewing socialism as a popular challenge, neither as an historic inevitability, as in Kautsky, nor as something to be seized, as per Lenin. State and economy mattered, for Gramsci, but citizens inhabited civil society, which was henceforth where socialists might direct their attentions. The struggle for socialism, for Bauman as for Gramsci, is the struggle for a new culture (1976a: 65–8). But Gramsci, of course, appeals also to intellectuals, not only because he was one, but also because he takes intellectuals seriously; we know one of us when we see one. Popular culture counts, then, but so do the intellectuals who are its cultivators. While Kautsky viewed social democracy as the confluence of socialism and the working class – an idea and an agent – Gramsci more accurately conceived it as the project of a potential class alliance or new historic bloc including intellectuals and workers. To acknowledge the importance of the intellectuals, as Gramsci did, was also potentially to foreground them as a problem, as the aspiring social ventriloquists ready to educate and to speak for the uncultured proletariat. At least, on Gramsci's view, we would be spared the pathetic comedy of intellectuals masquerading as pantomime proletarians, at the beginning of the long drama which ends: 'we rule you; we fool you; we eat for you; we shoot you, we serve all'. The Bolshevik experiment acted on the possibility that economy, not culture, still ruled; that to solve one problem would still imaginably solve the other. Yet the spirit of marxism, as Bauman concludes, was not about the management of the economy, and not even about forms of ownership, but about the activity of the masses. Lenin took the baton, but was unable to run with it (1976a: 76); perhaps he was actually running somewhere else.

The history of marxism, in any case, was transformed by the Bolshevik initiative. The Soviets were compelled to make a modernity of a particular kind, rather than a socialism of a marxian kind. This meant that the Soviets were faced with an impossible challenge: not only to generate a modern economy, but also a modern culture and forms of legitimation with it (1976a: 81). This was exactly the feature which Gramsci had discerned, later and at a distance; seizing state power, as in the Soviet experience, was deceptively easy; the problems came later, and were grounded rather in civil society, or perhaps in its weakness in this case. Nevertheless, in Bauman's eyes, one major problem in pre-revolutionary Russia was to be located in the fact that the marxists belonged to the emerging civil society rather than to the state; state power was not thrust upon them, but the change in mentality across the two spheres was nevertheless dramatic (1976a: 83).

Lenin identified his party with the people, against the actually existing population. Both the people, and the individual were occluded in that process, conceptually and politically. Seeking to sidestep the stage of individuation, as the Bolsheviks did, could only lead to the complete subjugation of the individual by a totally alienated social power (1976a: 89). No individuals, no possibilities for democracy. Yet the Soviet experience was a path through modernity, of a particular kind. It was a modernizing revolution, bringing together industrialization, urbanization, nation- and state-building, which compressed and out-achieved earlier capitalist processes of primitive accumulation.

The dominant image of socialist utopia was thus transformed, industrialized, flattened out; utopia was realized, in a sense, and therefore lost.

> It was no longer a utopia on the other side of the industrialization process. . . . On the contrary, it is now a utopia of industrialization as such; a capitalist utopia with no room for capitalists, a bourgeois utopia in which the private tycoons of entrepreneurship have been replaced by the grey, smart conformity of the bureaucratic octopus. (1976a: 91)

Socialism, after the Soviet experience, says Bauman in 1976 is a 'populist' version of the old bourgeois utopia. Yet the Soviet claim is not simply capitalist, even if the opposition between those who control and those they control is a similar kind of bipolarization to that evident in capitalist class relations (1976a: 93). One key difference, in the 1970s, remains in the way that politics is directly militarized (1976a: 96; see also Castoriadis, 1981). Politics, in the classical sense, is notable in its absence; but unlike capitalism, it is not economics here that sucks up politics, but rather the militarized political realm which controls the economy. Bureaucracy rules here, not capital. A good ten years before the western radical rediscovery of civil society, Bauman suggests that it is only the emergence of civil society alongside the end of scarcity which would potentially open this Soviet scenario up in a socialist direction.

Viewed from the perspective of utopia, however, the problem is even less shiftable; for the Soviet experience has aligned socialism with capitalism, whereas its critical role is caught up with the idea of socialism as the counter-culture of capitalism. The hegemony of the Russian Revolution within socialism has meant the closing of radical horizons, the relative disappearance of alternative points of view or judgements of value. Socialism's 'success' was now also to be measured by the number of factory chimneys, by the dominance of work discipline, puritan morality, by all the indicators of industrial progress. The Soviet system came to measure its own perfection and its own progress in the 'building of socialism' with the help of a bourgeois measuring rod (1976a: 100). Socialism, like capitalism, became a dystopia, neither a no-place nor a good place. Socialism, therefore, must start over (1976a: 108). The narrowing of modern common sense into its capitalist confines means that the mere possibility of social alternatives needs to be established again. What began as an idea in search of a constituency now becomes a constituency in search of an idea (1976a: 109). Socialism in a sense has become real, practically embodied in both east and west, and therefore has lost its defining, visionary capacity (1976a: 112).

The role of marxism in all this also becomes problematical. While the young Marx imagined a radical solution in a utopia back beyond capitalism and alienation, the Marx of *Capital* already opened this route in explaining the self-reproduction of capitalism. No amount of guarantees about the negation of the negation could solve this (Bauman, 1976a: 137). Marx's own vision thus shrinks across the path of his thought. Hope, then, needs more than vision or insight. Marx's vision ultimately fell too low, too close to the reality of capitalism. Marx, and marxism begin to emerge, finally, as part of the problem, not only part of the solution.

Socialism: The Active Utopia (1976a) is an inconclusive study. It is a report on the desirability and difficulty of socialist hope. Three themes emerge here which have especial significance for Bauman's later work: labour, order and intellectuals. The arguments about labour and socialism in this text plainly connect back to *Between Class and Elite* (1972), and stretch forward, to *Memories of Class* (1982) and beyond. Written in the mid-1970s, *Socialism: The Active Utopia* still persists in connecting labour and utopia, even if its referents are often more to the 1960s period – Marcuse, André Gorz, more generally Gramsci. Yet the impetus of the labouring utopia seems already exhausted; labour is increasingly part of the problem of modernity. Socialism, then, is a utopia or a culture more than a movement; the labour movement is not a utopia in itself, except in the most immanent sense. Yet the problems of the labour movement, and the value of labour, nevertheless remain central, and the coming eclipse of the moment of production by that of consumption changes none of this; problems of working life remain central to our spiritual and material existence. For socialists, still today, the idea of utopia cannot be reduced to the problems of labour, but that utopia which has nothing to say to work or labour is useless. The larger problem here is that already in this book the closure of socialism itself can be anticipated. If utopia remains possible, at the end of the book, then the future of socialism seems considerably less certain (see Beilharz, 1992, 1994b).

The problem of order is also foregrounded in *Socialism: The Active Utopia* (1976a), though its centrality only emerges fully in hindsight. Order shifts further into central focus in *Legislators and Interpreters* (1987), where it is intellectuals who seek to legislate order on behalf of the masses, and finally in *Modernity and the Holocaust* (1989a) and *Modernity and Ambivalence* (1991a), where the quest for order becomes the central problem of modernity as such. In *Socialism: The Active Utopia* the idea of order remains both less developed and more ambivalent. The impulse to order is one fundamental motive in the utopian project; utopian intellectuals seek to redesign and rebuild the world, and, as radicals, we cannot but help being both attracted and repelled by these ambitions. Perhaps we are more attracted by the possibility of the thought-experiment than by its prospects for realization; for the point, ultimately, may be less to seek actually to change the world than to know that the possibility exists, that we know we can live differently, that alternative ways persist. For Bauman, in any case, the negative credentials of the utopians as budding social engineers are here posted; the intellectuals are warned, but not yet damned for their open-ended legislative ambitions.

That famous propaganda image of Lenin did have him wielding a broom, sweeping away the parasites, the vermin, the scum of the earth; and the Bolsheviks were, of course, part of this problem, seeking to clean up the world for once and for all. The Bolsheviks were less gardeners than surgeons; ultimately this part of their project, as Bauman will argue later, is in direct sympathy with that of the Nazis, only where Nazis seek to exterminate Jews, for the Bolsheviks the vermin is a class enemy, the Kulaks. But both social forces wage civil war against one particular part of the project in order to cleanse the world. Neither are driven by intellectuals, but seek to destroy them.

The debate about the intellectuals is an old one, and it shows no signs of abating. Intellectuals, those who take themselves really seriously, have a residual problem with democracy. For if they, we, know better, why should we not rule the world? As Bauman indicates, this kind of mentality rests on a spurious scientistic and godly fantasy about mastery, as though the human world were amenable to 'fixing'. The Bolsheviks remained unable to transcend these barriers; Lenin agreed with Kautsky that workers would always need to be led, and Trotsky never escaped from the fantasy that the real crisis of marxism was only ever a crisis of leadership. The Western discovery of Gramsci in this context was a phenomenon in its own right. For Gramsci's marxism began from the recognition that everyday life was an extraordinary mixture of intelligence, habit and prejudice and Gramsci therefore insisted that in principle all citizens were intellectuals. Of course it remained the fact that some were more intellectual than others; yet it remained part of the socialist utopia, for Gramsci, that the marxist image of the future presumed that there was no genetic distinction between leaders and led. Gramsci, however, never escaped entirely from Bolshevism, or from the Jacobin way of thinking. When push comes to shove, marxist intellectuals who became professional revolutionaries cannot jump off the locomotive of history; democrats become demagogues, thinkers and interpreters become the legislators and hooded magistrates of history.

Yet just as Bauman remains ambivalent about the problem of order, to this point, so does his critique of intellectuals remain suggestive. For Bauman was also on the verge of making the transition out of marxism. His next book is directly continuous with these themes, even if it seems like something of a departure from socialism, into the realms of social science.

Hermeneutics and Social Science

In 1978 Bauman published *Hermeneutics and Social Science: Approaches to Understanding*. Obviously the text stands in its own right, but is also a key connector through to *Legislators and Interpreters* (1987), as the hermeneutic model begins to jostle with that of critical theory as a way to proceed in the intellectual world. For when Shelley proclaimed that poets were the legislators of the world, his sense was evidently metaphorical; ideas ruled, not those who articulated them. Even critical theorists could not entirely escape the sense that their thought should rule, ideologically at least, over the philistine and commodified world they were born into.

Hermeneutics and Social Science might seem at first glance to be only scholarly, a diversion, a different path from socialism. Yet Bauman's purpose in this book both cuts across those of *Socialism: The Active Utopia* (1976a) and anticipates the 1987 turn in *Legislators and Interpreters*, interpreters, by extension, being hermeneuts. Just as Gramsci became a major source of inspiration for western marxism, so the rediscovery of hermeneutics was a major, if marginal trend in critical thinking. Swamped by the more popular French trends in structuralism, then poststructuralism and deconstruction, hemmed in on the other border by the stern second generation critical theory of Habermas, hermeneutics has remained, ever since, something of a lost cause. Nevertheless, the image of knowledge as a conversation or dialogue between reader and text, where a 'hermeneutical circle' works both ways between the two, remains one of the richest of the available repertoire of interpretative tools in the human sciences and it does seem actually to describe how we work, whether we choose to recognize it or not (see for example Rundell, 1994).

If hermeneutics has remained somehow invisible, then, Bauman's challenge is to show that much of our common sociological culture, from Marx to Schütz, is nevertheless recognizably hermeneutical in its approach. Yet hermeneutics has a longer history as well, which Bauman traces from its classical focus upon the text through to its romantic obsession with the author (1978: 10). Like structuralism, much later, hermeneutics encouraged the idea of a depth-reading. Unlike structuralism, hermeneutics maintained a concern with the author, or with intention. Whereas structuralism, at least say per Lévi-Strauss in one sense sought to mimic natural science, hermeneutics sought to focus on the interplay between actors, readers, texts and writers (1978: 12). Knowledge is circular, repetitive if partial; it consists in an endless recapitulation and reassessment of collective memories, ever more voluminous, but always selective (1978: 17).

The hermeneut, as interpreter, is a translator across time or place, a cultural messenger or broker who mediates between text and context. In this sense, all sociology is practically hermeneutical, as it seeks to connect or compare moments or cultures, movements or ideas, to link up sympathies or experience (1978: 29). Hermeneutics is therefore definitionally intersubjective, yet its process is also cumulative; interpreters can know more than the author, authors count but they are not gods. The interpreter approaches what is familiar to the author as though it is foreign or unknown; the hermeneutical enterprise resembles anthropology in this regard, that it seeks out resonances and dissonances between inside and outside, older and more recent. The interpreter is therefore a messenger, only the message is not self-evident; for contemporary hermeneutics the interpreter is the receiver, and not only the agent of transmission. The hermeneutic circle is the process of constructing understanding which holds up culture, makes it possible. Hermeneutics opens up as it develops historically, from text to culture, for to understand is also to value (1978: 34).

Bauman's purpose in *Hermeneutics and Social Science* (1978) is less to track this movement comprehensively than to identify its significance in this moment of the late 1970s. This is also one measure of his achievement; his purpose is less to master hermeneutics than to capture its importance as a symbol. For these kinds of reasons, Bauman detours his path through Marx. While Marx's work is fundamentally sympathetic with hermeneutics, its usual lineage would be traced rather from Schleiermacher through Dilthey to Weber, Heidegger and Gadamer.

Why Marx? Bauman's approach to hermeneutics is broad and symbolic rather than narrow or literal in scope. The theoretical affinities are with the early, existential Marx of the 1840s. Marx's early work, historicist and humanist, runs a parallel path to that of the history of hermeneutics, for which meaning is created, exchanged, recycled and transformed as well as inherited. One difference is that Marx locates the roots of miscomprehension not in the mind of the cognizing subject, but in the object of cognition, within the structure of domination which constitutes the object (1978: 58). Thus, as Bauman observes, Marx transforms hermeneutics or epistemology into sociology (1978: 58). Herein lies the possibility of the critique of political economy, the exposé of commodity fetishism which is the peak of his achievement. Marx's work runs alongside hermeneutics, in this particular if idiosyncratic way; for here interpretation leads to or results in

revolution. Yet where Marx figures in Bauman's cast as the young revolutionary, Weber now appears as the institutional voice of mainstream
sociology. Bauman knows that knowledge is perspectival; as he says later,
in discussion of Husserl, as 'in the case of every great work, there are many
sides from which Husserl's contribution may be approached, and many
contexts in which its significance reveals itself' (1978: 111).

Bauman's Weber, in this text, is not the existentialist Weber whom, say
Karl Löwith aligns with Marx in his famous 1932 essay, *Max Weber and
Karl Marx* (Löwith, 1982). Weber's voice here, then, is less the sober or
black gaze of the soul who looks into the abyss and sees the future as the
iron cage, than the detached analyst of objectivity. It is difficult not to
suspect that at this point of his own biography, Bauman's personal sympathies are still more evidently with Marx, the romantic critic of reification,
rather than with the stoical figure of Weber. For even though Weber's
position is more sympathetic with the distinction Bauman later crystallizes
between legislators and interpreters, Bauman at this point observes the
distinction between spheres of value in Weber and proceeds to focus mainly
on the claim to objectivity. This Weber seems more decidedly American
than German, as sociological rather than philosophical or existential in
stance. For Weber's distinction between scholarship and politics exactly
anticipates Bauman's between hermeneutics and legislation, as it anticipates
the later foregrounding of ethics as the realm where no one can decide but
the subject, him- or herself. Intellectuals have to recognize that they have
no right to lead, or at least no right more than any other citizen. Weber is
thus both the analyst and the critic of rationalization (1978: 73–4). The
problem, of course, is that sociology is in the meantime turned into science,
losing the better sense of its own limits and claiming exactly that right to
legislate which Weber was wary of (1978: 86).

The further characters in Bauman's procession of hermeneuts are more
predictable, perhaps with the exception of Parsons: Mannheim, Husserl,
Heidegger, Schütz and ethnomethodology. Imaginably, were the book
written today, it would include Gadamer and Ricoeur. But as I have
observed, Bauman's purpose is less to establish a catalogue of victorious
heroes than it is to seek to capture the aura around their shared idea or
practice. Through the discussion of Heidegger the register of discourse
seems to shift. 'Things must go wrong' before they can reveal themselves as
problems (1978: 163). Later Bauman quotes Schopenhauer, to the same
end: 'If I talk of happiness, it is because something makes me suffer' (1978:
194). This way of thinking is later extended in *Freedom* (1988), where the
argument opens with the sense that freedom and dependence are mutually
constitutive, or chained together. The larger claim, characteristic of
Bauman's entire project, is that there is no such state as happiness; it is only
a moment, or moments in the struggle against the state of suffering. This
claim, sympathetic again with the anthropology of the young Marx, echoes
out through Bauman's work on class, dignity and deprivation. Within the
horizon of arguments concerning hermeneutics, its immediate connotations

are more precise. Within the realm of understanding, Bauman argues, it is incomprehension which is the norm. Understanding is nothing more than the struggle against incomprehension. The image of understanding is the negative of the experience of incomprehension: '*It is only the experience of incomprehension which makes us, in a flash, aware of the task of understanding*' (1978: 195). Incomprehension is the norm, understanding the exception, not because we are stupid, but because our means of proceeding are habitual, customary, ritualized, routinized. It is consequently only in the breaking of these habits and rituals that we momentarily glimpse the possibility of other ways to live or to proceed: 'We perceive the knowledge of "how to go on" as a task only when we do *not* know how to go on' (1978: 195). Again, Marx's presence can be felt behind the shoulder, for this is why change is the precondition of understanding, even if this is not always change of our own choosing. Bauman's is not an argument for revolution in permanence; but it does rest on the claim that by virtue of our nature as creatures of habit, the capacity to learn may be less natural than connected to changes in perspective, in sense of time or place, to juxtaposition of the uncanny with the familiar whether at home or afar. Certainly the whole of Bauman's *Hermeneutics and Social Science* (1978) is constructed within that sense of Vico, mediated through Gramsci, that what we know best is what we make or create; only this is not simply an occasional, accumulative process, but is also accidential and ruptural.

Alongside Vico, Bauman now turns explicitly to Montaigne, later to become the postmodernists' hero as essayist. It is not only custom or ritual in the general active sense but also in the mental or conceptual sense which hermeneutics seeks to place, as prejudice. Finally, Bauman introduces Habermas, rather than Gadamer, into this context, in order to discuss the image of communication. In this text Bauman probably spends more time discussing Popper and kindred problems of philosophy of science than he does Horkheimer and Adorno or *Dialectic of Enlightenment* (Adorno and Horkheimer, 1944). His enthusiasms for Habermas are also contained, though he evidently draws more from the early Habermas of *Knowledge and Human Interests*, and largely ignores the systematic-synthetic turn which Habermas much later takes into *Theory of Communicative Action*. Bauman's general claim here is that the epistemology of hermeneutics cannot be detached from the sociology of communicative action (1978: 244). It is less language that is central, than culture or in this sense communicative action. If sociology as a utopia were successful, then understanding and communal life would be more closely interconnected (1978: 246). Utopia would connect science and life, not suspend or submerge them.

Bauman thus closes his book on hermeneutics in a circular manner, as he began: for he socializes, or sociologizes hermeneutics, viewing it as a practical and social rather than cerebral or merely intellectual challenge. The focus, in other words, is on intellectualizing life and concretizing the life of the mind, rather than on cultivating a specific theory of reading or advocating an academy of eggheads capable of propagating it. Ordinary life is full of intellectual challenges; only in the twentieth century, in particular, political life is also inhabited by particular human problems called intellectuals, those for whom Truth is transparent and Progress a tributary path that is obvious. Ironically, in one way, this is a problem outside of hermeneutics, for the Road to Truth is more often or usually based on claims to natural scientific credibility, objective truth without subjects, which is the very approach that hermeneutics seeks to problematize and offer an alternative to. If positivistic claims to science are the norm, then hermeneutics is the exception. If explanation is the norm, understanding offers the hope of an alternative. The prospect of hermeneutics is thus like that of critical theory, marginal and tentative but no less compelling for that.

Structuralism, Semiology, Marxism

The intellectual profile of hermeneutics has always been marginal, partly because it is not a tool or method that can simply be operationalized, partly because its reception at least in English has been overshadowed first by structuralism and then by deconstruction. Bauman's work has a clearer proximity to hermeneutics, not least because the significance of interpreters becomes more prominent as his project proceeds. But he was not dismissive of structuralism either, or at least not of the structuralist activity. Semiology, likewise, is an open field for Bauman, as more primordially is the culture of marxism. These enthusiasms are detailed in three different and significant essays published through the late 1960s and into the 1970s.

Bauman's extended analysis of structuralism is presented in 'The Structuralist Promise' (1973b). Structuralism's appeal was apparent in its universalism, not least per Lévi-Strauss, combined with its sense of opening up into linguistics and semiology. The problem Bauman focuses upon is that anticipated already by Saussure in his 1916 *Course in General Linguistics*. Could the model provided by language itself legitimately be universalized across the social sciences? Just when the linguistic turn in contemporary social theory was taking hold, Bauman is already anticipating its conceptual inflation. Miscomprehension, as he argued earlier, is the norm. His own terms of criticism are strong and clear. Language is part of culture, and culture may even function like a language, but culture itself *is not* a language (1973b: 71). To identify language and culture is to do violence to both in the process. For even language cannot be 'pure communication'; meaning is as often contextual as it is indicated by the relation between signs or between signifiers and signifieds (1973b: 72). 'The empirical reality of each culture can be said to be full of "floating" signs, waiting for meanings to be attached to' them (1973b: 75). Communication ultimately works through ordering, rather than structuring; it is order, the central issue of *Modernity and the Holocaust* (1989a), rather than structure, which is predominant. Because communication is equivocal, it is better to speak of 'ordering' as the superior function of culture as a whole (Bauman, 1973b: 77). Culture rests upon the substitution of artificial order for natural order. Yet order itself is also highly variable in practice. Order is a graded notion: the level of order is measured by the degree of predictability (1973b: 79). The prospect of eliminating disorder remains illusory. Ordering works against an incertitude which itself is indissoluble.

The implication of this argument concerning order, then, is that the central frame of meaning is to be located in culture, rather than in language. Language belongs to culture, rather than the other way around. If, therefore, according to Bauman we need to direct attention to codes, rules or language then the interest in structure ought take us to system, to systems-theory rather than to structuralism as such. Language is a system; it cannot stand for the idea of system as such without risking the reduction of culture to language (1973b: 80). Thus Bauman's provisional conclusion regarding the 'structuralist promise':

> It is my conviction that the structuralist promise can materialize only if it is understood that the role played in linguistic analysis by the semiotic field is assumed, in the world of human relations, by social structure. (1973b: 80)

Social structure offers a cultural repertoire or field of action. But structural linguistics, as Saussure understood, is part of semiology rather than the other way around. Life also exists outside or alongside language; it can be silent, inert, or it can be rich in symbolic meaning of a non-linguistic kind. The habits of being in the world cannot be captured within or reduced to the spoken or written word. In the beginning, was activity.

Bauman chases the idea of culture further, via Marx, in his 1968 paper 'Marx and the Contemporary Theory of Culture' (1968b). Here Bauman rehearses themes which, like that of order in the foregoing analysis, will extend right through his later work. One such is the sense of culture as cultivation. Bauman begins with Plutarch's definition of culture as agriculture, as the combination of soil, seed and skill (1968b: 19). The project of perfecting the primitive turns the intractable into the tame. So far so good; for this is the beginning of the classical road to *Bildung*, or cultivation of the self. Yet danger lurks nearby: for the active striving for the perfection of the human being also presupposed a 'breeding ideal' (1968b: 20). For centuries, hitherto, it has been class domination which has provided the basic mechanism for the construction of breeding ideals. The distinction, of course, is of an elementary marxian kind, for class categories have for centuries coincided with the division between those who must work in order to live and those who live without working (1968b: 20). Culture thus comes historically to be associated with the immaterial, the spiritual, the intellectual. Much of this remains intact into modernity, only it is also, now, increasingly open to contestation. The nineteenth century socialist movement, however, was still in its thrall. The classical socialist argument concerned the universalization of high culture more than its transformation. *Bildung* for all was its cultural hope; culture should be democratized. This, too, was Marx's frame of reference (1968b: 21).

Culture itself is transformed when the old European continent 'discovers' the new world on the basis of the former's economic and military supremacy: 'Initially Europe was bound to the view of the newly discovered world as "primitive", as traditionally strange customs were interpreted as "lack of culture"' (1968b: 22). Cultural argument now emerged concerning the idea and fact of progress. Some, like Wesley, viewed civilization as an achievement at any cost; others, like Montaigne, the ideological precursor of romanticism in the Enlightenment, viewed the idea of European civilization as a puzzle, if not a contradiction in terms (1968b: 22). But these remained arguments about what was to be valued as culture, rather than arguments about the scope of the idea of culture in itself. Bauman credits Gustav Klemm with the achievement of opening the Pandora's box in 1848, for he was the first to apply the term 'culture' to everything produced by humanity rather than to the selected products of fine art alone. According to Klemm, culture included all those things which we add to nature, which would not exist without us (Bauman, 1968b: 22). Having viewed Marx in this context as S.S. Prawer would, as a cultural universalist in the European tradition, Bauman does not connect this sensibility to Marx's in *The German Ideology*, where culture in effect is human activity or history rather than the work of Goethe or Shakespeare alone (Prawer, 1978). Klemm thus anticipates the distinction that Bernard Smith was later to articulate as that between art in the general and art in the special sense (Smith, 1998). This was a kind of distinction at best incipient in the work of Marx, where the concept of culture as *Bildung* appears alongside that of culture as human activity in the anthropological sense.

The course of Bauman's argument takes him closer to the history of anthropology as such. Morgan and Engels remained evolutionary; it was not until Malinowski and Boas that cultures were valued and interpreted internally or relationally rather than comparatively in this hierarchical manner (Bauman, 1968b: 23). Only around this point the possibility emerges that everything is culture, in which case the category may literally become meaningless. On a practical level, the irony was different. For just as the idea of cultural value was being opened up or decentred away from Europe, western culture was permeating virtually every alternative culture on the globe (1968b: 25). Perhaps, then, it comes as little surprise that Bauman now empathizes with the Lévi-Strauss of *Tristes Tropiques*, for whom all of western civilization reduces to a scar on the preexisting landscape. Not because, for Bauman, the human experience is a waste of time, whose end we might celebrate, but because of this dissonance between what we are and what we achieve. In this sense, Bauman's immediate sympathies in this essay lie less with Lévi-Strauss the structuralist, than with Lévi-Strauss the romantic, the inheritor of the tradition of critique pioneered by Rousseau and before him, by Montaigne, where the problem is less culture than civilization (1968b: 26). Certainly this is a motif which recurs, not least later, say, in Bauman's critique of consumerism or of globalization.

For again in irony, Lévi-Strauss' own work deteriorates in the power of its insight from *Tristes Tropiques* to the later *Mythologies*, as it twists from critique of culture to the science of structure. In this way Lévi-Strauss' project, like that of other structuralisms, comes in the long run to value similarity over difference. Bauman's preference, in 1968 and long after, is to focus on activity and on culture rather than structure. In the 1960s, very clearly, it is Marx whose theory remains central to Bauman's vista, although his argument already proceeds through the articulation of the views of various others, anthropological, sociological, semiological and linguistic.

The centrality of Marx is foregrounded more systematically in another essay from 1968, 'Modern Times, Modern Marxism' (1968a). Already it beckons, to those of us who read it now 30 years later, in the direction separately followed by Stuart Hall, to the last years of *Marxism Today*, around Postmodern Times and Postmodern Marxism. This is an astonishing essay, the content and logic of which have barely aged across the three decades in between. Bauman opens the first few pages evoking, if not always directly naming, those central themes in sociology which we would associate with Marx, Simmel and Weber. First, he insists that Marx counts, but not as any kind of economic determinism, for marxism cannot be rendered as any kind of single-factor analysis (1968a: 400). Economy might be viewed as primary by Marx, but only or especially in the anthropological sense, that humans must first of all make a living, produce and consume. The second reference, to Simmel, is implicit in Bauman's introduction of the themes of social scale and complexity (1968a: 401). Large-scale organizations generate unmanageable 'noise' in communication channels. Organizations run through the logic of technical nationality, for managerial purposes. This leads then to the introduction of the third presence, that of Weber. For our culture in modernity has been transformed so that social science, too, is defined by quantification, and sober realism predominates (1968a: 402). Cultural problems become managerial problems; this is the theme at which Bauman arrives at this theoretical three-step via Marx, Simmel and Weber. This is the theoretical manoeuvre he follows, through critical social theory, even at his most marxist; it is never, in Bauman's case, marxist alone, and in this, it is most like Marx's own work, which draws together arguments from all kinds of sources too unholy for the most orthodox of marxists to swallow.

The issue that emerges at this point in Bauman's argument is conformism. Personal life also becomes a problem of management. Humanity is constructed from the viewpoint of the social system, rather than the other way around. But to the contrary, for Bauman,

> What is of primary concern is how to adjust society to individual needs, not the reverse; how to extend the range of freedom of individual choice; how to provide room enough for individual initiative and non-conformity. (1968a: 404–5)

Bauman's marxism is inconceivable without this libertarian thread, which connects his to the work of Castoriadis and, like that in Castoriadis, outlives his earlier formal commitment to marxism. Marxism, in this sense, is methodologically optional rather than compulsory:

> As far as research methods are concerned, their merits and shortcomings can be reasonably judged solely in the light of the volume and competence of the information they lead to. The choice of cognitive methods always is, or should be, secondary to the choice of problems one thinks important enough to be investigated. (1968a: 406)

Consequently, in theoretical or interpretative life, it all depends; structuralism, for example, may be a constraining theory and yet, in sensitive hands, it can generate insight just as well as hermeneutics or semiology can. Marxism, in this account, remains significant symbolically more than methodologically; its pertinence is bound up with the power of the themes and problems it identifies. Marxism is thematically useful or interesting, that is to say, rather than theoretically 'correct', because the problems to which it responds persist; and still do today. Since almost nothing has been done to prevent fragmentation of human action and human personality, to prevent the restriction of the individual's liberty to the sphere of consumer choice, to prevent the limitation of expression to the selection of goods offered by the market, marxist thought remains, for Bauman as in this context for his fellow exile Leszek Kolakowski, of profound contemporary importance (1968a: 407).

On Bauman's account, then, marxism is useful because it works on general problems of the human condition. Marxism is not unique in any sense rather than the incidental. For its theoretical attributes are variously shared by followers and representatives of other critical trends. Marxism, and by implication Marx's own theory, possesses originality only in the way in which it integrates historically available principles or insights: 'That is why the very nature of Marxist theory makes it an open and developing system, existing only in permanent dialogue with the most modern of its scientific contemporaries' (1968a: 412). Yet Bauman's sense of marxism as social science remains weak, or hermeneutical rather than natural scientific. His distinction between knowledge that takes the managerial view (Parsons) and that which is anthropological in orientation (Marx, Gramsci) aligns his own thinking with Alvin Gouldner's later attempt to distinguish between two marxisms, those of science and praxis respectively (Gouldner, 1975). If Bauman's sympathies as a Polish marxist are evidently with Lukács, and more so Luxemburg and Gramsci, then his ontological focus remains both upon the individual (as in Schaff and Kolakowski) and upon the social relations of the historic bloc (Gramsci) (Bauman, 1968b: 414). Having himself recently been released from his bonds to the Polish academy, Bauman also here takes the opportunity to remind that marxism itself is endangered if it becomes managerial. Because it is political, marxism is obstinately opposed to the conformity of academic respectability. Marxism is oppositional and critical by nature: this is Bauman's moral in this paper, poignant as it sits, between the lines, of his academic dismissal and personal harassment by the Polish 'marxist' authorities. A political nonconformist by choice, Bauman is also now compelled not to conform – to rebel, to say no, to oppose that obsession with order which itself calls for compulsory conformism.

Legislators and Interpreters

Bauman's Polish brief as sociological interpreter had led to an impasse; the state in its mercy had decided not to shoot this messenger, but compelled him and his family rather to leave their homeland. They became exiles, like so many other modern intellectuals who insisted on their vocations. Bauman's working life took him through Tel Aviv to Canberra to settle, finally, in Leeds, where he was Professor and Head of Department for almost 20 years. By necessity, then, an academic manager of sorts, he obviously continued to write throughout that period. But it was on the cusp of retirement via a stay in Newfoundland that he produced *Legislators and Interpreters: On Modernity, Post-Modernity and Intellectuals* (1987). This is the next book, after *Memories of Class* (1982), of his own transition. Bauman's opening ambit is apparent. The idea of intellectuals coincides with that of Enlightenment. By this stage of the twentieth century, we have some justifiable right to be sceptical about the claims of both, whether separately or together. Part of this sensibility is openly Foucauldian. For it was in this era, when intellectuals and Enlightenment began to generate some mischief, that for Bauman the power/knowledge syndrome, that most conspicuous attribute of modernity, had been formed (1987: 2). A new kind of state power coincided with a new form of intellectual discourse. So far, however, it remains clear that the field we inhabit is modernity. And so Bauman makes it clear, that for him modernity and postmodernity are not phases or crystal-clear conceptual markers. The two terms, he insists, are not like 'industrial' and 'post-industrial' or 'capitalist' and 'post-capitalist'. Nor, more emphatically, is modernity the same as modernism. For both modernism and its shadow, postmodernism, refer largely to self-conscious cultural and artistic styles (1987: 3). For Bauman, rather, the point of distinction at risk in the difference between 'modernity' and 'postmodernity' is primarily a matter of intellectual style, or the difference in context in which intellectual roles are performed. Modern and post-modern, in this way of thinking, might then be periodized as successive historical sequences; but the real point of distinction is the dominant image or model of intellectual activity in each:

In referring to intellectual practices, the opposition between the terms modern and post-modern stands for differences in understanding the nature of the world, and the social world in particular, and in understanding the related nature, and purpose, of intellectual work. (1987: 3)

To use the conventional distinctions, however limiting they are, the postmodern is then a phenomenon aligned with spirit, or culture, or ideas and intellectual practices. The postmodern might then usefully be viewed as ontological or epistemological, philosophical rather than firmly historical or sociological.

Wherein then resides the difference between modernity and postmodernity? The two frames offer, according to Bauman, quite clearly distinct worldviews. Modernity presumes an image of the world as an ordered totality, open to the prospects of explanation, prediction and control. Control itself is bound into the idea and practice of social engineering, planning, and mastery over nature. Effectivity of control and correctness of knowledge are tightly related. The typically postmodern worldview, in contrast, generates a plurality of models of order. Truth claims are connected to communities of meaning rather than higher or necessarily external goals. Localism and relativism rule, as they implicitly did before the modern. This then is the background against which types of intellectual activity are to be defined. For the typically modern strategy of intellectual work is best characterized by the metaphor of the 'legislator' role. The legislator possesses final authority and ultimate knowledge; his power rests on the social distinction between those who know, and those who do not. Legislation calls upon general and schematic knowledge which, as Weber said of bureaucracy, can be generalized in order to anticipate all future developments (as if!). Such is the extraordinary traditionalism of modernity. In contrast, again, and though Bauman does not summon up this precise word here, the typically postmodern strategy of intellectual work is hermeneutic. The postmodern intellectual is a translator, not an arbiter. He or she translates statements, made within one communally based tradition, so that they can be understood within the system of knowledge based on another tradition. Interpreters do not decide on behalf of others; they seek, rather, to facilitate communication between different autonomous participants. The postmodern strategy, in this way, might in one sense be imagined as closer to the practice of a certain kind of anthropology than to mainstream sociology. Yet these kinds of distinctions are bound to blur, for as Bauman insists, 'the post-modern strategy does not imply the elimination of the modern one; on the contrary, it cannot be conceived without the continuation of the latter' (1987: 5). As Bauman explains, there are levels of meaning at work here which make all this persuasive. For while, say, the postmodern strategy entails the abandonment of the universalistic ambitions of the intellectuals' own tradition in-the-world, it does not abandon the universalistic ambitions of the intellectuals towards their own traditions (1987: 5). Interpreters maintain a great deal of power or influence. Fundamentally, Bauman's is a Weberian or Kantian case seeking to reclaim the distinction between proper spheres of analysis or activity. For the real issue is the public claim of the intellectuals to power, as legislators, as phoney representatives of Reason or the People when in actuality they have their own agenda to bear.

Legislators and Interpreters is, then, an attempt to reconstruct a hermeneutical circle of its own, where hermeneutics can be brought to bear on the problem of hermeneutics and its eclipse by managerial or legislative forms of knowledge and power (1987: 6). Yet the position of critique is not yet entirely clear, as Bauman insists that he does not want to view the shift from modern to postmodern as necessary or progressive. He does not, at this point, further entertain the possibility that the hermeneutic then might be a return, rather than a progressive or regressive shift. Instead, Bauman returns to and departs from an earlier topic, the aetiology of the intellectuals. Through an extended discussion of the analysis of primitivism in the work of the anthropologist Paul Radin, Bauman arrives in effect at two provisional definitions. Intellectuals are ideologists; and they are defined relationally, by the role they perform in the reproduction and development of the social figuration (1987: 19). Again, the frame of reference is reminiscent of Marx's discussion of the emergence of the division of labour in *The German Ideology*, though Bauman does not invoke it here. Rather than referring here to Marx's priests, Bauman introduces Foucault's critique of the 'pastoral', for it is the power/knowledge nexus to which he draws attention here. Marx's was still, ultimately, an argument concerning economy more than culture, leading to the focus on exploitation rather than domination. Here, for Bauman, it is domination that counts.

Not that the road from interpretation to legislation was simple, however. For as Bauman emphasizes, one model for the intellectuals-in-formation was the 'active utopia' of *les philosophes* (1987: 24). The *philosophes* were not intellectual entrepreneurs seeking to sell a paradigm. Thus the ambivalence of the entire problem to hand; intellectuals are never only just power-hungry experts in the making. The root of the contradiction can nevertheless be located within the field of education. For the long change associated with Enlightenment privileges reason over experience, coming to the conclusion that humans most need instruction in what lies outside, or beyond them: 'To acquire excellence, men must be taught. They need teachers. They need those who know' (1987: 33). Bauman thus opens one possible path to his later discussion of the Holocaust, and then ethics; for whatever we can learn outside of us, whatever procedures and rules we can learn or are taught us, they cannot teach us how to act, or when to say no.

In this, modern society nevertheless resembles images of traditional society, where proximity and the relative transparence of social relations ostensibly went together with higher degrees of stability and control. The process we have made familiar to ourselves under the name of the Industrial Revolution changes this, by generating a category of vagabonds or 'masterless men' and their attendant institutions of disciplinary control, from the school to the poorhouse, the hospital and asylum. What Bauman adds to Foucault's adoption of Bentham, here, is a heightened sense of actors within these formative institutions. For the far-reaching consequence of the asymmetry of surveillance is the demand for a specialist in a position of supervision, which equals super vision. The practice of surveillance itself depends on the existence of a category of surveillors (Bauman, 1987: 47).

But at this point, Bauman changes metaphors, from Panopticon to gardening, or cultivation, and replaces Foucault as his marginal authority with Ernest Gellner. Whence comes modernity and its penchant for regulation? It is as though the gamekeepers of an earlier moment become gardeners; and it is the specific image of cultivation which here draws out Bauman's critical ire. For the emergence of modernity rests on the process of transforming wild cultures into garden cultures. The sensibilities underlying this critique seem to be recognizably romantic, valuing nature over culture; but this is also the beginning of a case in Bauman that leads to *Modernity and the Holocaust* (1989a), to the exposure of Nazi theory and practice in anti-semitism constructing the Jew as the weed. Nazism, too, is based upon the attack on nature, not only on rhapsody or rhetoric sung in praise of the weedless Black Forest.

The gardening state opens the way for eugenics. The power presiding over modernity (the pastoral power of the state) is modelled on the role of the gardener (Bauman, 1987: 52). The gardener becomes the image of that pattern of social engineering which in turn defines modernity. All of nature needed to be civilized, including the vagabonds and the motley members of the dangerous classes. The great unwashed would have to be re-educated, in their own interests. The specialists had arrived just in time to save us all; experts, teachers and social scientists in their vanguard (1987: 67). Education would arrive to free us all of our prejudices. The good citizen could be grown, like a grafted tomato, or the blue rose. Before our eyes, historically speaking, we see now the *philosophes* turning into legislators. Whether this is a fair representation of Enlightenment, however, is another issue; for the Kantian idea of regulation as self-regulation seems to disappear from these pages. Its central figure, in Bauman's argument here, is rather Rousseau forcing people to be free (1987: 74). The men of Enlightenment doubtless had the contempt for the rabble which Bauman describes; the critical question, however, is whether this exhausts their contribution to modern culture. If the project of Enlightenment is reduced to its tutelary outcome in education or instruction, then we are all in consequence far poorer indeed. Yet it is indubitably the case that, if the west has given us for example the modern project of democracy, it has also simultaneously given us the civilizing project in its dirtiest sense. The singular ideal of 'civilization' has always pitted itself against the actual contents of other, actually existing civilizations (1987: 93). And in this regard, as Bauman intimates, to civilize is not qualitatively different an act than to enact culture, or to cultivate. The pox of humanism here meant not only that nothing could be left alone, but that everything was open to change:

The forms human life and conduct assumed did not seem any more part of the 'nature of things' or part of a divine order which would neither need nor stand human intervention. Instead, human life and conduct appeared now as something which needed to be formed, lest it should take shapes unacceptable and damaging to social order, much like an unattended field is swamped with weeds and has little to offer its owner. (1987: 94)

At this point of the argument, Bauman turns more directly to discuss ideology, including the humanist ideology of marxism.

Marx's own obsession with changing the world, rather than merely interpreting it, places his legacy squarely within the tradition of thinking which Bauman here is rejecting. For Marx, too, knowledge could lead to a certain kind of collective mastery. *Savants* wanted not only to explain the world, but also to save it. Yet this was also part of the worldview which had sustained Bauman from the 1940s to the 1960s. What, then, had changed? Marx now appeared to Bauman, as per Marshall Berman's portrayal in *All That is Solid Melts into Air* (1984), as an unqualified modernist (1987: 112). For Bauman, in other words, the later Marx loses the balance which earlier sees him weigh up the respective gains and losses of modernity. For Bauman, as for Castoriadis and Baudrillard, marxism became the mirror of production. Entrapped within modern significations, marxism then became a theory of state-planned modernization. Bauman in turn discusses the image of Faustian man, but connects him here with Nietzsche rather than Marx; as I shall suggest later, it seems to me that it is Faustianism rather than humanism which best deserves Bauman's critical contempt. It is the Marx that stretches out through Trotsky who turns most fully from the spirit of Prometheus to that of Faust the developer (Bauman, 1987: 113; Beilharz 1987, 1992). Marx, in any case, remained I think both a romantic and a classicist as well as an ideologue and a revolutionary modernist. At this point in Bauman's own project, however, Marx begins to appear at least as much as the problem than as the resource for its interpretative solution.

Yet it is Marx whose visage remains on Bauman's study wall in Leeds, and it is Marx's critical spirit which animates much of his work. For our new world, brave or not, remains continuous with these older worlds and their problems. What becomes open to question is whether the classical sociological interpretations, from Marx to Simmel, either managed to determine the uniqueness of modernity or the continuity of its concerns with all hitherto existing social forms. Bauman's sense of sympathy with classical sociology of this critical kind is high, yet his sense is also that from our vantage point, a manic century on, the world also looks rather different. Or more precisely, the ways available to us to look at the world seem more diverse and contingent in nature. How so? Three factors are involved. First, the critical classics tended to assume the irreversible character of the changes which modernity signified or else brought in its wake. Second, the critical consensus conceived of modernity in critical terms, as an essentially unfinished project. Third, the critiques of modernity were all 'inside' views.

The philosophical discourse of modernity became both self-referential and self-validating (1987: 115–16). The idea of the postmodern is significant if only because it offers a margin for critical manoeuvre or detachment from these positions. At the same time, as Bauman consistently is given to emphasize, there is in another sense nothing 'outside' the modern or the global. So the postmodern is necessarily continuous with the modern, both in historical and in conceptual terms. Thus the irony, often, of various postmodern critiques of modernity which insist on their own novelty and nevertheless reproduce, for example, the first attitude of classical sociology, its principle of the irreversibility of change. The postmodern often presumes an end to the conception or epoch of modernity, a view which itself is quintessentially modernist in substance (1987: 117).

For Bauman the postmodern refers usefully not to an alleged change of epoch, nor to the arrival of 'postmodern times', but to this change in attitude or self-consciousness. The postmodern is a manifestation of the crisis in modern, and modernizing mentalities:

> The post-modernist [*sic*] discourse . . . is about the credibility of 'modernity' itself as a self-designation of Western civilization, whether industrial or post-industrial, capitalist or post-capitalist. It implies that the self-ascribed attitudes contained in the idea of modernity do not hold today, perhaps did not hold yesterday either. The post-modernist [*sic*] debate is about the self-consciousness of Western society, and the grounds (or the absence of grounds) for such consciousness. (1987: 118)

The emphases are characteristic of Bauman's thinking, and are worth dwelling upon. First, the postmodern is a debate about, or a critique of, culture rather than, say, economy or history in the first instance. Second, the argument looks back as well as forward; we may never have been modern in any thoroughgoing sense, indeed the modernist or boosterist model of modernity may be impossible, less unachieved than simply unachievable. But this would also mean that the 'premodern' is probably 'modern' in various different ways; for if high modernity is not modern, neither is early modernity; in which case, what does it mean to speak of modernity at all? Perhaps it is rather the case that we have always been modern, or open to change. And third, even though the argument here refers primarily to culture and has an historical inflection, its ultimate message is ethical: for it is not practically the case that culture thinks through subjects or actors, but rather that they, we, think through culture. The postmodern is also, then, a question of how we see ourselves; and as Bauman shows so painfully in *Modernity and the Holocaust* (1989a), there is at least one way in which the most modern of totalitarian actors and subjects are also the most excessively traditionalistic, or morally dutiful.

To put it in plainer terms, the postmodern attitude reflects a basic unease with high modernity and its humanistic claims of individual perfectibility to be achieved through social engineering. At century's end, we – many of us; or western middle class radicals in particular? – are no longer convinced that these ends are either possible or desirable. The ethical problems raised in a global register by these kinds of claims have long been identified as Eurocentric. It is as though we, the privileged, further down the path to the abyss of futile consumer hedonism, cannot resist calling back to those behind us that it only gets worse, the further we progress. Yet it is also this unease with our worlds and ourselves that drives the critical enterprise which in turn sustains sociology. As Marx observed somewhere, one cannot but help from time to time contemplating whether we have generated too much civilization, this for all concerned, north and south. What we cannot do, for Bauman, is to translate this interpretation directly into legislation. We do not have the ethical right to decide for others, if this means trying to help others avoid their own mistakes. It is as though for Bauman this should be the primary universal right, the right of all peoples to make their own mistakes. To behave otherwise, is to behave as though it is only the other who is capable of mistakes, or of evil. It is this sense of difference which has been lost in the rush of modern intellectuals to become legislators of taste, or of the world. Even so, the final claim of intellectuals remains Luther's, to speak the truth as we see it; we can do no other.

The implication is clear: intellectuals should embrace, again, the logic of interpretation, so that what we or others routinely call the postmodern also includes the practice of hermeneutics. This would mean to recognize that if we all inhabit the one world we also at the same time occupy different life-worlds. In this scene, avants-gardes whether artistic or political are bound to collapse, as the absence of all clearly defined rules of the game renders innovation impossible, which explains the predominance of the images of pastiche or collage; even surrealism is no longer iconoclastic (Bauman, 1987: 130). Yet in this situation the ethical problem remains. For if the intellectual obsession with classification also always carries with it the act of valuation, the question remains, how should we live? and the tradition-alistic, and modernist insistence remains with it, that the moral respon-sibility of intellectuals is to tell others (their readers) how to live. Whereas the unpalatable truth in the story told by Bauman is different: all we can tell others is the hardest thing, that they have to decide for themselves. The ultimate register of decision, then, is ethical rather than aesthetic, and this regardless of whether we view ourselves as modern or postmodern. The point is not that we should each of us cease to judge, but to the contrary that the fragility or provisionality of judgement be recognized. So this is a call for more debate and argument, not less; only for a different style of dispute, whether in politics or aesthetics.

Bauman's own debating partners in this are various, but they include the relativism of Rorty and the hermeneutics of Gadamer, both of them traditionalisms of different sorts (1987: 144). The issue then becomes one of community, and whether we inherit or make the communities we inhabit or hope for. Philosophers, henceforth, can behave more authoritatively in their own communities of scholars than they can in the community at large. Intellectuals, in other words, ought no longer dream of themselves as heroes. Bauman proceeds to connect this theme to Weber's Protestant Ethic, which he presents as a sociological myth, or at least as a myth made for and by sociologists. To view the arrival of capitalism as something other than intentional is one thing, for Bauman. What is more striking, to this critic of Weber, is the sense that the intellectuals, more than anyone else, liked Weber's tale immensely: 'In the myth of the Puritan, they immortalized a mirror reflection of themselves' (1987: 149). If the noble captains of industry were the obvious tragic heroes of this story, the projection involved revealed the interpretative heroes to be we sociologists, hardworking, righteous and stoical. Bauman's interpretation of Weber here is stunning, and reveals perhaps more clearly than elsewhere his relative indifference to the formal corpus of Weber's work, at least in its philosophical dimensions. His interpretation is as shocking as it is idiosyncratic. Yet a moment's reflection also reveals its immense power of suggestion. For Weber plainly is nostalgic for a lost world inhabited by great men, and he himself aspired to greatness. The Protestant Ethic, in that sense, involves a projection, just as by extension we could say that Marx's critique of alienation includes a projection, for this new world of capitalists is one that denies him a place in history, and not only the proletariat. The critique of alienation also indicates Marx's own sense of having been misplaced by a history out of joint.

Against the sociological projection of Puritanism, Bauman calls on the support of Richard Sennett and John Carroll. Whether the Puritan was the figure of the capitalist or of the sociologist, or whether he was entirely fictive, the dominant cultural model today is rather remissive or hedonistic. The contrast implied is nevertheless difficult to avoid: that if the modern or postmodern personality is hedonistic, it is the figure of the sociologist that acts as the censor or Puritan (1987: 152–3). The sociologist has become the Man of Reason, which is exactly the thesis of Bauman's book, interpreters become legislators in other words. Culture is tragic, rather than humanizing; the surplus of its achievements, as Simmel argues, serves rather to numb than to enable us (Bauman, 1987: 156–7). We drown amidst our cultural achievements because their abundance blinds us to each other. Ours is the story, still after all these years, of the sorcerer's apprentice. As intellectuals, we cede our autonomy into the institutions which control us, at the very same moment as we style ourselves as independent, mavericks, puritans or outsiders. We end up looking like the Marlboro Man, auratically strong and independent yet held up by the highway billboards of the culture-industry, supported by the very agent that poisons us. And even postmodern culture, this new critique of critical criticism, is delivered up to us daily by the market like toothpaste or cornflakes (1987: 163).

But if Bauman seeks to avoid the narcissistic self-projection of the sociologist as hero, he is clearly not in all this giving up the right to judge, and to judge harshly. For the undercurrent in Bauman's worldview remains, and it involves both a sense of loss and some sense of continuity in the form of anthropological street-wisdom. Bauman criticizes sociology persistently, but never deserts it; there is an insider/outsider dialectic at work here of the most extraordinary quality, and for us – as creatures of ambivalence – it is exactly this which appeals. It is as though the sense of loss encountered in modernity is precisely civilizational or in that sense, cultural; as though it constrains us powerfully and yet brings out the best in us, as creatures of habit, persistence, routine and innovation. Modernity becomes second nature, as it were, but it does not impinge directly upon our souls, for human beings are smarter and more resilient than that. We may be fools, in this way of thinking, or creatures of habit, but we are not idiots. We retain our need for dignity and freedom, and this is what generates the critique of modernity and its illusions. For consumer culture can only satisfy our second natures. We do see ourselves in the mirror of consumption, but we do not recognize the whole of our being there. Thus Bauman here damns the world of consumption but also decries the exclusion of the poor from its apparent rewards and riches. There are now, he concludes, still two nations in Britain, as there were when Disraeli first discerned the dichotomy in *Sybil*. If the market economy now is the kingdom of freedom, then the striking social division is that between those who can participate in this world and those who are excluded from it. The two nations are no longer Disraeli's, or Marx's, exploiters and exploited, bourgeoisie and proletariat (Bauman, 1987: 169). Our two nations are those of the seduced and the repressed. 'Without the second of these two nations, the picture of the post-modern world is totally incomplete' (1987: 169). Thus our most ambivalent of sociologists returns to the path of sociology; for the postmodern must also be viewed sociologically, precisely because, in the old language, it is a culture which is delivered (or denied) through an economy.

The irony about the way in which intellectuals identify with History or Progress, however, is that they also insist on insinuating others into the picture. So it is, for example, that peasants or proletarians become portrayed as stereotypical heroes. The flaws of the socialist imagination and those of sociology are often connected. Indeed, while the history of sociology should never be reduced to that of marxism there is nevertheless a particular sense in which their fortunes across recent times have been intertwined, for better and for worse. So here Bauman's thinking connects back to *Memories of Class*, where the 'Progress of Reason' involves a process in which the fact of factory confinement is substituted for what memory held alive as the image of the freedom of the petty producer (1987: 174). Only this dream of reason could not hold, even if this fact, in turn, was until recently too painful for us to recognize. The middle classes, socialists included, were so entranced by their own civilizing mission as to occlude their vision when it came to popular desire. Lenin agreed with Kautsky, that, left to themselves the proletariat would fail to come up with much; probably they would rather kick a football than get really serious. Marx's views were more complicated, but remained ambiguous; he presumed that the working class were capable of self-organization but analysed the problem away in what Lukács later constructed as the epistemologically privileged proletariat, positing alongside this the simultaneous sense that only those who had really understood Hegel could respectably call themselves marxists (Bauman, 1987: 175).

Bauman does not use these words here, but his arguments are caught up with representation and social ventriloquism. Marxists have long claimed to know, and to represent the interests of the workers better than they could themselves; there is, therefore, a kind of weird sense in which marxists magically become the proletariat made articulate, in a kind of substitutionism which even the young Trotsky might have marvelled at. But at the same time this is an issue more easily identified than resolved; for representation nevertheless remains a fact of modern life. If social ventriloquism is a moral problem, then institutional representation remains also a political fact. Bauman's purpose here, however, is less to resolve the issue itself than to argue forcefully for its recognition; for intellectuals are both narcissistic and yet self-denying. They both project their own problems and insecurities onto others and yet deny their interest in between those who rule and those who are dominated; they identify with superiors or inferiors as they choose, making invisible the specificity of their own project or ambition in the process. In other words, the ambiguity of legislation and interpretation is built into the position of the modern intellectual itself, which results in the combination of all rights with no responsibilities. The radical intellectual is the pantomime proletarian, the son of the people until the people get out of hand. If the proletarian therefore lets the intellectual down, this is only because the intellectual has constructed the proletarian in his own heroic image. The workers, in the meantime, stubbornly persist in identifying themselves as they will; they have better things to do than listen to the hectoring speeches of others.

And this is part of the problem, in turn, for the institutionalization of the working class by capitalism was never fully realized, and is now, again, unravelling, as labour is expelled from Fordist capitalism. Whereas marxists hitherto pondered the prospects of labour after capitalism, we today are faced with the puzzle of capitalism after labour, at least in the Fordist sense. That capitalism which vampire-like sucked the lifeblood from labour, in Marx's image, is replaced historically by the international mobile phone, don't-call-us of footloose finance (Bauman, 1987: 179). Today, we are locked into economic life less by the imperative to sell our labour-power than by the proliferation of things to consume. So class remains an actuality, as there is an apparent connection between personal income and expenditure, even as some categories of the population are redefined as economically redundant, surplus to the system's need. The old marxian theorem which indicated that the unemployed belonged to a reserve army, no longer then holds; and now Bauman begins to develop what becomes a standard claim in his work, that the dysfunctional can now be held up as examples, as human scarecrows as the rest of us scramble to keep up paid work. The new poor fail, on this account, to make good the transition from the old, productive way of life to that of consumptive bliss. They are not good consumers, or rather, their consumption does not matter much for the successful reproduction of capital (1987: 181). Even worse, they are known to consume outside of market circulation, an anti-social act if ever there was one.

For Bauman, then, this new postmodern population can either be seduced by consumerism, glitz and neon, or risk repression, harassment, being moved on endlessly at other people's insistence. So it is in this text, *Legislators and Interpreters*, that Bauman's work meets up with Jeremy Seabrook's, most notably *Landscapes of Poverty* (1985) (Bauman, 1987: 186). The virtual realities of endless orgasmic consumption, sex, lies and video generate a world which makes Weber's Protestant Ethic seem a universe, rather than merely a lifetime away. The outsiders, those without goods or hope are the cultural other of those elegant yuppies who spend money like there was no tomorrow. Yet this pair of others is not like that bourgeois and proletarian, set, as it were, against each other implacably, bearers of two difference cultures. The 'achiever' is rather a trend-setter, an example to be followed, 'a pioneer on the road everyone must aspire to follow, and a confirmation that aspiring is realistic' (1987: 187). Within these parameters it is impossible to criticize this endless noonward race; we can only be enjoined to catch up, to run faster.

But now it is time for Bauman to close this book. He does so by returning to the two possible optics before us, offering two conclusions, one each in modern and postmodern style. For while his purpose has plainly been to criticize the modern, his stated intention is also to avoid viewing the postmodern merely as its victorious or superior historical replacement. And as the foregoing shows, there will be ways in which the postmodern involves more senses of gain than loss, at least for some of us.

Bauman's modern conclusion to *Legislators and Interpreters* invokes the spirit of classical sociology with its core concern, that capitalism unregulated would erode society as we knew it. Markets rule; consumption replaces needs and transforms identity. Modernity in this sense has failed (1987: 191); or else, perhaps it has merely lived up to the blackest sociological scenarios anticipated by Weber or Simmel. To argue in this way, as Bauman recognizes, however, is nevertheless to hold open the principle of redemption. On this account, the 'potential of modernity is still untapped, and the promise of modernity needs to be redeemed' (1987: 191). Bauman's terms of reference in this modernist scenario are evidently Habermasian, which in a way surprises given the effective absence of Habermas' work from Bauman's analysis in this text. In any case, the coincidence is enough to make one wonder how much plausibility Bauman gives to this 'modern' conclusion. Yet Bauman does insist that the modern prospect remains open: we still strive towards the in-principle possibility that we could combine the dual values of personal autonomy and societal rationality (1987: 192).

Bauman's postmodern conclusion seems more resonant with the sympathies of his book. Here, the general scenario is that the Puritan gives way to the consumer, bracketing the poor and oppressed out of the social picture, socially or sociologically invisible, beyond redemption. The oppressed are no longer imagined as the antithesis of the system; rather, they are the failed attempts of the mediocre to fly (1987: 193). If, then Bauman's analytical sympathies stretch towards the idea of the postmodern as the critique of the modern, his personal sympathies are more old-fashioned. This is a world of hedonism where cynicism reigns. Bauman, the old utopian, must needs now protest; for even for moderns, utopianism ruled (1987: 194). It is as though Bauman recasts Durkheim's old insistence in *Elementary Forms of the Religious Life* (1915), where the implication is that the society which has no image of itself – no tradition or vision – will surely die. For Bauman, in contrast, that society which cannot sustain a plurality of imagined futures is already dead, closed, at least, to its own possibilities. So how can we do better, without endlessly retreading these old paths? The essential clue to the postmodern alternative in Bauman's work remains with the idea of interpretation, or legislation. The refusal of strategy is still, as he puts it in discussion of Rorty, a strategy in itself (1987: 198). Bauman's final conclusion is, in effect, to step out of his text altogether:

> Rorty's anti-strategy seems to fit very well the autonomy and the institutionally encouraged concern of academic philosophy with its own self-reproduction. Until further cuts, that is. (1987: 198)

Philosophers are permitted to abuse philosophy, for internal consumption, as it were; only then the postmodern huns arrive at the academy door, offering to confirm the diagnosis of the philosophers by closing the university. Thus do we speak authentically in one voice to our colleagues, and in another to our enemies, without undue fear of inconsistency; and in sociology it is just the same.

Conclusions: Out, towards Understanding

The path of the twentieth century may well lead from utopia to dystopia. Modernity opens the skies on our sense of possibility, even if it leaves us entering the millennium clutching only showbags or glossy brochures. The limit of utopia, in Bauman's argument, emerges as connected to its operationalizability. Utopia ought to remain in the realm of hope rather than programme, ending up in the brochure or in Disneyworld. The attempt to make utopia raises the question of the status of Jacobinism, discussed in Chapter 4 of the present study. Bauman's temptation is to identify Jacobinism and Enlightenment, or at least Reason and State with the project of *les philosophes*. We might choose to criticize this identification on analytical or historical grounds, only then the task of explaining modernity would remain. For we may well be prepared to grant that modernity is by nature ambivalent, but how does that help us explain the damage done in its name? Bauman's achievement in this context is to contribute more, I think, to the sociology of intellectuals than any other such writer in the twentieth century. Is this a confession on his part? as a lapsed marxist? No more so than the rest of us. It remains morally necessary for someone to call the injustices of the world we have made.

It is not Bauman's claim that we can do without intellectuals; in one residual respect his is only the Weberian reminder, that forms of authority ought not be inflated or illegitimately transferred from one sphere into another. Yet the messenger, the hermeneut will never only bring the mail. Some interpreters will also bear utopias, which we can accept or reject or pass on for the consideration of others. The point is that, at the end of the day, the political opinion of the intellectual is worth no more than that of any other citizen; and this is why we are bound to muddle through, occasionally shooting the messenger, metaphorically speaking.

In Bauman's work, in any case, it becomes apparent that language matters as communication, and not the other way around. Utopian horizons count along with traditional horizons, cultures, activities and habits whether real or imagined or both. The oddity about modernity, in this regard, is what centrality of place and value it has given to ideas and to their bearers, we intellectuals. Modernity truly is, or was, the age of ideology, but this holds true only as it reveals to us the worst and the best of its potentiality. We believed in the possibility of reform; we hoped for human perfectibility. As Bauman indicates, various interpretations or conclusions can be drawn from this assessment: more damning – what a disaster modernity has been; more modest, in turn – perhaps we need still to persist, do better. The latter, more powerful implication I think remains more resonant in Bauman's work. For contrary, say, to the legacy of aristocratic radicalism worked out through Critical Theory, Bauman's project seems to retain the sense that innerly humans do not fully internalize the disasters of the cultures or civilizations which they inhabit. Second nature remains misleading. We still retain our own ways of going on.

The Holocaust and the Perfect Order

Modernity and the Holocaust is almost certainly Bauman's most influential book. Winner of the European Amalfi Prize for Sociology and Social Theory in 1989, it has generated an extraordinary degree of interest, though perhaps not as much as Bauman might have hoped within mainstream sociology itself. For Bauman's purpose in this book was not to add another voice to those across Jewish or Holocaust Studies demanding that the ethical import of these events be recognized, nor yet was it another spin on preexisting cases or an attempt to draw new evidence to light. Bauman's insistence, rather, was that those practising the normal science of sociology were obliged to view or review the Holocaust as a central fact of modernity, of modern rather than German history, us and now and not just them or there. Modernity, on this account, was then and remains now as capable of generating barbarism as civilization. The message in the Holocaust, for Bauman, addressed the human condition in modernity. Sociologists could not afford to leave this to the specialists, even if this is exactly what could be expected in modern times.

Modernity and the Holocaust (1989a) is dedicated 'to Janina , and all the others who survived to tell the truth'. The Preface to the book tells the story of how his wife Janina's own work had such an incredible impact upon him. Zygmunt Bauman had not personally been directly touched by the Nazi Holocaust; Janina, in contrast, had grown up in the Warsaw ghetto. As Zygmunt Bauman puts it, to this point in his own life the Holocaust had been like a picture on the wall, tragic but neatly framed, a kind of closed capsule containing Germans and their abominations against Jews (1989a: vii). As these matters opened up on him, Bauman recast his image; for now the Holocaust appeared as a window, rather than a picture on the wall. It was a window on modernity.

Winter in the Morning

Janina and Zygmunt Bauman are a couple whose companionship is intellectual and political as well as personal and private. The significance of her work for his should not be underemphasized. *Winter in the Morning* (1986), her memoir of childhood, is an extraordinary book, impossible to summarize in its pathos and persistence, for its capacity to relate the horrors of life in the Warsaw ghetto is balanced by the ability to indicate that even in these depths, life and love went on. As overwhelming as passages in the book can be, Janina Bauman's own sense of ambivalence saves it from the unrelenting blackness which often compels readers of books like this to push them away, numbed, overwhelmed by the desperate hopelessness of it all. The book is an act of recovery. It restates not only the depravity of the institutionalized anti-semitism which was Nazism, but also reinstates the ordinary resilience of its victims, who had to go about making what they could of their lives in or outside the cast of the searchlight and the ever anticipated doorknock. The world of Janina Bauman's childhood changed, in effect, overnight. Its relative comfort gave way to hiding and starvation. The little things that held life together disappeared, were simply destroyed. So were the larger things; Janina's father died in the Katyn massacre. Under all these devastations, life continued; reading poetry and Descartes, or the *Communist Manifesto*, or *The Life of Termites* by Maeterlink, minding her mother and sister, worrying about love and boys while working in the cemetery or else hiding in those false compartments in backs of cupboards which most of us know about only from movies; these are extraordinary stories, told without self-pity.

As Janina Bauman puts it in closing *Winter in the Morning*, to look as a young Jewish girl upon the face of a German, a boy in this case rather than a man, left no sense of pity, or hatred, or joy, even though the war was over. Life returned to an earlier order, after a fashion, but in a different sense it was never the same. For while the enemies around her had shown Janina Bauman what depths humans would sink to, thieving petty personal belongings if not actually kicking Jewish heads, there were ordinary heroes aplenty fighting against them or merely offering compassion or a crust of bread. The message, if there is one here, seems to resemble Zygmunt Bauman's own sensibility (or perhaps it is the other way around) that humans are capable of all kinds of descent into inhumanity, and yet of snapping, shifting out of this as well (J. Bauman, 1986). The capacity for evil lies within each of us; and modernity compounds this, as Zygmunt Bauman will argue in *Modernity and the Holocaust* (1989a), by removing us from the face of the other. *Winter in the Morning* is an astonishing book, the enchantment of which cannot be conveyed; in order to understand Zygmunt Bauman's work, you must read it. For it contains the same kind of hope amidst despair, or sense of prospects among limits of the most severe kind, as holds up Bauman's sociology. The point is not so much, as it was for the redemptive young Marx, that everything is possible, as it is that anything is possible, perhaps even at the hands of the very same human actors.

How can we make sense of these human extremities? How can it be that humans could be capable of such violence and cowardice and yet of such compassion and sacrifice? For Zygmunt Bauman, the initial response was to look upon the Holocaust as a kind of radical exception, a gaping hole that had opened up in the fabric of what should have been a better history. Bauman tells us that earlier he still believed, by default rather than by deliberation, that the Holocaust was an interruption in the normal flow of history, a cancerous growth on the body of a civilized society, a momentary madness among sanity (1989a: viii).

But if the Holocaust opens all kinds of ethical or anthropological questions about us, and our propensity to do good and evil, then Bauman's major task in his book is more pointedly sociological. As he writes, it must also be a problem for sociology as such:

> *The Holocaust was born and executed in our modern rational society, at the high stage of our civilization and at the peak of human cultural achievement, and for this reason it is a problem of that society, civilization and culture.* (1989a: x)

Already Bauman hints at one aspect of his major thesis, that the Holocaust represents some kind of collusion between universal or transhistorical purposes and particular, technological means. Bauman early sets his argument against that view for which the Holocaust was a German, cultural problem without messages for all of us as humans or citizens of the planet. To compartmentalize the Holocaust, in this way, is to push it away, as though the other is elsewhere, rather than part of us. Bauman's hope, to the contrary, is to mainstream the Holocaust for sociology, for the Holocaust will surely tell us something about modernization, civilization, science and social engineering, and about us. Bauman begins from this claim, that 'the Holocaust was a characteristically modern phenomenon that cannot be understood out of the context of cultural tendencies and technical achievements of modernity' (1989a: xiii). What Bauman sets out to capture analytically is the extraordinary ethical ambivalence of the Holocaust as an event or process simultaneously 'unique' and 'normal'. Even those categories of contrast cannot easily capture the slipperiness of the phenomenon at hand. Bauman summarizes his case, in anticipation:

> *The Holocaust was an outcome of a unique encounter between factors by themselves quite ordinary and common; . . . the possibility of such an encounter could be blamed to a very large extent on the emancipation of the political State, with its monopoly of means of violence and its audacious engineering ambitions, from social control – following the step-by-step dismantling of all non-political power resources and institutions of social self management.* (1989a: xiii)

The provisos concerning politics and the sense of political contingency are worth emphasizing from the beginning. For even in bringing attention to bear upon the technological determinants of the Holocaust, Bauman is not offering an interpretation based on technological determinism. True, the Nazis needed the means to make the Holocaust, which was qualitatively and not only quantitatively more exhaustive than the hitherto-existing tradition of pogrom or random acts of violence against Jews. But it was the political will of Nazism which made all this happen; so that it is the combination of factors which begins to explain the event. It was not enough that the technological means of destruction were available, or that totalitarian political forms prevailed; it was also necessary that the Nazi Party actively set out to destroy the Jews as an ideal and real threat to their own project. Such is the sociological perspective which Zygmunt Bauman brings to bear upon the experience related by his wife in *Winter in the Morning*.

Modernity and the Holocaust

Bauman's project in *Modernity and the Holocaust* (1989a) is more than a little heretical; for he wants us to view it less as a sequence in itself, than as an opening onto something other. Invariably we can expect that his work will be criticized for failing to say enough about Germans and Jews as the specific actors involved. So why did this terror occur in *Germany*? and so on. Suffice to say, for the present, that Bauman eschews the kind of cultural particularism which informs a controversial work like Daniel Goldhagen's *Hitler's Willing Executioners* (Goldhagen, 1996; see also Beilharz, 1999). The distinction in approach is simple: where Goldhagen sees the Holocaust as a German accident waiting to happen, Bauman views it as an accident waiting to happen within the field of possibilities we call modernity. In any case, Bauman does not approach the problem of the Holocaust as an immanent problem or a local story. Why? Because it speaks to all of us, not just Germans and Jews; and because our discipline, sociology, needs to face up to this, for '*The Holocaust has more to say about the state of sociology than sociology in its present shape is able to add to our knowledge of the Holocaust*' (Bauman, 1989a: 3). Sociology has missed the boat, on this score, because it can only view the Holocaust as an accident, more specifically as the failure rather than the product of modernity (1989a: 5). Thus the stock western remedy for Nazism, after the fact, would be: more modernization, as though all that were modern were good, and all evil resulted from surplus traditionalism, or barbarism or ignorance.

Nor does Bauman seek simply to reverse this optimistic view of history and make the Holocaust the beast or the necessary result of modernity. The point is not, as the cynics would have it, that the Holocaust is the truth of modernity, but that it is one possibility within it. This is where both the analytical and the ethical challenge begins. Nazism is, among other things, inescapably modern. Auschwitz was also a mundane extension of the modern factory system, a sort of murderous Fordism in the making, a massive system of social engineering gone awry through reaching its own technical apogee. For Bauman, every element of the Holocaust was normal, in the sense of being fully in keeping with everything we know about our civilization, for civilization both creates and destroys. This contradiction, however, is exactly what is missing from most of the sociology of modernity, which identifies either dynamic progress or barbarism but not both, together.

Modern civilization, then, was not the sufficient but the necessary condition of the Holocaust. Without it, the Holocaust would be unthinkable (1989a: 13). Certainly the Holocaust would have been unimaginable outside not only the industrial image of production but also the bureaucratic model of rationality. Bureaucracy, of course, can be put to any end, can serve any master; and the instructions given did change historically across the history of the Third Reich. The early plans, to physically expel the Jews from Germany resulted in the Final Solution's diktat of elimination. Physical extermination became the most efficient bureaucratic response to the Jewish 'problem' (1989a: 17). The Final Solution knew nothing of the street passions of small town Germans; it was a serious business, guided by scientific management. The intersection of social engineering and instrumental rationality proves fatal, for the gardening posture divides vegetation into 'cultured plants' to be taken care of, and Jewish weeds to be exterminated (1989a: 18). Yet all these possibilities only begin to make sense of the Holocaust on the basis of something more elemental: the social production of moral indifference. Bauman argues per Herbert Kelman that moral inhibitions against violent atrocities tend to be eroded once three conditions are met, singly or together: when violence is officially *authorized*, *routinized*, and the victims *dehumanized* (1989a: 21). What is disarming about this list is that the first two features are already built in to so much of our institutional lives, yet the normal result of their combination is so radically different to 'ordinary' life. As Bauman observes, cooperation of the victims with the perpetrators of a pogrom is inconceivable (1989a: 22–3). The story of the Jewish police, in the Warsaw ghetto or elsewhere, makes all this difference through cooptation and routinization. The space for moral argument is closed, squeezed out, politically circumscribed by the anti-politics of totalitarianism. Arbitrary state power justifies violence as its own end. Indeed the state here becomes the object of Bauman's critical scrutiny as much as anything else.)

Why, then, ought the Jews be the particular object of the Nazi will to obliterate? Together with the Gypsies, they were self-evidently nationless, even though as Bauman observes the Jews were perhaps more fully accommodated into German culture, by the Weimar Republic, than any other such group (1989a: 31). Plainly the Jews could be fitted nicely into the category of the other. Here Bauman connects his thinking back to the themes of *Culture as Praxis* (1973a), where the conceptual Jew is analysed as *visqueux*, in Sartre's term, or 'slimy', in Mary Douglas', begging for expulsion in the lexicon of the Nazis (1989a: 39): '*The conceptual Jew carried a message; alternative to this order here and now is not another order, but chaos and devastation*' (1989a: 39). So the order/disorder, order and ambivalence issue is also posited here, though it is more fully elaborated upon later, in *Modernity and Ambivalence* (1991a). For the meantime, the Jew was an empty signifier whose identity could be filled up with anything or everything to which the mainstream objected. The Jew could be Bolshevik or bourgeois, socialist or capitalist, weak pacifist or ferocious warmonger, masses or elite, parasite or seducer, or all of these at once (1989a: 42). The figure of the Jew became a kind of floating signifier upon which all kinds of crimes or disorders could be projected as the meretricious immoralities of proletarians, aristocrats and shopkeepers alike. 'And so', Bauman summarizes, 'the Jews were caught in the most ferocious of historical conflicts: that between the pre-modern world and advancing modernity' (1989a: 45).

This is the fate of all of us, in different ways, given that modernity and tradition are always, ever complicit. Modernity and modernism become traditions, or habits at least. Fascism could therefore emerge not as a mere throwback to plebian demagoguery or Black Forest fantasy, but as what Jeffrey Herf would conceptually capture as 'reactionary modernism', a kind of hybrid necessarily combining high technology with romantic antimodern illusions of native teutonic grandeur (Herf, 1984). *The irony of history would allow the anti-modernist phobias to be unloaded through channels and forms only modernity could develop*' (Bauman, 1989a: 46). Only these ironies of history are normal, rather than exceptional, for modernity and anti-modernism always carry each other, as later do the modern and the post-modern (Beilharz, 1994b). The Jews, in particular, were also both of those things; traditionalistic, yet the epitome of the hated modernity itself. As Spengler had argued in *The Decline of the West* (1922), it was the rootless, cosmopolitan Jews who presented such a threat to the peace and stability, hearth and home warmth of *Gemeinschaft*. It was the Jews who in a sense represented the corrosive effects of modernity better than anyone else, for their identity was mobile rather than concretely rooted, though this was hardly a new experience for these people. Thus even socialists, like Werner Sombart, could end up anti-semites, on specific grounds of their opposition to usury or finance capital as well as those of generalized anti-modernism. As Bauman had shown in *Memories of Class* (1982), socialism could be reactionary as easily as it could modernist; and the path of reaction could travel in various different ways, some of them xenophobic or chauvinistic. Judaism became identified with money and power, indeed with 'the money power', for opponents left and right; anti-semitism made for some unholy alliances. For as Bauman observes, the way in which the Nazis forced the issue itself brought on the clarification of these political and ethical differences. It was not until the emergence of the Nazi movement that popular opposition to capitalism finally split and polarized, and the socialist branch finally adopted the uncompromising struggle against anti-semitism as one of the necessary elements in its attempt to stem the rising tide of fascism (1989a: 48). Anti-semitism had been the socialism of beginners. Even then, the question of remaining sympathies between Bolshevism and National Socialism was allowed to smoulder, or else was analytically avoided by resort to the categorical insistence that because of the agreed system of classification 'left' and 'right' could have nothing in common.

Bauman assembles his case here from all kinds of available materials, drawing perhaps especially heavily on those of Raul Hilberg and Christopher Browning. If there is a philosophical frame of reference which he relies upon more than others, it is likely to be located in the work of Hannah Arendt. Thus he proposes, invoking Arendt's memorable phrase, that in 'contrast to all other groups, the Jews were defined and their position determined by the body politic' (Bauman, 1989a: 50). The Jews were defined and then destroyed by the Nazi body politic; nothing in this was technologically given or culturally necessary. The decision to destroy the Jews was political, not economic. The Jews were unlike any other nation; they were also unlike any other foreigners; they were, indeed, the epitome of Simmel's *strangers* – always on the outside even when inside, as the sadness of their willing if contingent assimilation into German culture was to reveal. As Bauman painfully expresses it, 'there was hardly a single door slammed on the road to modernity in which the Jews did not put their fingers'. So they *'were the opacity of the world fighting for clarity, the ambiguity of the world lusting for certainty'* (1989a: 56). Only this local, Nazi world with global pretensions sought for certainty in tradition and not only through modernity, in the fantastic images of imaginary purity of a lost world destroyed as well as transmitted by modernity's ambivalent arrival.

At this point Bauman invokes again the image of the gardening state to symbolically represent the modern mania for a tight and final sense of order, as opposed to the earlier complacency of a social model more like gamekeeping (1989a: 57). Perhaps what is at issue is that the garden is bulldozed into nature, and only then 'naturalized'. For as Bauman argues, the elimination of the Jews was presented as a synonym of the rejection of modern order, yet it was achieved through that order. Racism as a modern phenomenon is unthinkable without the advancement of modern science, modern technology and modern forms of state power; racism as such is a strictly modern phenomenon (1989a: 61). 'Racism, in short, is a thoroughly modern weapon used in the conduct of pre-modern, or at least not exclusively modern, struggles' (1989a: 62). Now Bauman develops the argument that racism, itself, is an overinflated category which risks losing thereby its critical sting. Heterophobia is one thing; inter-group prejudice or resentment is widespread, and tends to stay this side of action. Racism proper involves less a personal attitude than a mobilization of political will.

> Racism differs from both heterophobia and constant enmity. The difference lies neither in the intensity of sentiments nor in the type of argument used to rationalize it. *Racism stands apart by a practice of which it is part and which it rationalizes: a practice that combines strategies of architecture and gardening with that of medicine – in the service of the construction of an artificial social order, through cutting out the elements of the present reality that neither fit the visualized perfect reality, nor can be changed so that they do.* (1989a: 65)

In other words, racism manifests the conviction that a certain category of human beings cannot be incorporated into the proper rational order, whatever the effort. In the modern world, distinguished by its ambition to self-control and self-administration, racism declares a certain category of people endemically and hopelessly resistant to control and immune to all efforts at amelioration. The consequence is inevitably associated with the strategy of estrangement (1989a: 65).

Racism, then, is an institutional matter, a problem of state policy, which in the Nazi case is mediated through social engineering on a grandiose scale. The very idea of social engineering raises again the question of Enlightenment. For Enlightenment deifies not only science, but also Nature. Arguments to nature, disguised so as to appear primordial rather than artificial, now become a standard strategy. It is within the realm of this social engineering neutrality that gardening and medicine supply the archetypes of the constructive (sic) stance (1989a: 70). Judaism becomes a problem of Political Hygiene; the Nazi task consists of safeguarding the good people from an overgrowth of the weeds. This in turn means that the people have to be educated about the threat to their wellbeing, for there will be a good chance that they do not know their enemy and need warming up on the issue sufficiently to follow their Aryan leaders with the appropriate levels of frenzied enthusiasm. This is exactly what necessitates some formal distinction between racism and heterophobia, for where heterophobia is a fact of daily social psychology, racism is an institutionalized form rooted within modern neutrality and modern social organization (1989a: 81). Modernity cannot explain the Holocaust, but it did make it possible. Modern genocide is political, in the sense that it is goal-orientated. It seeks to destroy an adversary, but with a specific purpose in mind: to achieve the grand vision of a better, and radically different society; so that Stalinism, too, depended upon a particular kind of genocide, this time directed against a class rather than a race. The kulaks or rich peasants, like the Jews in Germany, are the weeds which choke up the lives of those whose birthright it is to inhabit the garden. This, according to Bauman, is because modern culture is a garden culture: it defines itself as the design for an ideal life and a perfect arrangement of human conditions.

Put in more general terms, modernity has yet to come to grips with its others; to this point in time, it tends rather to grip them by the throat, or as Bauman will later suggest, either to expel them or to devour them. Modernity espouses the value of difference, as against the traditionalistic insistence on Oneness, Unity or *Einheit*; yet the very nature of modernity or at least of moderns is to lapse always back into traditionalism. Modernity, or its inhabitants, in any case reinvents the other over and over again. Partly, as Bauman will detail in *Modernity and Ambivalence* (1991a), this is bound up with the way we think or are encouraged to think. But as Bauman insists, this does not cast us inevitably in the pattern of hopeless repetition; if modernity is not exactly the history of progress, then it is not coextensive with totalitarianism either. Totalitarianism, to the contrary, is a specific political form available within modernity; it is one pattern of an alternative modernity, offering a different route, say, to liberal capitalist democracy, Fordism or welfarism. So while Bauman wants us to draw the horrible image of Auschwitz closer, so that we can also see ourselves in it, he does not want to argue that we all live our daily lives 50 years later on Auschwitz principles:

> From the fact that the Holocaust is modern, it does not follow that modernity is a Holocaust. The Holocaust is a byproduct of the modern drive to a fully designed, fully controlled world, once the drive is getting out of control and running wild. Most of the time, modernity is prevented from doing so. Its ambitions clash with the pluralism of the human world. (1989a: 93)

相
衝
突

The Holocaust is unique because it brings together some ordinary factors of modernity which are normally kept apart.)
(Is not modernity then after all a pattern of decline? This is nevertheless the logic of Bauman's work, that the substitution of civilization for nature leads us down the road to ruin. Civilization does not replace violence; it both institutionalizes and represses it. We learn to be more civil to each other at the very same time as we become progressively more indifferent and nasty (1989a: 95–7). Modernity provides us with the means or practical forms which enable us to be less human towards the other. Now Bauman turns his critical attention to the distancing effects of the division of labour. All divisions of labour create distance between persons by establishing links which take us away from the face of the other.) These result in levels of opacity never before encountered; the decision-makers do not actually witness the outcomes of the processes which they bureaucratically initiate (1989a: 99). These processes are universal in modernity; they are as apparent in the working of capitalist corporations or instruments of the welfare state as they are in Auschwitz. Imperatives are inserted into the top end of these social machines, and statistical (and human) results come out the bottom end. The result is the irrelevance of moral standards for the technical success of the bureaucratic operation (1989a: 101). The complexity and scale of modern divisions of labour mean that morality and competence are redefined as obedience. Bureaucracy generates dehumanization. As Musil has one of his characters say in *The Man Without Qualities*:

> This system of indirection elevated to an art is what nowadays enables the individual and society as a whole to function with clear conscience; the button to be pressed is always clean and shiny, and what happens at the other end of the line is the business of others, who, for their part, don't press the button. Do you find this revolting? It is how we let thousands die or vegetate, set in motion whole avalanches of suffering, but we always get things done. (Musil, 1995: 696)

Bureaucracy works, even as it generates dehumanization.

At times in Bauman's book it is unclear whether it is bureaucracy or politics which emerges as the main culprit. Perhaps it is both. For Bauman argues that it was ultimately Nazi policy, as politics, which made the Holocaust; yet bureaucracy, he says, is programmed to seek the optimal solution, so that bureaucracy is a determinant even regardless of the policy which is inserted into it. Certainly bureaucracy, and bureaucratic conceptions of 'efficiency' become defined as goals in themselves. Bureaucracy thus paved the way for fascism: '*Bureaucracy which acquitted itself so well of the task of cleansing Germany made more ambitious tasks feasible, and their choice well-nigh natural*' (1989a: 105). The visionaries of National Socialism made all this happen; for bureaucracy picks up where visionaries stop: 'But bureaucracy made the Holocaust. And it made it in its own image' (1989a: 105). Perhaps it is bureaucracy that delivers the nightmare, and the visionaries who imagine it, triggering the process of Holocaust through their possession of State power. For if bureaucracy is intrinsically capable of genocide, then the process of its development also depends upon the gardeners, those particular utopians whose image of the good society depends on the expulsion of a social curse, a race or a class which symbolizes all that which the new order seek to transcend. It is this fatal combination which has such devastating results (1989a: 106).

The greatest complacency available to us here comes of the conceit that we are, indeed, civilized. What Norbert Elias called 'The Civilizing Process' is an inevitably compromised process, extending Freud's claim in *Civilization and its Discontents* (1930). Civility is never more than a veneer; the prospect of violence and cruelty always rests just beneath that surface. The Scientists and Sociologists of Nazi Germany were only too happy to ride on this train. Now again Bauman insists that the direction of this story is primarily political. Social dislocations may differ in form and intensity, he says, but they are invited by the general effect of the *pronounced supremacy of political over economic and social power, of the state over society* (1989a: 112). Modernity remains the frame within which all this becomes possible, for Bauman, though the characterization he offers here sounds more like modernism – an age of artificial order and of grand societal designs, the fantasy of Faust, the era of planners, visionaries and 'gardeners' who treat society as a virgin plot of land to be expertly designed and then cultivated and doctored to keep to the preordained form (1989a: 113). Modernity *becomes* modernism fulfilled: perhaps this is the conceptual message which Bauman urges upon us here; all its other prospects become closed or blocked. As Bauman summarizes, three major factors here come in to play: the design or vision gives the modern holocaust the legitimation; state bureaucracy gives it the vehicle; and the paralysis of society gives it the 'road clear' sign (1989a: 114).

Subsequent developments, Bauman notes, make the present scenario even more cheerful. Information technology – the electronic battlefield – takes the face of the other even further away. The face of the other today wears the mask of Saddam Hussein. The psychological or moral distance between actors now becomes entirely absolute, or opaque. Bauman reminds us of Jacques Ellul's famous caution, that anything technologically possible will now be done, just because of this possibility (1989a: 116). It is as though ours is a civilization altogether out of control. What is surprising, in this sense, is the singularity of the Holocaust, rather than its specific occurrence.

For Bauman also wants to argue that the Holocaust is an extraordinary example of the irrationality of modern rationality. Thus the Nazis sought to exterminate the Jews rather than to enslave them; to destroy, rather than to take advantage of them. As Bauman proposes, this illustrates the perverse ability of modern, rational bureaucracy to induce actions functionally indispensable to its purposes while jarringly at odds with the vital interests of the actors (1989a: 122). This led both the Jews to participate in their own destruction, and the Nazis finally to create theirs, in turn. The victims soiled themselves, as their perpetrators did all along. But if the ethics of survival in the camps were extreme, the norms of the oppressors were more conventional, and this remains Bauman's primary orientation in *Modernity and the Holocaust*.

Bauman opens his discussion of the Milgram experiments by quoting Dwight Macdonald. Macdonald warned in 1945 that we would now have to fear the law-abiding person more than the one who broke the law (Bauman, 1989a: 151). The Holocaust forced upon us this universal message: faced with a morally impossible command, what should I do? Fascism did not result from chaos, from the heat of madness, but was administered through an impeccable, faultless and unchallengeable rule of law and order. The good Nazis were, after all, those who like you and me did what was expected of them, followed orders. If they did it, so could we. They were not monsters, even if they acted monstrously. Thus Bauman summarizes this most pertinent of conclusions: '*The most frightening news brought about by the Holocaust and by what we learned of its perpetrators was not the likelihood that "this" could be done to us, but the idea that we could do it*' (1989a: 152). It is exactly this kind of claim which Bauman must make in order to centre the Holocaust within the field of sociology; and it is just as likely this strategy of cross-reference which will also anger those working in Jewish Studies or Holocaust Studies, for whom the problems of Germans and Jews remain ever-present. Bauman's purpose is rather to generalize the Holocaust as a universal event. So he argues, for example, against the precedent established by Adorno and his colleagues in *The Authoritarian Personality* (1969), where it seems that only some types of people are capable of such terror. Adorno's vision divided the world into born proto-Nazis and their victims: 'The dark and dismal knowledge that many gentle people may turn cruel if given a chance was suppressed' (Bauman, 1989a: 153).

The message is continuous with that indicated by Janina Bauman in *Winter in The Morning*:

> During the war I learned the truth we usually choose to leave unsaid: that the cruellest thing about cruelty is that it dehumanizes its victims before it destroys them. And that the hardest of struggles is to remain human in inhuman conditions. (J. Bauman, 1986: viii)

Adorno's vision, like Goldhagen's, particularized or culturalized the problem, ascribing cruelty as it were to some categories of the population rather than others, emerging with a neat and simple image of victims and oppressors, good and bad citizens. Bauman's sociological curiosity and his ethical mission here is to highlight cruelty as an activity, rather than as a character-type. Individuals may well be classified as more, or less cruel; what is striking about the Holocaust, and in Bauman's frame, about the Milgram experiments, is rather how cruelty correlates with the relationship of authority and subordination.

Bauman's interpretation thus points in two different directions at the same time. It is sociological, in that it claims that inhumanity is constructed and practised within human relationships. As those relationships are rationalized and technically perfected, so is the capacity and the efficiency of the social production of inhumanity. But it is simultaneously ethical, for this claim opens the sense that there is an inverse relationship between the readiness to be cruel and the proximity of its victims (1989a: 154–5). *Modernity and the Holocaust* not only turns the Holocaust from a picture into a frame; it also opens the more direct engagement with the face of the other that culminates later in *Postmodern Ethics* (1993a).

Distance, however, is one thing; the problem which Bauman draws to our attention here is rationalized, or modernized distance, for the more rationalized is the organization of action, the easier it is to cause suffering – and to remain at peace with oneself (1989a: 155). It is this mechanized detachment and anonymity which makes the option of cruelty so readily available to those who would never harm the person whose breath you can hear. To put it more abstractly, action is removed from the senses, and from the senses of consequence. The suffering inflicted upon others disappears from the field of the senses of the perpetrator. Guilt is closed or blocked. Obedience becomes the substitute for conscience; law or morality offer pregiven circuits for individuals to follow. As Bauman summarizes it, '*Bureaucracy's double feat is the moralization of technology, coupled with the denial of the moral significance of non-technical issues*' (1989a: 160). When, to argue in sympathy with Weber, we blur the lines between ends and means or between ethics and instrumental action both practices suffer in the process. Morality as a matter of personal judgement seems to disappear at the very same moment that everyday life becomes moralistic. The point about the Milgram experiments, once viewed as an optic on the life of totalitarian societies, is that:

> the readiness to act against one's own better judgement, and against the voice of one's conscience, is not just the function of authoritative command, but the result of exposure to a single-minded, unequivocal and monopolistic source of authority.
> (1989a: 165)

Like Goffman's 'total institutions', the mechanisms of Nazism and fascism deprive or seek to deprive citizens of alternatives or senses of room for manoeuvre. Thus this most extraordinary traditionalism of these most modern, bureaucratic societies, where progress and development depend so directly and necessarily upon conformism. Modernity, in this way, depends upon the most robotic of human processes, and consequently is capable of delivering levels of human destructiveness at hitherto unimaginable levels.

Bauman's conclusion is as simple as, in a different way, this analysis is complex or paradoxical. Pluralism is the best preventative medicine against morally normal people engaging in morally abnormal actions. The voice of individual moral conscience is best heard in the tumult of political and social discord. This is the liberal, but more emphatically the libertarian voice in Bauman's writing at its most powerful; it is the voice of Albert Camus, or that of his characters, saying no, refusing to go along but not, for this reason, engaging in heroism, or at least not of any other than the most ordinary kind, like the Gentiles who help Jews under Nazism because they can do no other. If this is a call for strength in adversity, then, it is at the same time a social critique rather than a singular gesture towards psychology. For Bauman insists that if there is one central theme following from the Milgram experiments, it is that cruelty correlates with certain patterns of social interaction much more than it does with personality features or other individual idiosyncracies of the perpetrators: 'Cruelty is social in its origin much more than it is characterological' (1989a: 166). Bauman's purpose here is less to explain human cruelty as such than to throw light upon the social practices and forms of cruelty which add up to make a public regime of cruelty like Nazism. Institutionalized patterns of impersonality, humiliation and indignity become the cultural frames of totalitarian activity. Totalitarianism is a barred window on modernity.

Society as a Factory for Morality

Contrary to a whole tradition, say, of 1960s radicalism, then, Bauman here argues against the idea of the policeman in the head as the primary source of social reproduction. If society is like a factory for acceptable morality, then this is also only partly because factories make us work; they also generate other responses. Fascism does not, for Bauman, result from the little man that lives in all of us, or from what Etzioni called the 'latent Eichmann' in each head (Bauman, 1989a: 167). This is not to deny that we are all capable of cruelty, treachery, betrayal; to say that there is no alien-like gremlin awaiting within each of us is not to substitute for this the image of the internal angel. Bauman's critical point about the controlled experiments of Milgram or Zimbardo or the social-engineering regimes of Stalin or Hitler is rather that it is these vicious arrangements, and not the individual viciousness of the participants, that call out the orgy of cruelty (1989a: 167). What matters is that some people were given a total, exclusive and uninterrupted power over some other people: 'If there is a sleeper in each of us, he may remain asleep for ever if such a situation does not occur. And then we would never have heard of the sleeper's existence' (1989a: 168). This response on Bauman's part may not resolve the ontological status of evil; but then this is not the task which he has set himself. His frame remains the more conventionally sociological one, centred on problems of action while opening the door to ethics which lies on its other side. For this reason Bauman pushes away the idea of the Nazi Sleeper as a 'metaphysical prop', but only after he has inverted it, in order to make the observation that whether it exists or not, there is a sense in which those who resist are also sleepers in the first instance: 'Their capacity to resist evil was a "sleeper" through most of their lives. It could have remained asleep forever, and we would not know of it then. But *this* ignorance would be good news' (1989a: 168).

As Bauman proceeds to indicate, his argument leads towards the problem of the social nature of evil, or, more precisely, of the social production of immoral behaviour (1989a: 169). Plainly this is a substantial interpretative challenge, for the social scientization of sociology has effectively expelled morality from the field, reentering it by the backdoor as moralism. As Serge Moscovici argues in *The Invention of Society*, sociology becomes a practice characterized by institution-blaming (Moscovici, 1996). Whenever something goes wrong it is the fault of the school, the parents, television, the police or the welfare state; no one is ever responsible for anything at all these days. In Bauman's terms, talk about morality is subject to sociological reductionism, or the premise which runs from Montesquieu to Durkheim that moral phenomena can be exhaustively explained in terms of the non-moral institutions which lend them their binding force (1989a: 170).

Having established his curiosity about the Holocaust as a frame for making sense of modernity and the complicity of sociology in these fields both as part of the problem and potentially as a means of its explanation, Bauman now turns more fully into the analysis of sociology itself. This is a fascinating moment in terms of Bauman's own relationship to the classics. Deeply impressed by, yet increasingly distant from Marx, he remains deeply ambivalent about the contribution of Weber. Though there are senses of fundamental sympathy with Weber's Kantian critique of the way in which modernity generates its own self-destruction through the implosion of separate spheres, Bauman also seems to view Weber or Weberianism as part of the problem itself; the strength of his opposition to bureaucracy and its consequences pushes him away from this source of ambivalence in Weber's own project. Of Freud, there are various resonances especially perhaps later, when it comes to *Civilization and its Discontents* (1930); and Simmel's sociology is ever-present, though more as a kind of spiritual *Doppelgänger* than as an explicit model. But in this section of *Modernity and the Holocaust*, it is Durkheim whose legacy comes most powerfully under scrutiny. The problem in Durkheim's work, in a sense, is obvious; for it is Durkheim's work that calls out the critique of 'oversocialization'. Durkheim's identification of morality with social norms is in this way more potentially poisonous than anything that Marxists or Weberians could legitimately draw out of the work of their masters. For Durkheim initiates this modern sociological reduction par excellence, where society gives you morality and morality gives you society. The younger Durkheim may have well been a socialist, and the wealth of meaning in the later reflections of *The Elementary Forms of the Religious Life* (1915) may still remain unexhausted, yet there persists around Durkheim's work an aroma of conformism enough to make even the mildest mannered libertarian twitch. For if society (=?) determines what is morality, what, in turn, is the basis of either the critique of society, or of ethical conduct within that society? There is more traditionalism of a certain frightening kind in Durkheim's modernism than in either the Renaissance-utopia of Marx or the liberal stoicism of Weber:

> If anything, Durkheim's revision had rendered sociological reasoning about morality more circular than ever. If the only existential foundation of morality is the will of society, and its only function is to allow the society to survive, then the very issue of substantive evaluation of specific moral systems is effectively removed from the sociological agenda. (Bauman, 1989a: 172)

How should we live? – as we are told to? If each society has the morality it needs, what is it that enables us to speak out, or to think for ourselves? Ultimately the clever insight in Durkheim's maxim backfires: if such actions are evil as are socially prohibited, rather than social prohibition reflecting the social sense of evil, then god really is society, and our only duty is to conform. In this way Durkheim's sociology is both too traditionalistic, because conformist, and too modernistic, because relativist (1989a: 173). What Durkheim misses, then, is the possibility that while society might exercise a moralizing function, it may also act as a morality-silencing force (1989a: 174).

The conclusion to be drawn is not that Durkheim's sociology is worthless, but rather that it confirms the possibility that morality or ethics can be explained as a systemic function or secretion rather than as a human activity. On this score, the moral challenge posed by the phenomenon of the Holocaust to the discipline of sociology is frontal. The good citizen, law-abiding and civic in his or her obedience, will be the first to head the queue of would-be gardeners, all ready and too willing to do their duty in the name of the state or the will of the people. With a slight shift of emphasis, Bauman argues, the challenge of the Holocaust to law or right is deafening:

> *In the aftermath of the Holocaust, legal practice, and thus also moral theory, faced the possibility that morality may manifest itself in insubordination towards socially upheld principles, and in an action openly defying social solidarity and consensus.* (1989a: 177)

The good citizen may henceforth be he or she who stands against the *diktats* of compulsory *Gemeinschaft*. As Hannah Arendt argued, in effect, it now became incumbent upon us to contemplate the problem of moral responsibility for resisting socialization (Bauman, 1989a: 177). The ordinary relativism in morality generated by communal difference does not apply to the human capacity to differentiate between right and wrong (1989a: 178). Something must, on this account, precede socialization or the *conscience collective*; and this is why solidarity as such is not a good thing, but can be good or bad, as social solidarities can be constructed for different reasons and put to different ends, exclusive and xenophobic as well as warming and inclusive. Moral capacity, in this sense, must be located in the social, but not the societal sphere; or it must be practised in the realms of civil society, rather than in the state (1989a: 179). Morality results from being with others, not from rote instruction or code lists; we may find morality acted out within institutions, but it does not originate within the loci of such structures.

Enter Emmanuel Levinas, this most saintly of theorists. And Bauman begins in this company to anticipate some of the larger concerns he will extend into a fuller canvas – or is it window? – in *Postmodern Ethics* (1993a). Bauman's turn to Levinas is both necessary, and yet partial. Necessary, in one way, in that Bauman has insisted on the centrality of ethics to sociology and has demonstrated the hole in our disciplinary heart, so that the power of the critical diagnosis calls for a strong remedy, which is what Levinas offers with his insistence that ethics comes before ontology. For Levinas, as Bauman indicates, we are always with others; and the sociologists from Marx to Durkheim would agree, but it is as though they have not understood or dwelled sufficiently upon the profundity of their observations, as though they have shifted focus too soon to the level of seriality or group to take stock of the elements between you and me. According to Levinas, however, this is exactly the level upon which responsibility works – not my responsibility to class or nation or professional group, but to my immediate other: '*Responsibility is the essential, primary and fundamental structure of subjectivity*' (Bauman, 1989a: 183). Responsibility, however, arises out of the proximity of the other which modernity modifies and totalitarianism removes. Responsibility is silenced once proximity is eroded; it may instead result in resentment for the abstract other (1989a: 184).

It is the impossibility of absolute totalitarianism which allows moral leakage between the hostility to the abstract other and its actually existing bearers. Thus, as Himmler had cause to lament, too many ordinary Germans – even devoted Party members – could work up a lather about the abstract Jewish menace and yet still know their own, personal, 'good' Jews (1989a: 187). Again, it is the social production of distance which facilitates the manipulation of morality here. For evidently, moral inhibitions do not act at a distance; they are inextricably tied down to human proximity (1989a: 192). This also helps explain the apparent fragility of totalitarian politics, in flashpoints such as 1945 or in 1989; for though totalitarianism rests on violence, we can never be sure that it is completely internalized ideologically by its subjects. If it is the culture and institutions of Nazism which license and advocate attacks on Jews, then Germans will also be capable of other responses in other settings. A certain amount of pretence, or masking, or playing along is involved; as in the old Soviet empire saying, 'you pretend to pay us, we pretend to work', extended later into 'you pretend to govern, we pretend to believe you'. Obedience, or at least going through the motions, here replaces any other claim of modernity to human autonomy.

Ethics, in this regard, is less connected to matters of good and evil in Bauman's *Modernity and the Holocaust* (1989a) than it shadows problems of autonomy and obedience or heteronomy. The shadow of Kant's essay 'What is Enlightenment?' seems perpetually present in Bauman's work, as it does in that of his soulmate, Castoriadis. Only Bauman, as we have seen in the discussion of *Legislators and Interpreters* (1987), is less a robust enthusiast for the idea or project of Enlightenment, too critical of its dark side to fall in behind Kant's image of the upright man. Kant, and in different ways Marx and Weber, all seem in common to connect autonomy to the individual; Bauman makes it clear here that he wants to start from the image of the other. Marx and Weber are both individualists, of distinct kinds; Durkheim socializes the individual, projects the image of the multi-faceted individual out onto society. Bauman seems to harbour suspicions that the good citizen might be as open to the extremes of individualism as to those of conformism. His sympathies seem rather to be with Nietzsche's aphorism, that who demands morality is really asking for obedience. These are issues which Kant posits in 'What is Enlightenment?' but is not yet able to resolve; the good remains something which might be innerly motivated, but could also be governed by concerns with respectability or external experience.

More generally, Bauman is less concerned here with philosophy than with sociology. His puzzle is guided by the problem of acting, and only then thinking. Humans are not good or evil, but hold both capacities within them. The Holocaust becomes a prism on these matters because it distorts and magnifies them. For the shift against proximity is also a move towards increasing complexity, itself made manifest in elongated chains in divisions of labour or command, bureaucracy and democracy. Moral people can be driven into committing immoral acts even if they know, or believe these acts to be immoral – providing that they are convinced by experts or leaders that such actions are necessary (1989a: 198). For Bauman this means turning back to, or at least remembering the Sophoclean distinction between moral law and the law of society (or state). The image is more powerful than it at first seems, for having referred to Sophocles, Bauman proceeds to develop the case that what put the Holocaust apart was its bizarre pursuit of self-preservation at any cost (the extermination of others) (1989a: 199, 205).

> *The inhuman world created by a homicidal tyranny dehumanized its victims and those who passively watched the victimization by pressing both to use the logic of self-preservation as absolution for moral insensitivity and inaction.* (1989a: 205)

Me, or you – you murderous bastard! is the logic which destroys the other, which can only make a threat of the other. This is exactly why the significance of the Holocaust reaches out beyond Jewish Studies, into sociology, for it contains a lesson for the whole of humanity, moderns not least of all. Evil needs neither enthusiastic followers nor an applauding audience, though Nazism supplies them both; the instinct of self-preservation will do: 'by lying low, I can still escape!' (1989a: 206). This is what happens, or can happen when rationality and ethics point in different directions, when the technologies of destruction and the will-to-power of Fearless Leaders are upon us. Yet the tenor of Bauman's sociology, and of his own personality, is always to tell us the darkest truth and then to offer a glimpse of hope; for he knows too well that the truths of modernity can be numbing. Neither totalitarianism, nor modernity are all-encompassing, nor can they be: '*It does not matter how many people chose moral duty over the rationality of self-preservation – what does matter is that some did*' (1989a: 207).

Modernity and Ambivalence

To shift from *Modernity and the Holocaust* to *Modernity and Ambivalence* is to move from symptom to field. Yet Bauman's way of thinking and writing is not systematic – how could it be? – so *Modernity and Ambivalence* (1991a) is also quite literally an extension of Bauman's concern with the 'Jewish Question', as well as a return to and reconsideration of the modern or Enlightenment pursuit of the principle of order, whether theoretical or worldly. Let us cross the portal from one book to the next via Bauman's Amalfi Lecture in acceptance of the award for *Modernity and the Holocaust* in 1989, for there is at least one theme which connects them. This is the idea of adiaphorization, or the deflation of the realm of morality through the normalization of what was hitherto unacceptable to us through its reclassification as mundane.

The problem which animates Bauman's Amalfi Prize Lecture remains the way in which problems of good and evil have become social, or rather societal (1989a: 210). The problem with social organization is that it neutralizes the disruptive and deregulating impact of moral behaviour. Distancing and the will to punish the other through bureaucratic means eventually renders social action *adiaphoric* or morally indifferent, neither good nor evil, measurable only against technical and not moral values (1989a: 215). Some command; others execute; we all obey, and indifference prevails; we work, shop and die. Plainly we persist in encountering problems of recognition on the way; we are not merely molecules in motion. Yet our difficulties in recognizing each other go together with the astral capacities of the species now to constantly make and remake the world, or at least have it made for us by others or else by forces distant and unknown. The death of God has left us unable to discern the distinction between what is possible and what we ought do; again, we allow the technical capacities to generate their own ends as well as the means which might be appropriate to them.

When the planet is inhabited by Man and Man alone, anything is possible; yet the world made in our own image is also in a way its own self-negation, for the only measure of Man is abstract Man himself. This is the world which gives us the Gulag, Auschwitz and Hiroshima, as well as global poverty and misery on levels hitherto unseen. In high modernity, the classless society, the race-pure society, the Great Society become the task of man; somehow the project of caring for others and the self is too ridiculously modest (1989a: 218). Technology becomes as animated a force as Man, while we, in a sense, become passive recipients of the devices of the social order. Modernity and technology fuse to generate a culture and its attendant social institutions which are, in effect, closed. Bauman cites Jacques Ellul: technology today develops *because it develops*: if we can do it, why on earth should we not (1989a: 220)? The whole world is reduced by us in the process to objects of utility or else discarded. Thus do we divide the world into objects of value and rubbish; even humans can be accommodated into these nice distinctions.

Modernity and Ambivalence (1991a) opens with a discussion of language, culture and thinking which reaches back to the more directly political concerns of *Legislators and Interpreters* (1987) via some of those indicated in *Hermeneutics and Social Science* (1978). The key concept in this key book in Bauman's project is the idea of ambivalence itself. In one way the very idea of ambivalence is obvious, expressing as it does a commonplace about us and our world. We love and hate both it, and ourselves. Bauman's concern is more directly with the consequences of the principle of endless motion and its freezing by our language, culture and social institutions, the latter, of course, including the discipline of sociology itself. Ambivalence, as Bauman puts it, is the possibility of assigning an object or an event to more than one category. It is a language-specific disorder: a failure of the naming, segregating function that language is supposed to perform. 'A' is self-evidently not 'B'. But ambivalence also indicates ambiguity; sometimes 'B' really looks like 'A'. These kinds of uncertainty, according to Bauman, generate anxiety; we have a right to presume that 'A' and 'B' are distinct. Ambivalence therefore feels scary, like disorder. Yet, Bauman insists, ambivalence is actually not pathological, so much as it is normal. It arises from one of the main functions of language: that of naming and classifying (Bauman, 1991a: 1).

To classify, then, is to set apart, to segregate; it signals a human activity, a human presence among the abundance of phenomena and things that go to make up our world. To classify is to confer meaning, to give the world a structure or pattern, to make it open to the prospect of predictability. We are animals that seek out routine or habit, who form conventions and common senses which enable us to go on. We seek to reduce risk or randomness through constructing routines or repertoires: 'Because of our learning/memorizing ability we have vested interests in maintaining the orderliness of the world. For the same reason, we experience ambivalence as discomfort and a threat' (1991a: 2). Yet the risk – for risks remain – becomes that the naming/classifying purpose embroils us in the linear paths of instrumental reason; makes us think like bureaucrats. Thus Bauman's characterization of naming/classifying has an uncanny resemblance to Weber's characterization of bureaucracy, where all becomes the effect of precedent and routine, and all difference or creative capacity withers. For as Bauman has it, the ideal implied by classification is a kind of universal filing system, or, to change metaphors, a map of the world the same size as its object.

So why the fuss about classification? And how does the strength of this critique echo back into marxism, class theory and its own obsession with classification? Classifying consists in either exclusion or inclusion. Germans and Jews; bourgeoisie or proletariat. All acts of inclusion imply others, of exclusion. That these acts may be arbitrary is one thing. Bauman wants to make a stronger claim: that invariably, 'such operation of inclusion/exclusion is an act of violence perpetrated upon the world' (1991a: 2). Thus the tragic ambivalence of those Jews who were also assimilated Germans, or the more comic classification anomalies generated by capitalists like Engels who want to be with their proletariat, or working-class tories who despise nothing so much as their class peers.

Bauman's next move in *Modernity and Ambivalence* is characteristically clever: now he introduces the problem of modernity into the picture. Modernity is both the object of his book, the field within which the quest for classification really takes off, and is itself a category full of ambivalence: for we can be modern, modernist, late modern and even postmodern all at the very same time (1991a: 3). Modernity is a name, not a reality; it signifies something, perhaps even something highly evocative, but it cannot by its nature capture all of the illuminations and depths of darkness which we might investigate or visit under that rubric. 'Modernity' as a sociological term is not the same as 'modernism' or the 'postmodern', which we associate more variously with aesthetic or cultural forms; but all of these are 'quasi-totalities we want to prise off from the continuous flow of being' (1991a: 4). Humans, however, have a need for order which again becomes societally accelerated in the field we call modernity; so that while all peoples seek order, only moderns seek to place everything in order. Order becomes that which is not chaos; chaos is what is not orderly. But for Bauman, order and chaos are *modern* twins (1991a: 4). For we moderns have somehow come to convince ourselves that order is natural, rather than chaos or flux. We allow the distinction to become too firm, as though the alternative to order is not another order, but chaos.

Thus Bauman anticipates the general argument of his book: 'The typically modern practice, the substance of modern politics, of modern intellect, of modern life, is the effort to exterminate ambivalence' (1991a: 7). Of course, the quest is impossible, but this does little to prevent us from seeking after it with a vengeance. Bauman's characterization of our culture is stark: 'Intolerance is . . . the natural inclination of modern practice' (1991a: 8). Even tolerance is insipid, for it represents nothing more than the blind eye. Yet modernity, or modernism, is not only capable of self-reproduction. For there is also a love–hate relation between modern existence and modern culture. Modern culture both undermines and serves modern existence (1991a: 9). Bauman endorses the bleak image of our condition left us by Walter Benjamin: the storm irresistibly propels the walkers into the future to which their backs are turned, while the pile of debris before them grows skyward; 'this storm we call progress' (1991a: 11). Only Bauman's claim is less stoical, more incisive. For ambivalence seems to become the accidental result of this, like Benjamin's debris: 'If modernity is about the production of order then ambivalence is *the waste of modernity*' (1991a: 15). Waste; it could be the stuff of modernity, for our discards are hardly unworthy; or it could be rubbish, excrement, mess, dirt. And then there is the problem of the status of the concept of modernity in this claim; for if modernity is the field within which this tragedy occurs, then modernism is the force which drives it so relentlessly forward. Ambivalence must in this way itself remain an ambivalent category. Bauman anticipates this issue here in insisting that the category of the stranger is ambivalent, rather than simply negative, as the idea of the outsider might at first suggest. At the same time as he embraces the pathos of Benjamin's image of history, Bauman also endorses the more provisionally optimistic view of Agnes Heller, that it might remain possible for us to transform contingency into destiny (Bauman, 1991a: 16).

More generally, Bauman observes here that the central problem in *Modernity and Ambivalence* relates back to the theses of Adorno and Horkheimer in *Dialectic of Enlightenment* (1944). This acknowledgement in turn points in at least two distinct possible directions, for the darkest interpretation of the Enlightenment as modernity's nemesis in Adorno and Horkheimer coexists with more balanced, niggling curiosities about the ambivalence built into Enlightenment. In other words, *Dialectic of Enlightenment* is a text which also carries its own traces of ambivalence, even if the mainstream reception of the argument is that modern history has come to an end through the power of self-destruction. Fifty years after that test, however, Bauman's concern is not only to hammer the Enlightenment but also to show its own capacity to generate a postmodern legacy. Critical thinking, in Bauman's interpretation, is not only self-destructive; more emphatically, it is also destructive of the worst conceits of modernity, or modernism – its blind arrogance, high-handedness, and its endlessly ambitious legislative dreams (1991a: 17).

The event which called out *Dialectic of Enlightenment* remains that which is the pretext for *Modernity and Ambivalence*. Bauman sets off on this journey from his last stop, in *Modernity and the Holocaust* (1989a). In its German edition Bauman's Holocaust book directly evokes Adorno and Horkheimer: it is translated as *Dialektik der Ordnung*. Why do we feel compelled to resist the lessons of the Holocaust? To marginalize, or exoticize it as peculiarly German (1991a: 19)? The problem, again, is more general; it has to do with a way of thinking and being which result in the practice of the gardening state, the global compulsion to Order. The specific connection which Bauman wants to draw here is that provided by eugenics. But eugenics was also a European and transatlantic phenomenon, by no means peculiarly Germanic or unique to the Nazis. What is astonishing about eugenics before 1933 or 1941, as Bauman observes, is not who enthused for it but who did not. Eugenics was an extraordinarily influential movement, bringing together ideologically speaking Nazis and Fabians, liberals and social democrats. Bauman points the finger at Beatrice Webb, and especially at H.G. Wells but also at T.S. Eliot in the English setting. Order, cleanliness, hygiene, race-breeding, all these things went together in the interwar years, across typically political boundaries (1991a: 34–5). What is more disturbing, perhaps, is the way in which such thinking crosses over with the utopian horizons which Bauman also wants to defend. For genocide is necessarily connected to that desire for rational social engineering which is so ubiquitous within utopianism. More, all visions of artificial order are necessarily asymmetrical and thereby dichotomizing; there is inevitably an in-group and an out-group, or a problem and an imaginary solution (for example, eliminate the social parasites and improve life for the people). Further, the connection between eugenics, ordering and utopia is apparent in the fact that the imagination of the rationalizers or social engineers is tempted by the prospect of a state of ultimate and stable perfection (1991a: 38–9). The predominant figure of utopia suspends historicity or change, and thereby elevates some image of stasis in its stead. But where there is stasis there can be no life, no struggle for freedom or for dignity. Only death offers stasis.

This social science fiction, like its natural scientific parallel, suspends the presence of the other from its purview. Genocide becomes a fact of modernity, for modernity is its necessary condition. Consequently the sole factor capable of counterbalancing the genocidal potential dormant in the instrumental capacities of modernity is the pluralism of powers, and hence pluralism of authoritative opinion (1991a: 50–1). Conceptual pluralism will not lead to pluralism in everyday life, but the second is implausible without the first. For it is, of course, practical rather than merely formal ambivalence which is Bauman's political concern here. What really matters is the social construction and legitimacy of ambivalence. This is Bauman's cue to introduce the theme of the stranger, for the stranger also represents the third. There are friends, and enemies, and then there are strangers. Friends and enemies work together as insiders and outsiders, whereas strangers inhabit the liminal zone in between (1991a: 53). All these categories represent the other, but in distinct ways. The friend is the outsider for whom I am responsible before they reciprocate, and regardless of their reciprocation. The enemy is the other who is beyond the pale, regardless. Following Simmel, Bauman identifies friendship and enmity as forms of sociation; friends and enemies represent the other as subjects, like or unlike us.

Strangers are different because they represent the undecidable, as in Derrida's discussion of the *pharmakon*, both remedy and poison (1991a: 55–6). The third term is difficult, threatening, yet it is ubiquitous, part of the very condition of ambivalence itself.

Some strangers, in Bauman's understanding, are not just in transition, yet to be decided; rather, they are undecidable: 'These are the true hybrids, the monsters – not just *unclassified*, but *unclassifiable*' (1991a: 58). The stranger is, or represents anomaly. The stranger is a constant threat to the traditional world's order; and given that modernity is a tradition of its own, the stranger's status in modernity is still uncertain, even in the society of strangers. The stranger is not only strange, but unknown; strangers are not original, they were not there in the beginning. By violating history, the stranger also violates time, and not only place (1991a: 59–60). By arriving, the stranger represents the possibility of an end, the end to our normality or stability. The stranger represents modernity's scope of freedom, sexual, geographical, political. 'Even here, however, the treacherous incongruity of the stranger does not end' (1991a: 60) for the stranger also undermines the spatial ordering of the world. The stranger is a walking contradiction, by the standards of the cosy *Gemeinschaft* of the sociological imagination: the stranger is both physically close (too close) and spiritually distant. This incongruity is what makes the stranger ambivalent; for this reason, the stranger is the 'bane of modernity' (1991a: 61).

What can Bauman mean by this claim? His guiding shadow, Georg Simmel, would rather have suggested that even if the stranger is a novelty, he or she is paradigmatic of modernity, less its bane than its expression or symbol. What the stranger violates is less modern boundaries than the traditionalistic bifurcations of inside/outside. The stranger may then violate the historical experience of modernity, yet nevertheless embody its idea or spirit. Bauman, however, does not want to slight tradition in order to save modernity. At the same time, he is plainly wary of the kind of compulsory *Gemeinschaft* which moderns often project upon their own image of tradition. *Gemeinschaft*-claims substitute images of friendship, or intimacy, or family, for all other kinds of sociation; the family often thus secretly becomes the image of the good society, contrary to what many experience as the constraints of the family, and against the very spirit of the good society as a political form of association. This, in turn, makes Bauman twitch because it indicates the presence of a certain kind of ideological organicism, where the 'natural' is valued over and against the social; it is a line of argument which remains widely influential in contemporary thinking, from deep ecology to national socialism. Bauman despises those who want to garden us into shape, but he also remains deeply suspicious of the opposite claim, that it is nature rather than society or culture which makes us what we are. He is a kind of ambivalent modernist, where all the markers or categories begin to break down, for neither tradition nor modernity, the modern nor the postmodern can abstractly or absolutely be defended against all other competitors or classifications.

Who, then, is to blame for the human condition? modernity or post-modernity? or us? Surely it is us, as actors or subjects; only Bauman's cautionary note is that the prospect becomes more dangerous as the means of destruction expand and escalate in high modernity. Nor do they decrease in postmodern times, even if critical narratives turn our eyes away from totality and towards the fragments. The dominant metanarratives, or ideologies or cultures might enable some outcomes to be advantaged over others, but they are not actors in themselves, unless, perhaps, we sign over our own responsibility to them.

How could we reasonably be anything other than ambivalent about modernity? As Bauman puts it, modernity, after all, is a rebellion against fate and ascription, in the name of omnipotence of design and achievement (1991a: 68). 'There is, therefore, a genuine contradiction at the heart of modernity' (1991a: 69). Now Bauman turns the case towards problems of assimilation. How do we deal with strangers? If we are tolerant of them, our inclusion of strangers remains half hearted. Moderns may shift historically from policies of stigmatization to those of assimilation, but this is merely to offer a more humane alternative to fascism, to soak up the other rather than destroy them. Assimilation offers domestication rather than difference. But this kind of modern offer to the outsider – 'enter, be like us' – remains essentially traditionalistic, for here identity remains singular and genetic in origin; fellow travellers will always be second-class citizens, because they are inauthentic. Modernity remains deeply traditionalistic in its residual commitment to the image of the national citizens as sprung from the ground or from its previous generations. Now we are all strangers, Poles in Britain as much as Germans in Australia, or Indians, or Brazilians in New York City. Only some remain stranger than others (1991a: 97). Modernity, in Bauman's usage, opens such problems but cannot resolve them. Postmodernity in his lexicon seems to mean living with, or even embracing ambivalence. Where a philosopher such as Heller identifies the possibility of pluralism with a modernity which is escaping from its own habitual traditionalism, Bauman seems rather to identify the prospects of such realization with the postmodern. For Bauman:

Postmodernity is modernity that has admitted the non-feasibility of its original project. Postmodernity is modernity reconciled to its own impossibility – and determined, for better or worse, to live with it. Modern practice continues – now, however, devoid of the objective that once triggered it off. (1991a: 98)

Postmodernity is modernity come of age, modernity without illusions . . . modernity without modernism? Only modernity without modernism – without the will to power, the will to make, reform, destroy life – this really would make no sense. Bauman suggests that the postmodern maxim to replace that of moderns or Enlighteners is 'liberty, diversity, tolerance' rather than 'liberty, equality, fraternity'; and progress may even be possible if tolerance is reforged as solidarity (1991a: 98). Diversity replaces oneness, so far so good; equality disappears, or resurfaces as the challenge of solidarity, and here Bauman himself solidarizes with the pragmatic minimalism of Richard Rorty (1991a: 101). Postmodernity always runs the risk of extending modernity's other claim, not to social engineering, but to the decency of liberalism.

As in *Modernity and the Holocaust* (1989a), however, Bauman's argument in *Modernity and Ambivalence* (1991a) works both on the plane of the critique of modernity and on the modern tragedy of the Jews. This moment in Bauman's life's work may be more about the Holocaust than about modernity as such, even as he urges the painful connection between them upon us. Assimilation, again, is the narrative link in Bauman's argument, for it covers not only the more specific problem of the Jews but also the general proclivities of modernity to swallow up difference, to devour and to indigest. Assimilation represents a declaration of war on difference, on semantic ambiguity; as Bauman argues in the opening to this book, it is therefore both a cosmological or epistemological and a political or practical matter. It is one, mental precondition of modern barbarism.

Assimilation and After

Bauman recommences his story by focusing upon the travails of the German Jew. This is a tale of paradox waiting to unwind. Contrary to the popular pre-Nazi adage 'Be a Jew at home, and a man in the Street', the Jews as would-be Germans felt truly German only at home, where they could play their game of illusions undisturbed by the kicks of the Gentiles passing by in those streets (1991a: 121). But emancipation cannot come of assimilation, especially not with a hostile agent as host. Only there is a twist in Bauman's narrative, for just as later under the influence of Janina's work he returns to the image of the gypsy as the outsider, so here does he shift to the case of the less prominent Jews, the *Ostjuden*, the less civilized Jews from the other side of the river, not from Weimar or Berlin but from Poznan or Budapest (see also J. Bauman, 1998). The *Ostjuden* were less well assimilated, and therefore embarrassing to others who chose to leave their ethnic idiosyncrasies behind. The Jews of Eastern Europe were in a way even more liminal, for they were refused a category of their own, being cast rather as failed German Jews (1991a: 132).

Readers of Bauman's work will therefore find that a key issue for *Modernity and the Holocaust* (1989a), the nature of the Jews as a category, is more fully defined in this other book, *Modernity and Ambivalence* (1991a). The outer frame of a sociology of modernity dominates the first and returns in the second, again, because assimilation as we know it is a modern phenomenon. Assimilation is necessarily bound up with the 'nationalization' of the state, or the construction of national identity and nation-building upon claims to geographically bounded originary belonging (1991a: 141). With typical irony, Bauman notes that the definition could also be reversed: what is at risk is perhaps less the modern nationalization of the state than the statization of the nation. Or to put the human problem in terms of its organizational corruption, the assimilants found much to their own despair that they had in effect assimilated themselves solely to the process of assimilation (1991a: 143). The policy of assimilation was the front line of social engineering, the cutting edge of modernity's advancing order (1991a: 149). Within the horizons of fascist thinking, this was precisely a matter of fabricating a tradition, often inserting romantic claims within the most advanced technological forms of organization. In this way, at least, the reactionary modernism of the Nazis was somehow especially representative of modernity itself. Bauman's purpose is to establish and to probe the nature of this connection. To reduce or to identify modernity and fascism is not his claim, for indeed this would be to commit the very mistake of conceptual assimilation which he wishes to force upon our attention as the common underpinning of Nazi and modern traditionalism.

Is not then Bauman's own position, by contrast, some kind of romantic enthusiasm for chaos or what went before as the sole alternative to these new kinds of murderous order? Bauman's is not an other worldly rejection of modernity, like that in Illich or Marcuse. We can expect, instead, that Bauman would enthuse for the third term if for anything. The only choice cannot be between state-sponsored order and non-modern chaos; the challenge must rather be to make your own order. Nor can there be any happy choice between the alleged alternatives of racism or assimilation, outright rejection or innerly dilution of the other by the social system.

Sociology, meantime, became part of this state-sponsored project; contrary to the myth that all the good-hearted sociologists fled from Germany together with Freud and the Frankfurt School, many stayed and took their orders from Hitler. Yet here, again, ambivalence reigns, for as Bauman reminds us, sociology was early on identified precisely as a dangerous, because dirty Jewish discipline (1991a: 167). Our discipline, bless its ambivalence, is both willing servant of modernity and its critic. Simmel survives here as the representative of critique, more even than Marx, for Marx's followers took his desire for systematicity out of the British Museum and made it into the operational principle of Soviet state power. Simmel's famous motif, by comparison, was the fragment, or the very absence of the ongoing motif. Simmel's sociology remains on the level of phenomenology, it is manoeuvred through the perspectives of the human condition, like Bauman's own work; it does not take on where it left off, or channel all problems through one or two core conceptual concerns (1991a: 185). In this sense, it could be said that it is not sociological at all, for it avoids that temptation to the analytical reductionism of the 'single fix' which is so characteristic of sociological endeavour ('it's the economy, stupid!').

Nevertheless, Bauman's path in *Modernity and Ambivalence* goes out through the mall, the supermarket and therapy, what together he refers to as the privatization of ambivalence. The conclusion to this book accords with the later strategy common throughout his writing: the bad news ends with the exhortation to do better, at least to maintain hope. Bauman opens his closing by standing together with the modest humanism of Agnes Heller: the future is by definition open; we might still transform contingency into destiny, not as masters of the universe, but as actors in our worlds, both shared and personal (1991a: 231). As moderns, or postmoderns, we have available to us a repertoire of choices or fields of action which we choose either to exercise or else to neglect. Modernity is a field of possibilities: why then have we, or others, chosen to work on the most paranoiac rather than the more modest? Humans will always be tempted by the fantasy of rational mastery; again, it is our misfortune that modernity delivers up the means to make the Frankenstein fantasy possible. Postmodernity, understood in the sense that Bauman values it, as modernity without illusions, this is a chance of modernity. Tolerance, he says, is a subsequent chance of postmodernity. And solidarity is the chance of tolerance. Each is preconditional for the next; which is to say, as Bauman acknowledges, that the friends of solidarity do not seem to have much cause for cheer (1991a: 257). The problem is that one downside of the postmodern sensibility is a kind of numbness that goes together with the occasional attack of euphoria. Solidarity, care for the other, sometimes seems to look distinctly old fashioned in a world of speed, gratification and self-development. Hence the recurrent irony of modern utopia, which draws its animus from the horror of difference and impatience with otherness: 'And yet they also offered a chance for genuine concern with the plight of the wretched and miserable' (1991a: 257). The sense of contingency makes it possible to imagine the world as other, as changeable. The ordinary humanist impulse to change or reform signals all this in its essential ambivalence: the world needs to be changed, for too many suffer too much unnecessarily; so *we* must change the world for them.

As Bauman puts it, it is not that we have no contemporary equivalents of the great early sociological muckrakers, like Mayhew or Booth or Riis. The real difference is between the explosive effect that the revelation of human misery once had, and the equanimity with which it is received today (1991a: 257). Today we feel morally numbed in the face of other people's suffering, not least because our proximity to them has declined, or else has been transformed by the virtual realization of television thinking: what is the difference between a homeless person on *NYPD Blue* and the one you climb over off Broadway? As Bauman has insisted, our second natures at least have been corrupted by adiaphorization. So much that hitherto repelled us is now tolerated, and this is the negative aspect of toleration. Morality, meantime, is reprocessed as the moralism of politics or sexuality as soap opera, as in the Bill and Monica Show. This is a central issue for those who would enthuse for postmodernism, alone, without any sense of ambivalence. For postmodern tolerance goes wide and far, and includes tolerance for those who choose homelessness as a lifestyle. The arguments being developed by Bauman here connect back directly to those in *Socialism: the Active Utopia* (1976a). Today, socialism is inert, or inactive, and this may be a blessing for some, in that we are relieved of the endless complaints and hectoring from the moral highground of those who know better. On the other hand, if it is truly the case that anything goes, then there is no forum any longer in which we might even begin to argue about what the good society might be, and who exactly has right of entry to it. This represents a closing of the political imagination, or more literally, of politics, for the very idea of any notional common good is lost in marketized lunges after self-interest. It hurts, but as Bauman suggests, it is only too easy for postmodern tolerance to degenerate into the selfishness of the rich and resourceful. Indeed, such selfishness is its most immediate and daily manifestation (1991: 259).

This is not all there is to the postmodern world, for it, too, bears its own ambivalence. Sociologically speaking, it carries within it the traditionalism of modernism as well as the flexibility of the present; and this traditionalism itself will always cut both ways, for we cannot simply presume that tradition is good or bad in itself; some traditions offer balance, others constrain us. So the postmodern will also cut both ways. As Bauman captures the contradiction in one place, the 'postmodern world of joyful messiness is carefully guarded at the borders by mercenaries no less cruel than those hired by the managers of the now abandoned global order' (1991a: 260). What used to become dissent is now personal anxiety. Postmodernity is therefore simultaneously the site of opportunity and of danger.

Exit from Modernity, Stage Left

Bauman's work is often received as, or translated into, the postmodern. There is a certain sense in which Bauman's project becomes increasingly postmarxist, with the emphasis on both terms; and certainly it is also postmodern, but not with any illusions of rupture after modernity. The content of *Modernity and Ambivalence* (1991a) may surprise, as it returns to and develops arguments apparently central to *Modernity and the Holocaust* (1989a). As I have indicated, the critical onslaught against the logic and politics of assimilation or identity-thinking which opens *Modernity and Ambivalence* then tracks the Jewish Problem from west to east, via the *Ostjuden*. Bauman then turns to the analysis of new forms of oppression, or exclusion through the postmodern market and its culture or mentality, and evokes socialism or utopia as the ambivalence of modernity. So, now, does he return in concluding the book frontally to discuss 'Socialism: Modernity's Last Stand'. Bauman begins by restating his earlier conviction, that modern socialism is best understood as the counter-culture of modernity:

> Like all counter cultures, modern socialism performed a triple function in relation to the society it opposed and serviced: it exposed the deceit of representing the achieved state of society as the fulfilment of its promise; it resisted the suppression

or concealment of the possibility to implement the promise better; and it pressed the society toward such better implementation of its potential. (1991a: 263)

Socialism is Her Majesty's Loyal Opposition, both therefore responsible for the status quo and yet free of all blame for its failings. Socialism in this way was an alternative modernity, even if its modernity was necessarily a variation on the more powerful capitalist theme. Socialism in the west played out its role on the oppositional level; in the east, it took the social engineering prospect to new heights, even if they were paralleled elsewhere, in Nazism and in the New Deal. Socialism's own project was a version of that of modernity. Socialism was the idea of a radicalized modernity, a finished off and polished capitalism; the idea of socialism as radical democracy had to await the 1960s' rediscovery of democracy as another good idea which the bourgeoisie had failed to deliver on, rather than just another bourgeois slogan. Capitalists had failed to make good of modernity; socialists vowed, as the other football team, that they could do better. Socialists, in all this, claimed not only that capitalist modernity was inefficient but that it was unfair.

'Socialism found nothing wrong with modernity' (1991a: 265); apparently this refers to marxism, for marxism became the loudest voice and the fiercest opponent on the left, especially after the Russian October. Bauman here reads socialism as, like history, something that proceeds by its bad side; the emphasis is similar to that on the bad side of Enlightenment in *Legislators and Interpreters* (1987). In a way Bauman's force of attack is entirely appropriate: for among socialists and Enlighteners, the social engineers won; modernism, if not modernity, became the playground of the modernizers, turning the romantics into airy handwavers, dazed nostalgics for worlds we have lost. Socialism became historically identified with that monstrous Faustian project of remaking of the world articulated by Trotsky, the loyal oppositionist, and authorized practically by the fearless leader, Josef Stalin.

Might there then be something like a postmodern socialism, where socialism refers more to culture than to politics, to critique and opposition than to the will to power? (Beilharz, 1994b). Bauman's emphasis here is more on the postmodernity of modernity than on its modern residuals. It is difficult in this wasteland to see what possibilities socialism could have at all, in any significant form. Communism as a specific experience, however, is more precisely understood as an alternative experiment in modernity rather than a counterculture, as it was in the west (Bauman, 1991a: 266; see also Arnason, 1993). Lenin substituted socialist revolution for bourgeois revolution, rather than viewing socialism as the extension of capitalism. Postindustrialism in effect pulls the mat out from under these communist aims of outindustrializing the west; Gorbachev was a would-be modernizer and, in this post-Brezhnev context, was therefore a postmodernist, or postmodernizer (Bauman, 1991a: 268). Communism was an attempt at constructing a non-differentiated modernity, a mono-organizational society where the Party saw all and ruled all. It was a dictatorship over needs. Bauman endorses that critical category developed by Fehér, Heller and Markus in their 1983 book of the same name (1991a: 268).

Is then all hope gone? Social engineering in the megalomaniacal sense stands damned. But this discrediting adheres to its Faustian excesses: 'To abandon social engineering as a valid means of political practice means to discard . . . all visions of a different society; even makes it difficult to *imagine* another way of living or of organizing our lives and our priorities' (1991a: 269). There is always a risk here: to change the world may make it worse. To leave it alone, *laissez-faire, laissez-allez* is hardly any self-sufficient alternative. To allow this would truly be to authorize it. In any case, there are always social engineers, even when they do not proudly or noisily announce their own arrival.

Thus as a non-decision is a kind of decision, so is the non-celebration of the planners a silent recognition of their perennial presence and power. Less has changed than the publicists would like us to believe:

> Nothing merely ends in history, no project is ever finished and done with. Clean borders are but projections of our relentless urge to separate the inseparable and order the flux. Modernity is still with us. (Bauman, 1991a: 270)

Modernity is still with us; let us beware of mistaking our own mental clarity or need for clarity with the way our worlds actually work. What strange creatures we become, that our needs for understanding develop such elaborate prostheses that we no longer have any idea what it was we set out to interpret in the first place. Or else, we put all our best talents into explaining how to explain, not addressing what it is or was we set out to explain. It is as though the more we know, the more it intrudes upon the process of understanding. The argument is reminiscent of W.G. Sebald's more fictive musing in *The Rings of Saturn*:

> Perhaps we all lose our sense of reality to the precise degree to which we are engrossed in our own work, and perhaps that is why we see in the increasing complexity of our mental constructs a means for greater understanding, even while intuitively we know that we shall never be able to fathom the imponderables that govern our course through life. (Sebald, 1998: 182)

Ideas, words, theories get in the way; they do not only facilitate understanding, though yet again we cannot live without them. The problem, as ever, is in us, not in them, in how we use theory as dogma, in quest of certainty, to close our eyes against a world both shifting and shiftless. What we have learned, or stand to learn for Bauman, however, is that something significant has indeed changed. To speak of modernity as a project, as we now do is to confess that it is over, or at least determinate: 'Our ancestors did not talk of the "project" when they were busily engaged in what now looks to us like unfinished business' (1991a: 271). Even the idea of project starts to age before us, indicating some kind of concordance between intention and outcome which few of us would commit our lives to. Ergo the proliferation of posts, the sense that we have arrived after, after the enthusiasms or expectations of modernity, that our social dreams quite readily can be realized. Postmodernity expresses the realization internal to modernity that its own dreams were illusions, even if they were necessary illusions. It is as though we have broken the spell of our own illegitimate fantasy, for Bauman; as though we erred, fundamentally in ascribing reality to modern dreams rather than to everyday existence. The hopes which make us human, then, do not evaporate altogether; they shift register, from the paranoiac to the ordinary.

The fragmented society of postmodern capitalism now replaces the more centred world of western corporatism and communism in the east. Fragmentation of course also cuts both ways, dispersing power and responsibility. Even ambivalence becomes tokenized in this process; so that if Bauman argues throughout as though modernity cannot deliver or even tolerate ambivalence, he now senses that postmodernity turns it into little more than a stage prop (1991a: 279). Our survey of Bauman's work will have reason to probe further into the postmodern in the next chapter. To close this chapter, we will return to Bauman's diagnosis of Soviet modernity. The biographical path from which Bauman emerges is more powerfully informed by the experience of communism than by that of fascism, which he relays here in the first instance through the direct experience of his wife. Probably Bauman's increasing distance from the figure of Marx reflects a similar distance of his personal past with that interval of the history of Eastern Europe. Yet as Bauman says, nothing merely ends in history, no project is ever entirely finished and done with. Modernity is still with us, and so is marxism.

But marxism, today, is too caught up with this historical process to claim immunity from its own effects, intended or nay. Those of us who remain inspired by Marx therefore have to start at least to address the question how all this began, the Bolshevik pursuit of marxism as a paradise to be achieved. Bauman's views on some of these issues are available to us in his review in response to the epoch-making work of Fehér, Heller and Markus, *Dictatorship Over Needs* (1983). The Hungarians set out to establish what generations of marxists were keen to deny – that Soviet-type societies were *sui generis*, with a logic of their own. On this interpretation, the marxist blinkers of the mode of production type, which would insist that all societies must be either pre-capitalist, capitalist, or socialist told us more about the interpreters than the realities they sought to interpret. The Soviet Union may well have been historically enacted in the name of socialism, but its social forms displayed none of the dimensions traditionally associated with socialist claims to freedom or equality. But neither was the Soviet Union some kind of throwback to an imaginary oriental despotism, nor a mere duplicate of capitalism this time without capitalists. Fehér, Heller and Markus insist that Soviet-type societies merge particular modernizing and traditionalistic patterns; like Nazi Germany, they were not a simple denial of modernity, but represented different attempts to refigure modernity.

Bauman agrees with the Hungarians that the basic organizational aspiration of actually-existing socialism embodied in the dictatorship over needs was the imperative to control. To seek control at the level of the social system is first and foremost to seek the substitution of order for chaos, design for spontaneity, plan for anarchy, or else: control, control over both men and women and over nature (Bauman, 1984: 175). Bauman takes umbrage here at the early marxian fascination with species-being, and its capacity to crowd out the actually-existing individual subjects who ought really to make up socialism. In the spirit of his own work, and in sympathy, as often, with the views of Castoriadis, he suggests rather that the 'project of a rational society is, in other words, an idea of domination which sets itself goals no secular power dreamed of before' (1984: 175). Whether we choose to call it capitalist or socialist, this modernizing frenzy of utopia lives out the dreams of rationalism, or implicitly of Enlightenment. Socialism remains the counter-culture of capitalism, both born and lived out under the sign of Enlightenment. Organized socialism's primary claim came to be that it could rid capitalism of its own rationality. None of this, for Bauman, is explicable in class terms; rather, he summons up the image of 'pastoral power' (Foucault) to fill the gap: the Hungarians, for their part, remained allergic to Foucault, having learned about domination from Max Weber and Lukács. They would not therefore simply agree with Bauman when he blames the communist experiment on Enlightenment, or at least links the two necessarily, as when he says that 'the Soviet system can be seen as a practical test of the limits of Enlightenment utopia' (1984: 176).

As I have mentioned, Bauman's critique parallels that of Castoriadis, where the pursuit of rational mastery overcomes the only substantial alternative, the hope of autonomy. As in the logic of *Modernity and the Holocaust* (1989a), the logic of Bauman's critique of Soviet-type societies is to point out that they tell us more about modernity than about any specific variation on modernity. Yet the specificity, and limited longevity of totalitarianism as a form of modernity remains. Bauman does not endorse all the particulars of the argument concerning dictatorship over needs, though his sense of the significance of the *sui generis* case puts him in the same field. The logic of Bauman's case here, I think, is finally that socialism is so deeply bound up with capitalism as to return us to the earlier sensibility that it is industrialism, after all, which threatens to consume us. Modernity is still with us, and so is marxism, for better or worse. Alongside the persistence of modernity, there remains the persistence of stubborn subjects who say no, who refuse to accept that this world is made in their own image.

After Fascism and Marxism

Modernity, communism, fascism – all three inseparable. This has been our experience, the experience of the twentieth century, and it will haunt us still

into the new millennium. Bauman's purpose is to shift these from experience into theory, and sociology, as well – not as boundary issues or personal worries, but as core problems of our lives and thought. Fascism
emerges from Bauman's work less as the alter ego of capitalism than as a
possible logic, or political form of industrialism. Less predictable than the
experience of communism, nazism nevertheless tells a truth about modernity which makes us shudder. Communism, or socialism, in contrast was or
is the countercurrent of modernity as capitalism. The rise of socialism is, in
a sense, more predictable than that of fascism; fascism is among other
things a response to and against socialism, which is an Enlightenment
current reaching out of 1789. The Holocaust seems in Bauman's sociological imagination both to be a contingent historical event and yet somehow the silent secret of modernity, expressing the height of the crisis
generated by the crazy surplus of technical rationality. Communism seems
rather to represent the Faustian revenge of modernity's countercurrent, in
socialism. Socialism's world-historic excesses seem less controversial if more
puzzling than Nazism's; Nazism was an irrational rationality run amok,
whereas high Stalinism's motif was cold, immoral ambition which believed
in human perfection at any cost.

The historic collapse of fascism as a state regime in 1945 left its onlookers
and participants puzzled; what, actually, had held this monstrous fantasy
up? Communism lasted much longer than Nazism; its collapse also dis-
mayed, but more because of this deceptive longevity. 1989, for Bauman,
was thus in some senses a postmodern revolution; for the tide against
fascism was nevertheless a victory for a particular kind of modernity. That
nazism should collapse was predictable; that socialism would rise was
predictable, too, only its fall made less sense, not least with reference to the
demise of social democracy. Perhaps the citizens of communist and fascist
states eventually did little more than go through the motions. The anti-
communist revolution was a victory for the logic of consumption over that
of production, the old so to say Fordist circuit which held Soviet-type
societies together, some pretending to work, others pretending to consume.
The idea of postmodern, therefore, cannot be merely or exclusively cultural,
understood as an intracapitalist development where the sphere of culture
asserts itself more powerfully over economy. Postmodernism is also caught
up with the idea that the modernism of the planned or corporatist society
comes undone; consolidated in the 1930s and 1940s, it is loosened in the
1970s and loses its exemplar in the 1980s.

It is the irregular, or surprising nature of Nazism which explains I think
why it is that Bauman spends more space, and passion, engaged in interpreting the Holocaust than in the critique of the Soviet attempt at modernity.
Of course, there is more to the story than that. If *Modernity and the
Holocaust* (1989a) is a wilful critique of his own earlier self-understanding,
Bauman's critique of socialism is a less resolved, because deeply self-critical,
encounter with his own commitment to marxism. Bauman's explicit critique
of marxism is ruthless in its power and persistence; marxism as an historical

movement emerges as an alter ego of the despised capitalism which excels it only in the extent of its own illusions. The extent of Bauman's disillusion with modernity is a direct result of his fundamental disappointment in marxism. Bauman's worldview, however fragmented such a view might be, is postmodern because postmarxist. Marxism was everything, for years of this man's social life. Bauman's personal path in league with marxism slowly but surely inverted the imperative of the young Marx: marxism was everything, and became nothing. As Arendt says somewhere, however, we can never paste our own disappointments onto those who follow us, or let these things close us against the world or against hope, against utopia. Here we stand, we can do no other.

5   Touring the Fragments

Postmodernity, in Bauman's work, is first of all postmarxism, though in the long run it is also more than that. The postmodern first up here is the critique of the illusions of marxism. Bauman's line of argument is auto-biographical as well as theoretical. The certainties of modernity, the obsession with order, these were our socialist certainties, the mote or plank in our own radical vision. The semantics of critique in Bauman's work are distinct: modernity stands for modernism and marxism stands in for, or at least sometimes expresses modernity. But now, after marxism as a state form, after the Soviet experience, we feel weary, we feel somehow *after*. After fascism, after communism, in the midst of a consumer capitalism that seeks only to buy us off, in this setting it seems as though the project of modernity has missed its chance.

Bauman's social theory triggers through the sociology of power in *Memories of Class* (1982), and explodes into *Legislators and Interpreters* (1987); the point, hereon, is less to seek to change others than to interpret the worlds we inhabit. *Modernity and the Holocaust* (1989a) blows the whistle on fascism and anti-semitism but also on sociology and modernity. Elaborated through *Modernity and Ambivalence* (1991a), the Holocaust book leads directly into ethics; *Postmodern Ethics* (1993a) is the conclusion to *Modernity and the Holocaust*. After the book on ethics, Bauman's travels become more diasporic or essayistic again in kind, as witnessed in collections such as *Intimations of Postmodernity* (1992) or more projective ensembles like *Life in Fragments* (1995) or *Postmodernity and its Discontents* (1997a), which in turn begin to reach back to the critique of capitalism and western deprivation in *Memories of Class*. As Bauman moves progressively further away from classical marxism, then, the critique of capitalism is renewed rather than rejected or distanced; for our world seems again to become more bipolarized than social democracy after the Second World War had allowed. In this way Bauman negotiates the terrain he had initially inhabited, in the 1970s, as a critical marxist. If the silhouette of Auschwitz remains more prominent in this picture than the camps of the Gulag, this may well reflect the unalloyed barbarism of fascism as modernity. The experience of communism remains, in a way, even more elusive, for its own attempt at barbarism claimed as its credentials not only the victory of the proletariat but also the liberation of all mankind. The stark challenge presented by the idea of an imaginary sequel to Bauman's study of the Holocaust, to be entitled *Modernity and the Gulag*, stands before us; per-haps such a study would tell us even more about ourselves, those on the

left, than Bauman's Holocaust book does. Only it would likely be a st
of communism as modernity, rather than of modernity viewed through
communist experience.

Postmodern Ethics

There is a hole in the heart of modernity. It is called ethics. Moderns fill this
hole with order, with rules and regulations. Ethics was a chance given to
moderns, who have been unable largely to take on the challenge, for they
are still traditionalists at heart, creatures of habit, for whom the prospect of
autonomy is simply too much; easier to just follow the rules. By this process
morality or conventionalism is substituted for ethics, or care of the self and
others; and in turn moralism or hectoring replaces morality, or else
morality gives way to law: we let the magistrates and black letter law books
tell us how to live. This is exactly why Nazism is such an exemplary ethical
tale for modernity, for it rests on the appeal to heteronomy. The postmodern, for Bauman, then opens the prospect of starting over again with
ethics, and forward, rather than back, after the Holocaust, to Aristotle or
Kant. These are problems of ethics for moderns, not ancients; the social
contexts of action have changed, as generalized conformism has become an
attribute of modernity and moderns in general. Enlighteners have set out to
teach the people about ethics; perhaps they have to be untaught (Bauman,
1993a: 6). The legislators, in short, expected the worst of the masses,
presuming that their natural intelligence would always play into vice or self-
interest.

Bauman's beginning point in *Postmodern Ethics* is different. In the postmodern perspective, humans can be neither exclusively good nor bad; this is
a Jacobin residual, this older Manichean image of the world divided into
only two sorts of people, good and bad citizens: 'In fact, humans are
morally ambivalent: ambivalence resides at the heart of the "primary scene"
of human face-to-face' (1993a: 10). More, Bauman wants to suggest that
moral phenomena are non-rational, not governed by the canons of instrumental rationality, where any means can get us to particular chosen ends.
Moral behaviour is more like intuition than reason; we are not ignorant of
what is right and what is wrong, but we cannot always rationally justify or
explain a particular course of action or inaction. Further, for Bauman,
morality is aporetic, and complex, mixed; few choices are unambiguously
good (1993a: 11). It follows from this that morality is not universalizable.
Consequently moral responsibility – being *for* the Other before one can be
with the Other – is the first reality of the self, a starting point rather than a
product of society (1993a: 13).

Plainly the kinds of concerns established in *Postmodern Ethics* are philosophical, or more explicitly ethical, than sociological. *Postmodern Ethics* is
a philosophical detour which returns, in its closing moments, to more
properly sociological concerns located within social space and time, in the

context of culture and power, where vagabonds and tourists become the new tropes used to make sense of the postmodern stranger. The lack of a stunningly clear distinction between sociology and philosophy in turn manifests itself in the semantic slippage between 'morality' and 'ethics' in Bauman's work. The problem with the classification, like all others, is of course that realities slip and slide. Ethics slip into professional ethics, or code–lists; morality becomes moralizing, morality in the bad, because merely conventional sense. Both ethics and morality are therefore corrupted; the earthly practices of morality corrode the higher principles of ethics. This is a challenge, however, rather than a gloomy diagnosis, for the postmodern challenge is positive; it is not the 'anything goes' of cultural relativism, but it demands of us rather that we address formally the question of the Other. The issue forced upon us by the Holocaust is exactly that no one was responsible; it is this organizational theorem which we cannot accept as ethical discourse.

Postmodernity challenges us to be ethical, for the very reason that it is modernity without illusions, including Enlightenment illusions about philosopher-kings and law or compulsion as ethics (1993a: 32). Indeed, Bauman goes so far as to say that postmodernity brings 'reenchantment' of the world after the protracted struggle of modernity to disenchant it (1993a: 33). The allusion to Weber is not accidental, for Bauman here centres Weber in a way that he otherwise locates only Simmel. How do we respect the essential integrity of human experience while also recognizing that distinct fields of activity or spheres of life follow particular ethics appropriate to them? Weber understood the problem, and perhaps chose too emphatically the path of distinction. Bauman, here more reminiscent of Marx, wants to avoid a situation where there are always two sets of rules, one for life and another for science. But if difference needs to be registered at the societal or local level, so too does it disturb us globally. Since Montaigne, at least – perhaps since Herodotus – we have known about difference, though our habit has been to view difference as stigma or a sign of inferiority as often as it has been to view these others in wonder, or else to elevate them above our own cultures and institutions. As Bauman observes with reference to the work of Johannes Fabian in *Time and the Other*, imperial powers identify other places with other times; a certain kind of primitivism seems to be built into the logic of the civilizing process (1993a: 39). We now know these stories about the civilizing mission to be hollow, based on the superiority of violence rather than of culture or civilization. Thus the real challenge is to identify the universal in the particular of the face-to-face encounter (1993a: 43). Postmodern ethics is thus something, like solidarity, that is our responsibility: we have to construct it. And this is why Bauman shows so little patience for communitarians, for communitarians in turn seek to short-circuit claims to identity by referring to where allegedly we have come from, rather than where we might be going to. Communitarianism is tribal in its logic, for it reproduces the prescriptive patterns of tradition, where we must assume that my identity is deeply bound to race, place and tradition (1993a: 43). Communitarians want to rebuild the roots that different modernities have torn up; but we have to live, today, with dislocation and mobility. We are not bound to each other by similarity, but by difference, and in contingency. This means building the kind of moral proximity which modernity denies us.

Yet we are not saints, and the ethics of Levinas, which Bauman often relies on here, seem ultimately to be a saintly ethics. Who can always, or even consistently, put the other before the self? How am I actually to be responsible for the other, let alone for the third party? The practical implication of Bauman's earlier arguments in *Modernity and the Holocaust* (1989a) and *Modernity and Ambivalence* (1991a) is that tolerance may lead to solidarity; the mechanisms or institutions or social policies which might mediate between us remain unsighted, and institutions of this kind in any case remain shadowy in Bauman's thinking, where organizations sometimes seem like an excuse for a human solution to social problems. The other in postmodern times depends at least on toleration. Yet the social institutions known to us either swallow up strangers or else expel them. Here Bauman turns to Lévi-Strauss in *Tristes Tropiques*, and to his distinction between cultures that take in, eat up or devour the other, in the anthropophagic strategy, and those which expel or vomit out the stranger, in the anthropoemic strategy (1993a: 163). Bauman offers a modified insight based on Lévi-Strauss: societies actually combine both strategies, for this is not an historical or civilizational distinction. Societies reproduce themselves by excluding or assimilating the other, or by combining both strategies.

So where does this leave us, or the other? Bauman's optic in *Postmodern Ethics* returns to the social, and to the socialized. The real problem with modernity, or with the modern revolution, the revolution that is modernity, lies in the liberation of means from ends. If anything is possible, why should anyone in particular matter? (1993a: 190). Contrary to the widely shared view of modernity as the first universal civilization, this is a civilization singularly unfit for universalization. More, modernity cannot survive the possible advent of equality. It is a parasitic form of social arrangement (1993a: 215). As Hans Jonas puts it, and Bauman concurs, the scale of possible consequences of human actions has long outgrown the moral imagination of the actors (Bauman, 1993a: 217). By this stage, as it were, Bauman knows that he has spent such a long time staring into this black hole of modernity as to disappear into it. So he stops, and follows a strategy of intellectual brinkmanship common to much of his more recent writing. He brings us into the abyss that we, or our forebears or leaders have made, leaves us there to contemplate and then says . . . 'well?'. It is not Bauman's responsibility to fix this mess, especially not when we consider its extent: technology rules. Nor is it our prerogative to derive solutions from Theory or History and exhort others to apply them; for superior morality is always the morality of the superior (1993a: 228).

Postmodern ethics is therefore a possibility in a world where there seems to be little room to move, except as tourists, well-heeled, or else as vagabonds.

We cannot accurately be described as nomads, Bauman says, because they know where they are heading (1993a: 240). The whole world looks in this story something like Hotel California. Bauman's only hope here is that our seduction (or repression) into this Disneyworld is as shallow as the culture itself is. Humans have a striking capacity to learn, on this account, but this kind of sensibility only begins to allow for what humans might be, or achieve. For Bauman also wants to remind us that humans have intuitive wisdoms, some good, some bad . . . in sum, that the score is ambivalent; and to posit that if humans learn they can also unlearn. Such a human prospect seems daunting, but it is only perhaps marginally more daunting than the alternative.

One other interpretation at least of this dissonance between the larger pessimism and the more constrained optimism nestled within it might be ventured. If, as Bauman argues, all our thinking risks substituting prosthesis for closer intimacy, validating worldviews over the detail of our worlds, then perhaps it is the smaller message of anthropological optimism which shines more strongly than the elements of the negative philosophy of history of decline which frame it. The big picture is always too far away.

Life in Fragments

Postmodern Ethics seems to be viewed in some quarters as the pinnacle of Bauman's achievement. Why? Because philosophical, or abstract? Or fashionable, closer to the French philosophy which is still imagined by others to be the last avant-garde? I am unsure about this issue, and I do not want to be cynical about it. But it seems to me that *Postmodern Ethics* is far more symbolically significant than it is textually central to Bauman's work. Ethical life is the issue which emerges as vital from Bauman's analysis of the Holocaust. How does modernity make us conformists, when the Enlightenment brief was also to encourage us to think for ourselves? *Postmodern Ethics* pursues this line, but also in its positive register: perhaps the earth is now moving beneath our feet. This is an abstract concern because alterity is an abstract concern, at least until we learn to think of the sensuous other, the other as the man or woman literally on the street, or to puzzle over the third party or our concrete social responsibilities to others. Then, instantly, in Bauman's work as in our own conversations, the philosophical inflection gives way to the sociological.

Life in Fragments is subtitled *Essays in Postmodern Morality* (1995). Fragmentary it is in two ways, both in terms of its form, the collected essay, and its subject matter, which is more wide ranging. The field of concern is more sociological again; where *Postmodern Ethics* eschewed the discussion of particular forms of morality, *Life in Fragments* focuses on postmodern morality in the best and worst senses. Postmodern times make it both easier and more difficult to behave morally, or to think ethically; if in one sense the problems we face are more grave than before, then in another our scope for response is more potentially open. The horizons within which we live and struggle remain those indicated by Bauman in *Modernity and Ambivalence* (1991a); our worldly challenges have to do with problems of tolerance and solidarity. What is it that binds us when all that is solid has melted into air? What can we tolerate, or advocate, in worlds where the lack of discrimination is as disabling as the stigma of discrimination? How do we cope with chaos without succumbing to it?

Bauman's first conversation partner in this volume is Castoriadis. Castoriadis' work is in a way more central to Bauman's than, say, Levinas'; not because of influence, but because of affinity. Levinas is the main stimulant used by Bauman in *Postmodern Ethics* (1993a) to puzzle over the other. The significance of Castoriadis' work here is distinct, for Castoriadis is a soul-mate. What in Bauman is significantly connected to ethics, in Castoriadis is associated with the vital sign of autonomy. Autonomy, in Castoriadis, has the advantage that it is ambidextrous in nature: it refers both to the abstract, ethical goal for the good person or individual, and to the social value of the autonomous society (Bauman, 1995: 19). The converse value, heteronomy, similarly links the individual and the social; conformism is both a personal and a social issue. The line of tutelage-thinking that runs from Hobbes to Durkheim rests on a negative anthropology, where society (or ideology) becomes the policeman of restitution. Castoriadis' case is different not only from this lineage, but also from that which through Critical Theory culminates in Marcuse, where generalized conformism looks something like the natural outcome of modernity, where society still forms individuality and therefore conforms it. For Bauman, as for Castoriadis, it only makes sense to complain about generalized conformism because we know that there are other possible ways to live. Conformism is modernist second nature for us, learned and therefore unlearnable.

There are other stimulants here; and it is one of the watermarks of Bauman's thinking that its intellectual influences or traces are unpredictable. Christopher Lasch and Richard Sennett more predictably run through Bauman's footnotes, as critics of a modernity that routinely and necessarily fails to live up to its promises, as we do. Alongside Castoriadis here, we also find the presence of Schopenhauer, Nietzsche and Horkheimer, but more provocatively, we also encounter the voice of E.M. Cioran, the blackest Romanian follower of Nietzsche. Cioran is a thinker whose hallmark is cynicism, and this, too, is an antidote which Bauman employs against the wide-eyed optimism of the *Weltverbesserer* or world-reformers aspirant. Consistent with his own affinities, Cioran offers aphorisms that stop us in our tracks, which for Bauman is one thing that moderns need daily to do, to step outside the many paths of self-made progress and to contemplate the contingency of our world historic achievements. Thus Cioran: 'a definition is always the cornerstone of a new temple' (Bauman, 1995: 25). Cioran's echo of Nietzsche is unmistakable, and it is the presence of this kind of sensibility which sets Bauman's postmarxism apart from those other kinds of possibilities, where marxism is relieved of its Bolshevik

clothing but left with its Enlightenment brain intact. Cioran, in short, is for
Bauman a whistleblower; he may have nothing in particular to buy or to
sell in the bazaar of ideas, but he knows deceit when he sees it. Does this
make Bauman, then, an anarchist? The spirit of existentialism sometimes
seems to fit Bauman, and there is of course a kind of cooperative motif
which animates a certain kind of anarchist politics. Bauman is not
obviously a localist, or an explicit enthusiast of small-is-beautiful, although
the logic of smallness does point towards the kind of proximity which he
argues that we have lost, which condition is fundamental to modern
monstrosities like the Holocaust. Nor is it any accident, in all likelihood,
that Castoriadis was long viewed as a kind of hero not only by radical
marxists but also by those western libertarians for whom self-management
was the social goal. The difference in Bauman's case is that the local
(Leeds) coincides with various other sociological or geopolitical dimensions,
the region (Yorkshire) and the national (New Labour) as well as the global
(per globalization). The prospect of autonomy, in this sense, relates more to
a sense of the conduct of everyday life than to specific period images
or slogans such as self-management. The substance of everyday life, viewed
in one way, at least, in turn is chaotic: unpredictable, uncertain, given to
breakdown, relying on a kind of 'Plan-B' readiness to adjust and adapt in
the face of all this.

Conformism is not just a problem because of conventionalism, however.
Bauman's case is not for a generalized nonconformism; this would be a
mere reversal, a substitution of one bad situation for another. Bauman is a
freethinker rather than a nonconformist. The problem of conventionalism
remains, however, as Bauman indicates in discussing Nietzsche's idea of the
will to power. If truth or falsity is also, practically, a political issue, is not
truth itself merely a convention (1995: 37)? As Bauman indicates, however,
not even Nietzsche can stand, last man, outside this problem; for, he, too,
in turn validates some aristocratic prejudices against those of the mere
masses and their self-appointed middle-class do-gooder representatives.
Bauman for his part wants no truck with these potentially tyrannical
liberals, but nor will he endorse either the agnosticism or the aristocratic
radicalism of Nietzsche. Too much of Luther's stance remains: we must tell
the truth as we see it. Speaking and judging still count; only there are times
when we speak and judge too endlessly, when silence, or touch and not
words are called for.

We die, each of us, alone, but we are born and live together. In the middle
of our being we may make contingency into destiny. But the problem of
identity, for Bauman, is not always obviously the key problem for postmoderns. Identity, he says is exactly a modern problem, for identity is
identical within itself; identity as we know it is a modern phenomenon, as it
is relatively stable even though it changes. The postmodern problem of
identity is primarily one of avoiding fixation and keeping options open,
or more literally mobile (1995: 81). Modern identity, unlike traditional
identity, was creative rather than prescriptive; postmodern identity plays

with recycling, endlessly, involves consumption as production or as creation. Early modernity gives you the telephone, modernism the payphone, postmodernity the mobile phone. Movement is central both to modernity and postmodernity. It is not just identity but the sum total of social relations that are mobile in time and space, even where the sense of space itself is reconstructed by the acceleration of time. If identity is constructed by movement, in turn, then this for Bauman generates particular personality types or paths of activity in the present, two key of which are the vagabond and the tourist.

Even if mobility is a postmodern and modernist motif, there of course remain all kinds of actors who are not mobile every day of their lives. Just as tradition inhabits the modern which holds up the postmodern, so is inertia a good part of the human condition in many places and lands, even where immobility – being stuck – seems to be the worst oppression. Poor or rich, we can all stroll in the malls, but some of us will always be caught in the sticks, or on the edges of suburbs that run into vacancy. The vagabond is distinct in his or her absence of alternatives: these are excluded actors who are compelled to move on. The vagabond is a familiar character in the narrative of Bauman's sociology; when masculine, he is the masterless man of the margin, whose footprints trace the edges of *Between Class and Elite* (1972) and then later *Memories of Class* (1982). From the Elizabethan Poor Laws of the sixteenth century to the caravan under the flyover pass in the new millennium, the vagabond is always just out of the picture of modernity and its predominant social forms. The vagabond is not a nomad; the pattern of movement which life dictates is less habitual or predictable. The vagabond is, then, for Bauman, the archetypical stranger. His prospects of assimilation are always slim, regardless of personal intention or desire; 'he still smells of other places, of that beyond against which the homestead of the natives has been built' (1995: 95). Not a nomad, because nomads live clearly patterned lives, but also because the postmodern propensity for semantic anachronism is too high; to say that we are all, these days, nomads, that we are all 'homeless', is to obscure some quite dramatic distinctions across the differing life-chances available to individuals across the social scale. Thus Bauman introduces the category of the tourist, in order to hold open the tension, for tourists are travellers well of heel. Tourists choose to move; they reflect the restless ethos of modernity, and they manifest the means available to those who are at home both with the commodity-form and the money-form. They seek the all-too fleeting pleasures of new experience per tourist travel, via the amazing plastic card which opens all doors in the house of consumption. Utopia is Hotel California; the tourists are inside, or on their way, while the vagabonds lie outside the city gates, working out how to get in. This is the world intellectually videotaped for us by Mike Davis in *City of Quartz*, where it is evident to all that the way of life of the inmates is entirely dependent on the exclusion of the outcasts, where the ethical choice about the good society becomes an aestheticized or rather, sexualized, choice between the body beautiful and the derelict in rags. The postmodern body, like the city of Los Angeles, is an artefact, where a mirage, that of perpetual youth, still guides the image of the perfect face and body, while the face and body of the Other bring out nothing but offense and repulsion ('we worked for our money').

The figure of the stranger thus becomes more strange in postmodern times, not less. We may all be strangers, today, yet there are some strangers whose attributes are less exotic than repelling. Modernity is not only the circulation of strangers that Simmel had portrayed; it involves their accentuation, and not only assimilation. The stranger may well share our own sense of place, or locality; he or she may in fact have shared this region with us, or even preceded us here, as Australian aborigines precede all the other migrants to Terra Australis. The boundaries are new, commodified boundaries, the lives of distinction drawn by money more than strictly by patterns of speech, dress or ethnic derivation, though in the margins race still rules. The restriction of access is an old one: no admittance except on business. This is the high capitalist face of postmodernity. Modernity thus maintains its traditionalism, but also pushes hard in its Faustian imperative of change. This, in turn, makes modernity violent. Modernity is by nature a frontier civilization; civilization itself depends on growth, extension, on the barbarism that seeks to expel barbarism in the name of order (1995: 141). Violence can routinely be directed against the other, against the outsider, but it can also be inner directed, against the wolf who remains within modern man; for there is always in modern eyes a wild man lying in wait inside every civilized one (1995: 145). The levels of organized violence which we might associate with the modern state nevertheless remain somehow invisible, because protected by the aura of legitimacy; violence is something which in the popular imagination is associated with street culture, or else perhaps with domestic violence. Bauman's immediate concern is that post-modern violence escalates further and yet at the same time becomes even less socially visible, thanks to privatization, deregulation and localization (1995: 161). More, violence is reformed through the never ending assault on degeneration, disease and deformity. Modernism makes a good fist of this, exemplified in the eugenic strategies of the Scandinavian Social Democrats as well as the Nazis and American liberals; postmodernism again turns the attack inward, so that the imperative of self-reform takes the place of state-sponsored reform programmes (1995: 167–73). The self, like the kitchen, becomes the site of DIY. At the same time, this renewed individualism plays into neotribalism, the wilful discovery or invention of traditionalistic forms of identity-behaviour from the stock of the past. Here 'who am I?' is not the breathless question of modernism, 'who can I be?', but the older, nostalgic question, 'where did I come from – who was I, what have I lost that can now be recovered?'

The modern, postmodern obsession with identity thus throws up all the old definitions of modernism and traditionalism rampant. I cannot be what I am; I must be more, so I must be either what I was, or what I will be (. . .

everything). Both these life strategies play into the logic of the social ostracization of others, for if I am what I was then so perhaps are all the others – boundaries up! – and if I am everything, then they must be nothing, lest they cramp my space and style. But these local variations become really nasty at the level of state power rather than personal preference. As Bauman argued in *Modernity and the Holocaust* (1989a), whereas tradition gives you the pogrom it is really only modernity that produces genocide, for it generates the means alongside the ends. What this means is that the Age of Enlightenment culminates or ends in the Century of Camps; yet somehow this tells us little about Enlightenment, far more about modernity and the will to violence, or about the adiaphorization of ethics and morality in the modern world: '*Modernity did not make people more cruel; it only invented a way in which cruel things could be done by non-cruel people*' (1995: 198). The tactile senses of suffering simply disappear when we cannot see the face of the other, or else when the face we see looks like a mask for which we can only feel disgust and repulsion. If human dirt, too, is matter out of place then we, or the state, must move it. If, as Ellul says, we discover that we have the means, then we also discover that we have the imperative to act. But we could also discover that we have the power to act differently, if we have the ethical imagination. The 'risk society' – Bauman again endorses the category popularized by Ulrich Beck here – increases both the sense of threat and the possible horizons of hope (1995: 278–9). Postmodernity both accentuates the possibilities and the constraints within modernity; which dimension will we, as actors, respond to? Bauman's own horizons of expectation and limitation shift together with these sensibilities. Hope persists, even if it does not prosper.

Postmodernity and its Discontents

In 1997 Bauman published *Postmodernity and its Discontents* (1997a). The telltale reference to Freud in the title runs along with another message. Perhaps we jaded moderns are now, already, becoming weary of the postmodern. Around 1989 the idea of the postmodern still had the aura of a modernist mission, to save us from the stultifying past and high certainty that for Bauman characterizes modernity. Postmodernity seemed to offer so much; less than ten years later, a decade of living without an alternative, and the postmodern was beginning to look tawdry, having delivered little by way of new lives to either intellectuals or especially to vagabonds.

Freud knew, in *Civilization and its Discontents* (1930), that nothing came without a price. The cost of civilization was repression; yet the Other would ever seek to assert itself, to seek to break out of the newly refined state that modernity offered. There would always be the wolf in man. Freud remained ambivalent about this condition in a way that violated the founding Hobbesian sense that coercion was the price to be paid for order and stability; the alternative, anarchy and chaos, was always thought to be worse. Bauman does not call for wild nature, or clamour for primitivism rather than modernism; what we need, apparently, is a third term beyond the false choice of 'order' and 'chaos', or perhaps which combines them in something more mixed or ambivalent, like ordinary chaos. Modernity, however, sought out values such as beauty, cleanliness and order. This, for Bauman as for Freud, was the modern pact; for Bauman, its cost included the extremities of the gardening states of Nazism and Stalinism, and the more civilized repression of minorities and outsiders across the free west. Today, however, ours is the age of deregulation (Bauman, 1997a: 2). The conditions of the pact have changed, at least for some; the gains and losses have changed places: '*postmodern men and women exchanged a portion of their possibilities of security for a portion of happiness*' (1997a: 3; emphasis added). A kind of reversal has occurred across the postmodern divide. The discontents of modernity arose from the pursuit of a kind of security which tolerated too little freedom in the hope of individual happiness. The discontents of postmodernity, in turn, arise from a kind of freedom defined as pleasure seeking, at the expense of individual and social security (1997a: 3).

Bauman's collection of essays works across this terrain, from security to aesthetics. He begins with the greatest obsession of modernity, and its most frightening: the Dream of Purity. Security and aesthetics, indeed, are here connected: for the modernist obsession with order identifies the two, to the point at which the need for aesthetic clarity and safety combined in the final solution. No mess, no fuss; Jews away (1997a: 5). As Mary Douglas famously indicates, with Bauman's agreement, however, dirt or disorder is really only matter out of place; 'dirt', like 'weed' is not an essential but a relational or cultural judgement (1997a: 6). 'Dirt', 'weeds' . . . human weeds . . . strangers. This kind of utopia/dystopia is proverbially premodern, in that it elevates simplicity and stasis over complexity and change. This was the type of a perfect world, still, 'a transparent world . . . nothing "out of place"; a world without "dirt"; a world without strangers' (1997a: 12). Enter Nazism and communism as attempted utopias of purity, the first of race, the second of class; and the more civilized and modest democratic capitalist utopia of belonging and citizenship to the exclusion of all others, state and citizen as husband and wife. But the new, postmodern utopia is different; it has neither subject nor citizen, neither husband nor wife, only neurotic but risktaking, high adrenalin risktaker individuals. The new dreck are all the rest, those who refuse to risk life and limb or who cannot afford to impale themselves on hi-tech consumer goods; these Bauman calls 'flawed consumers', those who just can't get it right by the new criteria of conspicuous consumption (1997a: 14). Ours, today, in this recurring theme, is a world without limits – only the content of this proposition changes, so that we are no longer driven to Faustian projects so much as to endless shopping, seeing and being seen. The new revolutionaries of postmodern times choose Stolichnaya and black leather, but this is all that they have in common with the Bolsheviks. Modernity, according to Bauman, declared war (or permanent revolution) against modernity; postmoderns make permanent revolution a fashion statement (1997a: 16).

In *Postmodern Ethics* (1993a) Bauman offers a modest, yet ambitious challenge: that these new times might yet afford us the prospect within which to recognize the Other. By *Postmodernity and its Discontents* (1997a) the shine has disappeared off the postmodern, partly because of the excessive zeal of its intellectual advertising agents, partly because of the looming commodification process which threatens to gobble up the postmodern as well. Simmel, as Bauman variously has occasion to observe, is one kind of intellectual lifeline across this barren terrain, for he was the most postmodern of the early modern social theorists, and the most modern of postmoderns in his concerns with fragmentation, the metropolis, the stranger, and money or commodification. Simmel, like Weber, remains ever in our shadows as sociologists because he insists on asking the most fundamental of questions about personality: what does this (or any other form of) culture do to character? What is the relationship between social form or institutions and soul, or personality? How can we connect the social outside with the human inside? As I have tried to show for example in interpreting *Modernity and the Holocaust* (1989a), these remain essential questions and curiosities for Zygmunt Bauman. For we cannot simply deduce the inner from the outer, to conclude, say, that all Germans were inner Nazis; and yet the historic association suggests a stain, or strain, a connection of steel, as strong as it became later to be fragile and corroded.

The stranger, for Simmel, was a modern personality type. The postmodern stranger is more ubiquitous. The modern stranger, for Bauman, remained anomalous, ever a potential enemy of the modern State. The modern State applied those strategies earlier alluded to in order to clean up these nasty stains: devouring or vomiting, assimilation or expulsion (1997a: 18). Postmodern state strategies involve something different, licensing an ethic of personal achievement or personal self-perfection; the new imperative is neither any longer to fit in or get out, so long as you keep moving, and consuming, but fast. If the older, modern utopias valued stasis, the new, postmodern image demands speed, restlessness, dizziness not as an end-state (qua Stalin) so much as a way of life. Strangers, here, are our servants, or our enemies, those parasites who come from elsewhere and stay, at our expense, and even the otherwise decent communitarians tend to fall into this logic, where difference signified by race reinstates borders between us, the original inhabitants, and them, the invaders of our community, our space. Postmodern tribal particularism now stands in for the empty universalism of modern times (1997a: 32).

The postmodern strangers now either service the privileged, or else are incarcerated. For as moralism substitutes for ethics, and law for morality, so does law substitute incarceration for the roving movement of the unincorporated. As we can no longer 'afford' the welfare state, so do strangers definitionally transform before our eyes into enemies. With the privatization of responsibility goes the privatization of prisons (1997a: 37).

Those inside the wall project their fear about the Others outside upon them, resulting in the sense that we must strike first, before the aliens take their revenge on us. The social logic involved is that of the final solution, even if the means invoked differ. The enemy is within; they include the ranks of the flawed consumers and the dangerous classes, those whom we cannot allow access to the market, for we need our demons all the same (1997a: 39). Criminalization emerges as the consumer society's prime substitute for the fast disappearing welfare state provisions (1997a: 59).

Modernity, as Simmel understood, is primarily concerned with motion. Bauman picks up on this sensibility in 'Parvenu and Pariah'. We are all one, or other; new, in but not of a place; or else outside, looking in through the glass (1997a: 72). The postmodernist equivalents of these personality-types, for Bauman, are tourists and vagabonds. Tourists both belong and do not; they belong in their Hilton Hotels and limos; they choose to travel. Vagabonds also travel, but because others move them on (1997a: 93). One of modernity's most cherished illusions was that the pariahs might also come inside; the postmodern world depends again on the older image of master and slave, Two Nations, Mark Two. At least modernity still harboured such illusions.

Modernism, in contrast, saw not only nature but also modernity itself as a bitch to be whipped. Modernism could never escape from the military image of intellectuals or innovators as the avant-garde; and the modernist avant-garde, like its aristocratic predecessors, had little more than contempt for the aesthetically illiterate masses (1997a: 98–9). In this way not just modernity but modernism itself became a new traditionalism. Yet modernist art always reinvents itself, this time as postmodernism, and while the path of history is continuous, it is not self-identical: postmodern art and fiction offer us something different. Perhaps these other forms of creation offer us the sense of critique, creation or utopia which sociology, as a science, no longer readily can deliver upon (1997a: 119). But has cultural activity itself become democratized? We can each of us create, in principle, only just some of us can be received by others as we write, sculpt, paint, perform. Bauman returns momentarily in the context of this discussion to the tutelary legacy of the Enlightenment, symbolized in the kindred French, German and English notions of *civilization*, *Bildung* and *refinement*, each doubly elitist in that they presume that some rather than others are gifted with what it takes and conclude that this then confers upon them the right to instruct those others (1997a: 128). Culture, too, became like health or industrial commodities, something that was produced in a factory of order. Though the postmodern mentality still emerges from these pages as more tolerant than modernity, Bauman's critique of Enlightenment turns rather into the rejection of humanism, that stream of western intellectual history which precedes Enlightenment as well as informing it. Various aspects of the Enlightenment encouraged belief in God, or at least tolerated it; and belief in God, or the sacred counts here, as it always signals the limits of Man, or men. Where there is the sacred, there are limits to human activity or ambition. For humans are best equipped, as in Vico, to take care of things human. Therefore, the sole things that matter to humans are the things that humans may take care of (1997a: 170). In seeking to be as Gods, humans both reach beyond their own station and, at the same time, neglect the ordinary rituals and responsibilities of care for the self and the other.

In this interpretation, which Bauman here routes through the work of John Carroll, the problem with modernity is Humanism, this double sin of disrespect for the sacred and exaltation of our species. If men would be as gods, they would be neither; there would be nobody home. Carroll sees this maniacal missionary zeal as the downfall of moderns. Much of Bauman's Jeremiad-writing is consonant with this general sense, like that in Heidegger and negatively in Sartre, where the human propensity to project breeds monsters. Bauman notes that he follows a different emphasis to Carroll, for whom humanism is uniformly disastrous in its effects on western civil-ization (1997a: 171; 215, n.12). Humanists may have believed change to be possible, but they did not therefore believe that anything was possible. Even the heady romanticism of the young Marx – 'I am nothing and shall be everything!' – was moderated by the far more balanced sense that if human subjects in a sense made history, they did so within cultural and historical constraints over which they had no control. In the subsequent history of marxism, humanism, in turn, gives way to structuralism, which will hear more of these changes. If for John Carroll, then, humanism emerges as the ideological blight which makes for the disaster called modernity, for Bauman the devil looks more like Faustian man, the inexhaustible, mono-maniacal developer who will stop at nothing, the devil included.

Faustianism is a cultural trend, manifest later in figures like Trotsky, and like the latter it is also an expression of a personality-type which, as Spengler had it, is quintessentially modern and decadent (Spengler, 1922). This is the human model of creative destruction, where the latter is always more prominent than the former. All that is solid melts into air, and we are left awash in detritus as a result, the more progress, the more waste, both human and other. The frenzied pursuit of change necessarily violates any momentarily longer sense of constancy. The worst personal crime one can commit, in this scenario, is to remain the same, to risk missing out. Yet we need, as sociologists and as citizens, to remain still at least for long enough to recognize this process for what it is. Speed is a conspiracy against contemplation of any kind at all.

Having begun this book with Freud, Bauman returns to him in closing, and to monotheism. Oneness is dangerous: *Ein Volk, ein Reich, ein Führer, Einheit*, one true path or meaning, all this leads to the gallows (1997a: 201). Freedom requires something more than this; and as Bauman claimed in opening *Postmodernity and its Discontents*, it depends upon some modicum of security. Freedom is a social relation, which implies dependence, and therefore equality and justice, or at least the struggle against inequality and injustice. It is not Baudrillard who carries out the closing narrative of this text, then, but the less exotic figure of Beveridge, the radical if aristocratic liberal whose policy underpinned the postwar British Welfare State (1997a: 205). Baudrillard's influence on Bauman is recognizable, in his passing discussion of simulacra, in the use of notions such as repression and seduction. Like Levinas, or elsewhere Lyotard or Bourdieu, here Baudrillard is a stimulant for Bauman, but none of these offers any secret to Bauman's thinking, or any royal road into his social science.

Baudrillard's books literally sit alongside Bauman's on the theory shelves of the bookshops; perhaps there is then a connection that is osmotic? Bauman dedicates a separate essay to Baudrillard in the volume edited by Rojek and Turner, which turns Baudrillard's playfulness onto Baudrillard himself: *Forget Baudrillard* (Bauman, 1993b). Bauman's line in is the sense of smell, so everpresent in our lives and yet so marginal or irrelevant in sociology. For Baudrillard is a sensual writer. He uses words that are tactile and olfactory, or at least these are the words which call out to readers like Bauman. The connection is suggestive; for Bauman, modernity declares war not only on dirt, but also on smells. Smell is transgressive; it respects no boundaries. The other stinks; natives stink, the poor smell; as Orwell said earlier, you can smell class. Mortality, death, stench, decomposition, degeneration, a whole mobile army of metaphors stands ready to assault moderns equipped to defend themselves with nothing but industrial strength Domestos and the code-books of hygiene (Bauman, 1993b). The more common symbol drawn upon by Baudrillard for Bauman is visual, rather than olfactory – it is the image of simulacra, where commodity fetishism becomes absorbed in the larger society of the spectacle and our capacity to differentiate between surface and reality shrinks. Baudrillard's path out of marxism indicates other kinds of sympathies, or similarities, across his own path and that of Bauman; there are other associations, including a fondness for photography, where the visual matters regardless of how we value it against some other, sociological reality. Only that other, sociological reality persists far more powerfully in Bauman's work. This is not, in Bauman's thinking, because the postmodern is only a code word for the self-indulgent or playful; rather, it reflects the persistence of modernity, and therefore of capital, in a new world only apparently held up by culture and its consumption. Where for Baudrillard capitalism disappears, apparently, into simulacra, for Bauman simulacra remain the problem to be explained, perhaps even transformed. Freedom remains possible; and in sympathy with Beveridge, security remains desirable.

Freedom

To turn directly to the discussion of freedom is, textually speaking, to turn back ten years, to 1988, when Bauman published his book of that name. Freedom is, in a sense, both one of the most important modern concepts and the most elusive, or overlooked. Everybody knows that we are free to choose, when it comes to the ways of the marketplace, and yet many of us sense that we have no real freedom at all, or else that freedom of movement or action is so unfairly distributed as to be a mockery. The possibility of freedom remains vital to Bauman; like liberty, it is the third term that makes up his revised trilogy, together with tolerance and solidarity. As I have suggested, Bauman is no liberal, though he may look like a liberal against communitarians, whom he suspects of harbouring too much by way of traditionalistic prejudices and residues. Libertarian, perhaps; but this merely reflects the nay-saying sentiment in Bauman, sceptical of power and critical of those who claim to represent others while cultivating their own power in smiling silence. Freedom matters, for Bauman, much as does justice – not in the Rawlsian sense, where magical theorems like the veil of ignorance are contrived to provide conceptual solutions for practical problems, but as a counterfactual. Bauman endorses the logic of Barrington Moore's great work *Injustice* (1978; Bauman, 1988: 41–2). The hope is not that justice can ever be achieved, in any absolute sense; rather, justice is a category which is evoked in struggle whenever justice is denied. It is inequality which outrages us, as radicals, measured notionally against any non-specific image we might entertain of a more equal world; and so it is acts of injustice that drive us on to maintain our enthusiasm for justice. Freedom, as Orlando Patterson showed later in his magisterial study, is not just a western fig leaf but a kind of universal value which is asserted transhistorically wherever there is oppression or, especially, slavery (Patterson, 1991).

Bauman's approach to freedom is similar, but distinct; for Bauman, the idea of freedom passes us directly on to the associated value of dependence. Dependence is not the opposite of freedom, but its precondition. The fact that this necessary relationship between freedom and dependence is lost on mainstream political discussion, which dichotomizes so easily between liberalism and collectivism, is one reason why contemporary politics is so hopelessly equipped to deal with the ambivalence that is us. Not that the prospect of freedom is entirely illusory, but that it is deceptive. For freedom as we encounter it is formal; it is real, but its consequences may be quite different to what we hope, or imagine. We who are fortunate inhabit a culture with a relative absence of hard prohibitions; this is the classical negative liberalism named by Isaiah Berlin as 'freedom from'. Then there are positive freedoms, the 'freedom to', but these are the realms where our intentions may come to nought, or even turn in the reverse direction. Both these aspects of negative and positive freedom refer us to the other, and to the social, for while the idea of freedom is often associated with the misty realms of the abstract individual, freedom of action occurs within socially formed fields. Sociology, as the critique of modernity born of the critique of tradition, is the discipline which emphasizes the social, in this case, the constraints or limits within the spheres wherein we might expect to act freely. If all our social arrangements are in the first instance artificial, or legitimized by the ideology or culture which naturalizes them, then it makes sense that sociologists might focus on problems of 'unfreedom' rather than freedom; and indeed it is true that much of classical sociology takes exactly this path, with the marxian emphasis on exploitation, the Weberian trope of domination, and the less melancholy concern of Durkheim with the necessity of regulation. 'Freedom' appears especially elusive within the sociological classics, with their various implications that perhaps earlier forms of society were more free, at least for some, or at least for the more noble. To put it more plainly, sociologists simply do not believe in free will, and consequently they often speak a language much more like determinism (Bauman, 1988: 4). The natural, or rather the social bias of sociology is to refer everything to the social, and often unintentionally to diminish the potential autonomy of the subject or the individual in the process. Sociology veers between the 'cultural dope' or cipher or yes-man and the residual fantasy that romantic heroes, once painters or poets, now intellectuals or critical theorists, alone can rage against the machine.

So there is a ton of books on freedom on the library shelves marked philosophy, and roughly the same weight of books on the shelves in sociology on domination. Bauman casts the line of his own book somewhere in between, to take both the individual and the social into account. Summarized in a sentence, his curiosity is in the claim that the 'free individual, far from being a universal condition of humankind, is a historical and social creation' (1988: 7). Freedom is contingent, both historically and socially, but also practically; its effects in everyday life are more provisional than we would like to think (or are told). So Bauman sets himself the classical critical task in this book, not to debunk, but to denaturalize the idea of freedom: to render 'the familiar' strange, not as the explanation of how we live but as that which needs to be explained. Bauman sets out then to treat freedom as an anthropologist would, as though it were exotic rather than normal. For freedom is not universal; it appears, and potentially disappears, together with a particular kind of society (1988: 7). Freedom is a result, rather than a precondition; it is not the property of an individual, but rather indicates an asymmetrical relationship between individuals.

Freedom is not only an individual aspiration; it is also a factor in social reproduction and not only in ideological terms. This centrality of individual freedom as a link holding together the individual life-world, society and the social system has been attained with the recent shift of freedom or claims to freedom away from the sphere of production and into the sphere of consumption (1988: 7). Freedom has been reconceived, in recent times, as the freedom to consume. Together with the weakening of the older social democratic state, the freedom to consume can be seen as both an expansion (for some) and a constriction (for others) of freedom into postmodern times.

Freedom is therefore both an introduction to an idea, and an argument which runs along the back of *Legislators and Interpreters* (1987) into Two Nations: Mark Two. Like *Legislators*, it relies upon Foucault's rediscovery of Bentham's panopticon. But it is also, I think, more imaginative than *Discipline and Punish*, for the latter is a book that seduces its readers as much by virtue of its controversy and style as by its argument or message.

Bauman, for his part, begins not with the extraordinary spectacle of the public execution, but with the plainest explanatory device – a definition, and some context. What do we need to know about the idea of freedom, in order to begin to enter the labyrinth? Bauman's insight may seem Foucauldian to those who come recently to the festival of theory; it could also be seen as classically sociological in its emphasis on power. Nietzsche may have named the will to power, but he did not discover it; maybe Machiavelli did. Here the roseate aura of nobility or heroic resistance takes on a different hue:

> Freedom was born as a privilege and has remained so ever since. Freedom divides and separates. It sets the best apart from the rest. It draws its attraction from difference: its presence or absence reflects, marks and grounds the contrast between high and low, good and bad, coveted and repugnant. (Bauman, 1988: 9)

Freedom represents a coming-to-be rather than a stable condition or achievement, a movement rather than a fixity of place. Freedom, that is to say, emerges conceptually and historically from unfreedom. But more – and here Bauman anticipates the theme of alterity central later to *Postmodern Ethics* (1993a) – freedom only begins to make sense in relation to another: 'For *one* to be free there must be at least *two*' (1988: 9; emphasis added). The condition of freedom is unfreedom. Freedom can be an abstract universal, but in concrete terms it is exclusive rather than inclusive: we cannot all be free all of the time, any more than we can all hope to be happy all of the time. As Bauman explains,

> Freedom signifies a social relation, an asymmetry of social conditions; essentially it implies social difference – it presumes and implies the presence of social division. Some can be free only in so far as there is a form of dependence they can aspire to escape. (1988: 9)

Freedom means mobility, the freedom to go anywhere; freedom in this sense for the tourist is also freedom for the vagabond, even though these two freedoms are obviously less than identical.

If freedom is a loaded, or ambivalent category, so then is dependence. The master depends on the slave just as the slave depends on the master; but this is merely to refer to asymmetrical relations of power which are not only reproduced but formed without free consent. In our ordinary everyday lives we also agree to depend on one another, or to offer support, to lovers, to friends, to significant others. Dependence is also ambivalent, and it is the failure to register this in mainstream political discourse which allows the stigmatization of dependence as a 'female' value and the corresponding typification of independence (or freedom) as a 'male' value, whereas all human creatures in fact combine both values or positions in different ways. These are all problems and possibilities that become pertinent in modern societies; yet it is also a hallmark of modernity that it seeks out order, as the possibility of the absence of regulation threatens its own cultural sensibilities. Conformism is socially encouraged; freedom is reformed as conformism, the right to fit in, to be included. Enter Foucault, closely behind Bentham . . . or is he in front?

Bentham's Panopticon is a clever device, well-worked by those modern cultural pessimists for whom society is nothing more than a prison. Its presence in much negative critical theory is like the evil eye. We always wait for the traffic light to turn green – at least when we see the cop across the street. Is this because we internalize the message to follow rules, or merely because we know how to behave street-wise? Bauman goes for the interpretation which indicates practical credibility: the design of the panopticon is not concerned with what the prison inmates think, only with what they do (1988: 12). A different reading of Foucault would place the emphasis on internalization, that actors follow the policeman in the head, concluding therefore that indoctrination is more powerful a factor in social reproduction than coercion or outright violence. Bauman's image of modernity is not Orwell's dystopia in *1984*, where we need actually to love Big Brother, and not just pretend that we do. The dimension of pretence or acting out, rather, is vital to Bauman's choreography of action, where we can never presume any direct or causal connection between playing along and internal conviction. Humans routinely play along, even with Nazi or communist plots; their lips move, sometimes they might even goosestep, but these externalities tell us little about the life of the mind, or heart, chilling though the sequence may nevertheless be.

As is evident from works such as *Between Class and Elite* (1972) and *Memories of Class* (1982), Bauman knows about British political economy, and not only about French philosophy or the local antics of its Anglo enthusiasts. Consequently Bauman discusses Bentham here, more than he does Foucault. The connection is significant, for while Bauman's book is shadowed by the dialectic of master and slave developed by Marx out of Hegel, it is also formed under the influence of his ongoing concern with 'masterless men', those from the victims of the earliest manufactories through to postmodern vagabonds who can be held up to the inmates as social scarecrows, to scare the children. The controllers see, but are not seen; the inmates are seen, but are unseeing: 'The combination of the independence *from* and mastery *over* constitutes freedom of the inspectors *in relation to* the inmates' (1988: 15). Freedom is therefore one side of the social relationship which has unfreedom or domination as its other, though neither social partner can be entirely free, as the relationship is what is mutually constitutive of society writ small. As Marx says in *Capital*, no sovereigns without subjects, no subjects without sovereigns. Bentham's Panopticon is not therefore an image of society, but it may be usefully viewed as a parable for modern society, where the freedom of some makes the dependence of others both necessary and profitable, while the unfreedom of one part of society makes the freedom of another possible (Bauman, 1988: 19). Bauman goes so far as to suggest that within the history of sociology, Panopticon may be compared to Parsons' social system, with the singular difference that Bentham leaves culture to look after itself. Panopticon is an engine that runs on pure power; so here the parallel with modernity breaks down. Still the overall message to this point is grim: 'In the light of this analysis, freedom appears as the capacity to rule; as a bid for power. Freedom is power, in so far as there are others who are bound' (1988: 23).

Yet society cannot be a prison, or else there would be no need for a separate analysis of the prison as distinct institution in its own right, and citizens are not just inmates. The whole of modernity cannot be defined even symbolically by this particular part; freedom cannot be reduced to some kind of systems-category or institutional by-product. Bauman acknowledges this when we take leave of the silent realms of self-flagellation and enter the historical realm. Having begun with definition and context, via the Foucauldian narrative, Bauman turns now to history, to the sociogenesis of freedom. For inasmuch as the idea of freedom relates to activity or to movement, it also has its own history, this in a special sense; freedom only makes sense to us as a movement into new spheres of development, even if these are processes where achievements can also be reversed. This also serves to remind us of two of the most routine sociological observations concerning modernity, that it inaugurates new vistas of social and geographical mobility. Freedom as a modern motif is irredeemably caught up with the image and site of the city which is also the locus of the frustration of freedom, the emergence of new patterns of servility and entrapment. Henceforth the city would be the site of modernity's dreams and disillusions, that particular place where freedom would be offered to all and made available to each, according to their credit lines. Still amidst all this sense of swirling change, the bond between freedom and domination remains:

> The effectiveness of freedom demands that some other people stay unfree. To be free means to be allowed and to be able to keep others unfree. Thus freedom in its modern, economically defined form does not differ from its pre-modern applications in respect of its social-relations content. (Bauman, 1988: 45–6)

The weakness of moderns is their propensity to tell this story through its good side, as though there were no other, or bad side. The dynamic of rational mastery is presented as our collective opportunity and fate by the gushing boosterists of modernity, who are unmoved by charges of deceptive advertising. The more sober among the classical thinkers, such as Weber, start from a different premise: even if there were an abundance of social goods and esteem, there will never be enough to go around; only a social minority will ever know freedom in its more extensive dimensions (1988: 47). Freedom for some goes together with the dull conformism of bureaucratic regulation for the rest of us.

Yet freedom is an impulse that will not neatly follow orders, or flow perfectly through bureaucratic channels. The history of modernity is also the history of its other movements, of their struggles and consequences. At the same time, as we witness ongoing forms of collective action, however, individualism is rechannelled into consumerism, and this is not only a postmodern phenomenon: sociologists have been fascinated by the spectacle of consumption from Veblen through to Bourdieu. This is not only shopfront, or deception; indeed, modernity democratizes consumption by formally opening lines of money or credit and by weakening marketplace ties of ethnic identity or origin. Freedom to consume becomes the letout for lives lived under so many other forms of domination. More, as Bauman observes, consumption is no longer closed by monopoly claims to exclusivity. Consumer freedom is less a zero-sum game than many others we play; identities are not scarce goods (1988: 63). Yet this simultaneously devalues welfare, which in its postwar form has not been delivered through the market in terms of packages directed towards consumer 'choice' (1988: 70). Now the pleasure-principle rules, even in situations where the punters are unable to afford it.

Little apparent cheer emerges from the closing pages of *Freedom*; perhaps, paradoxically, part of Bauman's sociological purpose is to encourage us to consider unfreedom, in order to urge freedom on. The only apparent choice we face here, in 1988, prior to the collapse of communism, is consumer capitalism on the one hand or what Fehér, Heller and Markus (1983) call the dictatorship over needs on the other, less hidden hand (Bauman, 1988: 88). Symbolic variations on these choices, Bauman suggests, are offered in the images of Huxley's *Brave New World* and Orwell's *1984* – dull and brutalized collectivism, or else mindless hedonism; though perhaps it is the anaesthetized utopia of Rabelais' *Gargantua* which really captures the prospect – that place where enjoyment is the only duty, failure to enjoy the only crime (Bauman, 1988: 91). Yet the human need for autonomy is never sated, not even by the utmost cornucopia of consumer goods and services. This need for something other can be made manifest only as a need for abundance and endless consumption; second nature rules. Here Bauman agrees with Hannah Arendt that such civil privatization necessarily erodes the strength of the public sphere. Consumerism seems to bring us the worst of both worlds, in that it expands the influence of markets and shrinks that of the *res publica*.

Exit, via Budapest

Bauman's list of stimulating thinkers plainly includes Arendt, as much as on totalitarianism as on the separation of values. It seems to me that while the association is less than total, it is connections of this kind that are ultimately more suggestive than, say, those between Bauman and Baudrillard. One consequence of this is an apparent sympathy across the work of Bauman and that of Agnes Heller, which is addressed in Bauman's celebration of Heller in the essay 'Narrating Modernity' (1994). Bauman shares Heller's concern with the human condition in modernity. Where Arendt is the classicist and Heller the modernist, Bauman is the postmodernist. This human condition is an historical product, but it is not necessarily historically conditioned. To view modernity in this way is already to take a step beyond modernity, so that Heller's, like Bauman's, is a self-consciously postmodern story. Postmodernity is not a type of society but a way of responding to modernity: it is a type of historical consciousness, itself bound up with a sense of movement, of moving beyond (Bauman, 1994: 98). At this point, some differences emerge, of emphasis at least, between the two thinkers. Heller wants to insist that modernity both cultivates and frustrates difference, at the same time. Bauman's response is that modernity breeds difference unhappily, unintentionally as it were, or at least without enthusiasm (1994: 99). Heller, in contrast, is both sceptical and optimistic; she expects little of our moment, and is delighted to be surprised by the unexpected. As Bauman puts it, she revisits the house of modernity where the social sciences dwelled for most of their history, all the more wise for what she has seen in her travels; but she meets the residents on their own terms (1994: 111). She asks the question, where are we at home? and answers that this, like much else in our lives, is increasingly mobile, both in a practical and an existential sense. As Bauman confides, Heller's work is like a postmodern supplement to Arendt's analysis of the human condition (1994: 116).

Our lives, on this shared account, remain contingent, laden with possibilities which may never be realized, but rich for this nonetheless. Heller's own path took her from Budapest to Melbourne, to New York to take up Hannah Arendt's chair, now back to Budapest. The student of Lukács, she managed to take the best, to avoid the stranger parts of his baggage. Zygmunt Bauman's path also took him via Australia, momentarily, back to Europe, to the culture of tolerance we still call England. He was barely touched by Lukács, as the Hungarians hardly were by Gramsci. When I asked him in conversation about the influence of Lukács he told me that he had entered that room through the wrong door; his way in was via *The Destruction of Reason*, which Heller calls a two volume pamphlet connecting irrationalism and Nazism, a position beyond credibility to the author of *Modernity and the Holocaust* (Bauman, 1989a). Heller's general emphasis, I think, falls upon the bright side of modernity, the possibilities which remain before us; and Bauman finds this attractive as a symbol of hope within the scenario of a postmodern constellation which surpasses modernity only in its relative distance from the bestiarium. We cannot dwell for ever looking into this abyss; to ignore it, on the other hand, would be the kind of folly that only incurable optimists or modernist idiots could commit.

The image of entering the same room by different doors is one that recurs in Bauman's conversation and self-understanding. Perspective, accident, timing, contingency: they all matter. More closely aligned, what we call the modern and the postmodern together blur into one. Located outside of the enthusiasm for modernism, Bauman's perspective suggests something different. Postmodernity, in this view, cannot be judged by the moderns any more than marxism can be held against Marx. All those years after the Marx Renaissance across Eastern Europe, its messages still haunt us, as our voices collide with theirs and bounce back, like the echoes of a postmodern humanism, hopes smaller but surviving.

6   Following the Human Condition

The journey never ends; we never understand until it is too late. Perhaps this is the single most powerful self-understanding that modernity and its modernisms forgets, or destroys. Change will always elude us, as will understanding and the prospect of perpetual peace. Yet nothingness is what waits after life; the types of abyss into which we peer along life's journey together with Zygmunt Bauman are human and manufactured more than ontological or theological. The faces we confront in the street are not those of our own mortality, but those of our fellows, those we have allowed to suffer, those our forebears have killed or allowed to die. Death and suffering are constant presences in our lives, only we needs must push them away, just as we differently feel the compulsion to push the other away, to avert the gaze, keep on walking, don't look back. These are some of the themes that link the books grouped together in this chapter, on death, globalization and its figures – heroes and vagabonds – and on the prospect once again of opening the public space in which a politics might emerge that could encourage us to recognize our others, to deal better with the living even if we cannot escape our dead. *Mortality, Immortality and other Life Strategies* (1991b) is a peculiar book, in the context of Bauman's work, for it is more like a corridor that leads nowhere in particular than it is a bridge or door. This book enters the realm of death and then leaves it, with no obvious connection on, as say, *Modernity and the Holocaust* (1989a) leads to *Modernity and Ambivalence* (1991a) and that other windowless room of human precondition in *Postmodern Ethics* (1993a). The other books discussed here follow rather the pattern of thinking which otherwise characterizes Bauman's strategy of connecting rooms or entering the same room by different openings. *In Search of Politics* (1999b) is the reply to *Globalization: The Human Consequences*, or perhaps is its extension from sociology into the political. Yet there are also echoes across these works, not least those suggested by the occasional cartoon in the newspapers which sees us all disappearing under the mountainous detritus of endless consumer goods while the devil looks on, smiling. For if culture is something we use to push death away, then consumer culture is the latest counter-memory device forced upon us, to help us cope, symptomatically, with the future.

Mortality and Immortality

When, in conversation, I asked Zygmunt Bauman what his favourite among his own books was he answered without hesitation: *Mortality, Immortality and Other Life Strategies* (1991b). I remember being unsure as to what I expected him to say, but I did not expect him to say this, and I wondered whether perhaps this was, so to speak, the unloved child. For if Bauman is popularly imagined mainly as the author of *Modernity and the Holocaust* or perhaps of *Postmodern Ethics*, then this smaller, more difficult book has indeed been overshadowed or forgotten by his readers in the rush.

Mortality and Immortality is almost certainly Bauman's most difficult book. Dense, abstract and demanding both in form and content, it also takes on a field which is almost impossible, for it is by definition beyond us. It is a work of great courage and originality. The intellectual strategy which informs *Mortality and Immortality* is similar to that in *Modernity and the Holocaust,* for this is a book about death which is not a study in the sociology of death and dying (1991b: 1). Its object is not ritual, or the life path, nor even that of the changing vision of death pioneered by Phillippe Ariés. It does not address the cultural institution of death and dying. Its purpose, rather, is to blow the whistle on the marginalization of death within disciplines like sociology. Just as the Holocaust is sidelined out of sociology, into Jewish or German Studies, or else is pushed away as barbaric, a premodern residual, non-modern and therefore not our problem, so is the presence of death in sociology dealt with as though it is merely the area specialization of its own devotees. Bauman wants to argue, rather, that the presence of death is central to culture and therefore to modernity and its discipline, sociology. Death, therefore, is a kind of absent presence. It will not stay in its place, in the hospital or bedroom, in the cemetery or splattered on our television screens in the spectacle of accidents. The purpose of *Mortality and Immortality* is therefore to unpack the conscious or repressed knowledge of mortality in those human institutions, rituals and beliefs which in their own understandings have nothing to do with death (1991b: 2).

Death is difficult, difficult even to imagine. It is the absolute other of being, an unimaginable other, but it is not by virtue of that opacity actually so distant from us. Death is beyond comprehension, for it involves absolute nothingness; modernity's claim to be everything already therefore speaks to eternity. The cult of life itself necessarily rests on the denial of death. Death is an impossible puzzle inasmuch as the only death we can really intimately know, our own, is beyond communication. My death is subjective, not intersubjective in its most intimate sensibility. More, humans are the only creatures who not only know this, but also know that they know (1991b: 3). Nothingness hangs before us from the first moment of its realization. But these are not only personal fears or nemeses. As Bauman argues, the whole purpose of culture is, as Freud indicated, prosthetic; it is the artificial limit or artifice with which we push away not only savagery but also the prospect of death. Culture ultimately concerns transcendence and it relates to survival, not just to smug middle class concerns with proper speech, etiquette or decent aesthetics. If culture often is taken to reflect a whole, or larger way of life, then it also subsumes into it a whole pattern of obsession with death, or impermanence. Every waking moment of our lives, then, we struggle against death. We struggle to make a living, to make money, to leave a written or concrete legacy, to leave children, or students to follow us and therefore immortalize us. Bauman summarizes in characteristically direct prose: 'Without mortality, no history, no culture – no humanity' (1991b: 7).

The power of death is most powerful when it does not appear under its own name: this is Bauman's claim, and this is what makes the book difficult. More elusively than the strategy in *Modernity and the Holocaust*, which asks us to think from one historically and geographically specific experience into the field called modernity, *Mortality and Immortality* reminds us of Pascal's invitation to look under the plank that we find ourselves suspended upon. Bauman is looking under this plank, and urges us to join him; we do not know what we are looking for, and the demand to look death in the face sociologically is on first glance impossible. Though this approach has its existential aspects, it is not only a personal challenge that Bauman is issuing. The point is not only that God laughs at us, pathetic specimens, as we struggle to push away the inevitable. The creative point at issue is that in this process we together generate culture, and the nature of the challenge is such that this is a process without end. Meaning, therefore, is less impossible than it is contingent; culture is not merely a buttress, but a daily activity (1991b: 8). Mortality, and immortality therefore become approved and practised life strategies (1991b: 9).

The postmodern enters into this discussion only marginally, as a matter of emphasis. For Bauman wants to suggest that there is a difference between modern and postmodern life strategies, where the first attempts to push away death by declaring medical war against it, while the postmodern substitutes disappearance for the final irreversibility of death. The larger field of vision, however, is neither modern nor postmodern so much as it is sociological, for as Bauman emphasizes, his curiosity is not about the specialized discipline of death and dying so much as it is in sociological theory in general. As far as the postmodern is concerned here, it represents a query over the forms in which these problems manifest themselves socially:

> We do not live, after all, once in a pre-modern, once in a modern, once in a postmodern world. All three 'worlds' are but abstract idealizations of mutually incoherent aspects of the single life-process which we all try our best to make as coherent as we can manage. (1991b: 11)

Mortality and Immortality, then, is based upon a shocking gesture, like that which holds up Bauman's approach to the Holocaust, and, differently, like that which informs *Postmodern Ethics* (1993a). The shock in *Postmodern Ethics* is more in the noun than in the adjective, this not least for a genera-tion of sociologists who have been taught to imagine ethics as a matter of filling in forms before committing research upon human subjects. But ethics is less shocking because it is incomprehensible in pedestrian terms – ethics? After all, what is all the fuss about? Bauman's attempt to foreground death, in *Mortality and Immortality*, is more phenomenologically successful in shocking us – we can smell a problem here. Whereas ethics is somebody else's problem, the Grim Reaper has his uncomfortable habit of catching up with all of us. But as with the Holocaust, Bauman here demands of us that we peer again into the abyss.

So why should death matter as a central problem for sociology, and not only for us as itinerant individuals, whether tourists or vagabonds? Theor-etically speaking, death is the greatest affront because it is the ultimate defeat of reason. Reason cannot 'think' death, let alone shift it (1991b: 12). As Bauman argues elsewhere, modernity not least in its humanist or Faustian furies recognizes no limits; but here, there is one. Bauman quotes Edgar Morin, whose work on the 'sociology of the present' he visited earlier in *Towards a Critical Sociology* (1976b: Ch. 3) – 'the idea of death is an idea without content', and Freud – 'it is indeed impossible to imagine our own death; and whenever we attempt to do so we can perceive that we are in fact still present as spectators' (Bauman, 1991b: 13). Again, to connect back, say, to the theses of *Legislators and Interpreters* (1987), Bauman's under-stated critique is devastating: everything about modernist culture identifies knowledge and resolution. If we cannot 'know' death, we will be powerless to resolve it. If to know means to do, then we are done. Death is the scandal, the ultimate humiliation of reason. But this can never be con-tained, as though it were a cerebral issue. The practical consequences are powerful: 'Notoriously, societies are arrangements that permit humans to live with weaknesses that would otherwise render life impossible' (1991b: 17). Societies are not only symbolic, but also practical agencies of prosthetic care for our others. Culturally, three larger patterns emerge.

If death is absurd, then it is for Bauman open to denial. The first dominant pattern of denial is to be found in transcendence, whether religious or tribal; I may be mortal, but my god or my people both precede and outlive me, making my life meaningful as a link in the longer chain of being. The second, more modern response is in romantic love, where I identify with my chosen other, and project eternity upon my partner or upon our love. The third, high modern approach is less to deny than to launch a military-medical attack on death, denying it by desegregating it into various disease-conditions which can be treated individually. Death here is turned into illness, or illnesses; nobody just dies anymore, every-body dies of a particular diagnosable symptom or set of symptoms or diseases. The medicalization of death thus represents yet another case of classificatory imperialism, as per Bauman's critique in *Modernity and Ambivalence* (1991a). The easiest way to deal with the ambivalence of everyday life, for specialists, is to drive it away. And of course there now remains the fantasy-possibility of medical transcendence, best expressed in the realm of cryonics, where Faust's head can now be transplanted onto the cadaver of the Frankenstein monster (1991b: 25–6). Bizarre though the proposition may seem, we moderns still live entranced by the dream of eternal youth.

The more modest levels upon which we live through culture indicate something less disturbing – simply that culture works against the memory of death. Culture allows us to forget by placing us more emphatically in the past or future than in the present (1991b: 31). Later in the text Bauman quotes Schopenhauer, to emphasize the same point, for happiness: 'always lies in the future, or else in the past . . . consequently, the present is always inadequate but the future is uncertain, and the past irrecoverable' (Schopenhauer, in Bauman, 1991b: 90). The modernist fury at this sense of limits expresses itself in what Bauman, following Norman Brown, calls the Oedipal project, though it could also be called the Faustian temptation: humans feel compelled to behave as though they are autogenetic, either killing God or the father or else assaulting the mother, destroying the earth in order to remake it (1991b: 35). The lust for autogenesis succeeds however in bringing its own nemesis in the form of iatrogenesis.

The more modest approach, as signalled later in *Postmodern Ethics* (1993a), is simply to acknowledge that if I can only recognize myself in others, then this ought to inspire being for each other and not only being with each other (1991b: 40). Sociology, in this sense, is properly the realm of the other. But this will not relieve me of the responsibility to look inward, nor can it resolve the pain of existential solitude. One can tell about one's existence, but one cannot share it. Being with others does not relieve us of existential singularity. Proximity refers us outwards, rather than inwards (1991b: 42), though here, as in *Postmodern Ethics*, Bauman will only sit for so long with Levinas before returning to the social. For even eternity, and mortality, are asymmetrically distributed. Those who have the time or means to worry are more likely to value eternity; for the rest of us, our days are in the first and last place as a shadow. Eternity – Bauman quotes Valéry – is a form of leisure, so that the more cultured classes consume more of it than those who are daily preoccupied with keeping mind and body together (1991b: 65). Culture therefore means different things to different people, and so Bauman revisits the social history of how it came to be that high culture was pitted against mass, or vulgar culture; only the cultured will be truly immortal, memorialized in public monument as local heroes or flashed for 15 minutes of video fame.

Yet in one sense we are all existentialists. As Bauman puts it,

One of the most painful prices humanity paid for the comforts of modernity was the discovery of the absurdity of being. There was no room for the perception of absurdity as long as the monotony (experienced as *normality*) of being lasted. (1991b: 94)

The emergence of the unexpected as a normality of sorts generates a new kind of existential insecurity. New problems throw up new pretenders with putative solutions: with modernity there emerges a whole array of specialists with watches and clip-boards. Bauman quotes Gellner, who suggests even more powerfully than Foucault that

> at the base of the modern social order stands not the executioner but the professor. Not the guillotine but the (aptly named) *doctorat d'état* is the main tool and symbol of state power. The monopoly of legitimate education is now more important, more central than is the monopoly of legitimate violence. (Gellner, in Bauman, 1991b: 100)

The people, the citizens have to be made; they have not always existed; and this story is coextensive with the process of nation-building and modern state building. This is central to Bauman's concerns here because cultures have to be constructed as prostheses of differential kinds, as do nations; all three, nation, state and culture, are necessarily intertwined. To be more explicit, the nation-state becomes the dominant form of collective transcendence. The nation-state is the modern expression of group immortality, expressed symbolically in the new ideology of nationalism (1991b: 105).

Nationalism is, as the cliché has it, the religion of modernity, which for Bauman means that it is the racism of the intellectuals (1991b: 109). For nationalism is based on the older prejudice, that what binds us together is not negotiable solidarity but firmly fixed affinity, with intellectuals as legislators acting as the proven spokespeople of these great discoveries. The immortal nation thus has its own immortal representatives, its poets and historians, servants and scientists, national saviours all. The point, then, is not for Bauman simply that nations are imagined, or invented, that traditions are new rather than somehow miraculously primordial; his concern is with the social dynamics of this process, with identifying its immediate middle-class agents and its victims, and with prising open the issue of its internal dynamics, for the pursuit of collective immortality is part of this vain rehearsal of death. Every sign of construction, moreover, is also evidence of destruction; for it was not only the case that men (and women) had forged into citizens ready to slaughter their ex-neighbours across the other side of the newly-drawn boundaries, but this process also involved the destruction of other forms of sociation which preceded them (1991b: 114). Citizens then must be taught norms by us, the educated, once they have been stripped of their old understandings by science; luckily for all, however, second nature does not always run deep, and our new citizens learn how to play the game without giving too much away.

Now that we have lost our histories, we have to be told in turn what our history is, as monument, as museum, as 'heritage' (1991b: 121). History becomes the legitimation of state power. History is immortality. If sociologists become the chief reformers of Durksonian bent, then historians become the guarantors of civic identity, the genealogists of the present who can tell us who we are by virtue of where we have come from. So we are faced by new storytellers, or institutional hermenuets who give us the authorized goods, alongside medical specialists dispensing doctor-induced disease and sociologists tempted to ease our burden through the propagation of eugenics. Contrary to the earlier, notorious indication that societies are arrangements which help carry our disabilities or our disabled, it now begins to look like a good idea to dump them, while we reconstruct ourselves (1991b: 146–7). So far so bad, but all this is compounded by the adiaphorization of death itself: for while we seek to kill death medically, we also at the same time normalize it by emptying it out, so creating a world where television or video-game heroes are wiped out only to rise again unaffected, or where our children lose a pet (or a friend) only to expect immediate replacement. So do we lose our ability to mourn, or to face up to the abyss when it opens nearby us. Big Brother no longer watches us . . . we watch Big Brother, and have difficulty deciphering what the fuss is about (1991b: 195). Our culture has indeed become Faustian, when we collectively travel to hell together for demanding that the moment of our enchantment should last for ever; and this is the backhander in Marx's curious speculation in the *Grundrisse*, that modernity shows us the key to the anatomy of what went before, for civilization cuts both ways, and high modernity accentuates not only its spectacular senses of gain but its tragic sense of losses (1991b: 121).

Yet the quality of modernity, or of postmodern times is such as to display banality just as well as decline. So the phrase which holds together Bauman's postscript to *Mortality and Immortality* is one we would identify, thanks to the wicked talents of our advertising hermeneuts, with the pleasures of chocolate: 'to die for . . .' (1991b: 200). Beyond these cleverly manipulated aromas of Belgian flavour, Bauman's own conclusion is at once more simple and more moving, that the readiness to die for the other is the only truly ethical attitude, where ego and other face, where mortality and immortality fuse and we are back, momentarily, in the Gulag, or in the Ghetto (1991b: 207).

Mortality and Immortality is a great book, perhaps Bauman's most original and for that reason his most difficult. For while Bauman happily agrees with Wittgenstein that in principle there is much that we can or ought leave unspoken, part of the purpose throughout his writing is also to indicate taboo, where it matters. Ethics is taboo, for sociologists, whose general working banner is rather 'business as usual'; the Holocaust is out of bounds for working sociologists, too local or marginal to their concerns in other times and places beyond its shadow; and death is simply too difficult, while it is at the same time imagined by us as part of our private worries rather than as constitutive of our public lives. Bauman's case is just that, as freedom depends on servitude, so social life and culture depend on death and its consequences, that all of our achievements across the civilizations make sense only in the context of culture as prosthetics. Like second nature, like the phantom limb, this culture becomes part of the routinized repertoire with which we carry on. We must push death away, by the artifice of culture, we can do no other; yet we also need the sense of self-detachment sufficient to recognize ourselves in this process.

Globalization

Some of Bauman's work is of this nature, that is it is as it were solitary, preconditional, the result of that self-imposed isolation which allows contemplation and insight into problems of social being which in a sense precede sociology or critique. Across Bauman's work *Mortality and Immortality* (1991b) and perhaps *Postmodern Ethics* (1993a) are most like this, afterwords that really are prefaces. Other books, like *Between Class and Elite* (1972) and *Memories of Class* (1982), analyse particular social configurations of domination, though they too pursue the question of how these developments are formed within and exert influence upon the life of the mind and its inhabitants, we intellectuals. Some of Bauman's work follows Simmel's curiosity about the relationship between social forms and personality or character-types, tourists, vagabonds, strangers, lovers. Other books take on the tasks of bringing messages from some sociological cultures to others; here we might include *Towards a Critical Sociology* (1976b), *Culture as Praxis* (1973a) and *Hermeneutics and Social Science* (1978), or of introducing sociological narratives to altogether new audiences, as in texts such as *Freedom* (1988) and *Thinking Sociologically* (1990). Some interventions are more reactive, as in the contributions on the postmodern, or additive, as in the sociology of intellectuals in *Legislators and Interpreters* (1987), though the same codas apply; in one sense the reactive embrace of the postmodern is an attempt to register the possibility of a third nature, after modernity and its no longer convincing attempt to close on second nature, after modernism as the end of history no longer closed. *Modernity and the Holocaust* (1989a), *Modernity and Ambivalence* (1991a) and *Postmodern Ethics* (1993a) from a different perspective make up a triptych of their own; the logic which holds these arguments together is more continuous, as though they were instalments of a larger imaginary book or project entitled *Critique of Order*. Now in his autumnal years, still a frenzy of writing activity while at the same time an amiable conversationalist as chef in the kitchen, walking or drinking Scotch, the emphasis of Zygmunt Bauman's style has shifted more directly into the urgency of social and political affairs. His more recent triptych is held together less immediately by theoretical continuity than by style and voice: these are short, direct political interventions or contributions, less *für ewig* than to upset the happy complacencies of British sociologists who after the long night of Thatcherism can do nothing more imaginative than apologize for New Labour. This political triptych consists of *Work, Consumerism and The New Poor* (1998b), linked here in Chapter 1 to *Memories of Class* (1982), as its reprise, *Globalization* (1998a) and now *In Search of Politics* (1999b).

Globalization, like the postmodern, rapidly became flavour of the month or of the decade. Plainly the two are in some ways connected, at least in the public and scholarly imagination. The larger themes connect; sociology goes together with modernity and the nation-state, the postmodern gives you something after sociology and whatever comes after the age of nation-building, in our case globalization. Perhaps we should not be surprised that Bauman opens *Globalization: The Human Consequences* (1998a) with precisely these problems – the usual, for sociologists, for they involve questions of the extent of change and the extent to which nomenclature can stretch to discover the distance. But sociologists at the same time are always ahead of themselves, anticipating results yet to be shown, discovering new societies where others, more cautious, will merely discern emerging patterns or trends, whether postindustrial, postmodern or postnational. Yet the critical or interpretative challenge remains, for if we are well advised to associate new social trends with the desire of their self-appointed analysts, we ought also take our leave of those who, on the contrary, refuse to acknowledge change even as it bites them on the leg.

As Bauman recognizes, to begin, one initial difficulty here is that both the idea of a process of globalization and the word itself have become reified, and at the same time bipolarized. Globalization is either the problem or the solution, depending on who or where you are. And certainly this is one aspect of its reception, enthusiastic or cynical, for as Bauman writes, 'Globalization', the hybrid term used to keep open the sense of tension between the global and the local, may indeed distribute its benefits so asymmetrically that in result it means globalization or high mobility for some, and localization or domestic exile for others. But to begin with the word, Bauman evidently takes it seriously, yet also is dubious about its substitution for thinking:

> All vogue words tend to share a similar fate: the more experiences they pretend to make transparent, the more they themselves become opaque. The more numerous are the orthodox truths they elbow out and supplant, the faster they turn into no-questions-asked canons . . . 'Globalization' is no exception to that rule. (Bauman, 1998a: 1)

The problem is recurrent, built into the habitual nominalism we inhabit, where the identification of a problem is taken for an explanation. This is the bad side of culture, or more particularly of theory as prosthetic, where the word cancels out the problem. Bauman's purpose is to get the other side of the word, to the social roots and consequences of the globalization process. So Bauman begins from the premise that if globalization is widely encountered as something caught up with the modern or postmodern experience, it will nevertheless be encountered differentially, for these are problems that are caught up with time and space or region and class, gender or ethnicity, and globalization can be expected to divide as much as it unites (Bauman, 1998a: 2).

These are among other things old marxian wisdoms, that the pattern of industrial development since the Industrial Revolution encourages social and geographical mobility, but more for some than for others. Some can choose desirable regions or commute between cities, while others are locked into specific pockets or else like vagabonds are compelled to leave one limited location for others even worse or at best mixed in their consequences. As Bauman puts it, in this context, 'Being local in a globalized world is a sign of social deprivation and degradation' (1998a: 2). Those who travel freely do so at the expense of those who are corralled into particular areas; the latter either are physically excluded, or else service the rich. A new form of 'absentee landlordship' emerges, whereby the privileged are no longer tied to place or to those of their inferiors who are stuck there. The global elites are responsible to no one. Consequently the residual aspects of *noblesse oblige* which informed the modern welfare state are eroded; obligation to the social other is reduced by the absence of any proximity other than circumstantial (1998a: 3). This is the global version of tourists and vagabonds, for 'being on the move' has radically different, indeed opposite meanings for those at the top and the bottom of the new hierarchy. Those among the victims of the system who cannot be compelled to move on are instead institutionalized; the alternative to compulsory mobility, for those at the bottom of the pile, is criminalization, incarceration: the prison again replaces the welfare state (or more literally, the school).

Bauman's hope here is not at all to solve these problems, but to act as one messenger among others who bring the mixed news. As he puts it, in sympathy here with Castoriadis, the trouble with the condition of our contemporary civilization is that it has stopped questioning itself; more directly, its own forms of social evanescence mean that we risk becoming immune to the suffering of others. Our political obligation first of all is to question, just as our moral obligation is to care for the other (1998a: 5).

Globalization is one of those spheres of activity wherein the traditionalism of modernity stands exposed, and strong. The nation-state, Fordism, the welfare state all-together exploited the working class, but it in principle included them, and offered them the possibility of citizenship. In ordinary language, national capital was open to the claims of local loyalty; in Australia, for example, one of the few slogans which drew capitalists and workers together over decades was 'Buy Australian'. The threat of international capital historically was that it could and would go elsewhere; but now all major capital flows are global, and such loyalty as exists is to the peak shareholders, wherever they be, not to employees or suppliers, let alone the locality where a firm is housed or originates (1998a: 6). The formal or contractual bonds of reciprocity are undermined: whoever is free to walk away from the locality is free to walk away from the consequences. The whole idea of duty or responsibility is further weakened; not even the immediate producers benefit from reciprocity, let alone those outside production, the younger or weaker; the interests of future generations are even less pertinent. The nature of these shifts is historic, for the prospect of proximity to the face of the other is radically transformed by movement, by that fact of mobility which earlier alerted Marx and Tönnies and later Spengler and Schumpeter to the fundamentally corrosive power of modernity. Capitalist modernism is indeed a process of creative destruction; creation, or innovation for some, indicating destruction of the living conditions of others (1998a: 14). Change, put simply, is destructive, perhaps especially when its rate accelerates beyond our capacity to cope collectively or individually. This is not, of course, as Bauman repeatedly emphasizes, to return to the cosy call for more of the old *Gemeinschaft*; but it is, at least, to query whether the necessity of change coincides with the extent and nature of the specific changes that are foisted upon us, on risk of our own obsolescence. What worse threat is there than the idea of being left behind? (It all depends, I suppose, on the company and the context we find ourselves in.)

To summarize: Bauman's opening ambit is that rather than homogenizing the human condition, the technological annulment of temporal-spatial distances tends to polarize it (1998a: 18). The sterile enclosures of Apolline protected space in the yuppie fortress go together with 'no-go' areas where creative disorder of Dionysius reigns; and as we know by this point, Zygmunt Bauman is not much impressed by this *Get Smart* choice between order and chaos (1998a: 22). For what is worse in this process of social segregation is the disappearance of the hope that we used to call the public sphere (1998a: 25). There is no longer any space within which politics can occur; it is not just that we cannot agree and disagree together, but worse, that the ground of such possible meeting has gone.

The politics of struggle over resources does not only involve money and power; it also crosses over time and space. Obviously the politics of industrialism, as sketched in say *Memories of Class* (1982), is deeply implicated within the control of the working day and that space within which it is performed. This kind of micropolitics goes together with a more extensive series of struggles over space, which is apparent for example in regionalism and the battles of separatists against the consolidation of the nation-state as sovereign. The nation-state claims to control not only time, or memory, but space: mapping and naming is the first historical act of invaders and expeditionaries. The newly emerging agencies of the modern state cultivate their power by maximizing the extent to which they are the source of lesser units' uncertainties (1998a: 34). Not only Panopticon, figuratively speaking, or national mapping but especially city-design works out these principles (1998a: 34–5). Here it is our old fellow travellers, our friends the utopians, who again lead the way; for the utopianism of city-design itself embodies the early modern horror with the sprawling chaos of the spontaneously emerging cities (which were also planned, after their own manner). Uniformity and regularity were cardinal design-principles for utopians such as Morelly, as Bauman reminds us; there is a direct line, in effect, from Morelly to Corbusier. These utopians, however, thought of order as something that was unique within their own heads; like all natural tyrants, they could not recognize that disorder is a form of order, and therefore that there is always a plurality of orders both in other people's heads and within their lives.

The vital connection between utopia and space is as powerful as that connecting utopia and time, even if it is less well observed. Utopia in the strong sense is beyond time; it calls out stasis, which is its greatest flaw. But utopia also has a necessary relationship to space; so that the idea of utopia as 'no place' is misleading; most responsible utopians have a place in mind. The concrete social link binding together utopia and modernity, notwithstanding the essential romanticism or traditionalism of most utopian argument, is the city form and the art or science of architecture. Bauman quotes Baczko's radiant study *Utopian Lights*, where we are captives of 'a double movement: that of the utopian imagination to conquer urban space and that of dreams of city planning and of architecture in search of a social framework in which they can materialize' (Baczko, in Bauman, 1998a: 37). More, the image of the transparent city space held together by legislators and intellectuals, political actors and philosophers, is a kind of transitional programme at once practical and theoretical. All of which makes one wonder at the level of Foucauldian fury directed towards medicos, lawyers, sex-reformers and educationalists, while the architects of our lives seem largely to have escaped scrutiny. Perhaps at the end of the day, we have somehow second naturalized architecture as the way the world is, enabling its agents to remain invisible as the ur-designers of the physical institutions within which all these other abominations have been allowed to occur. Perhaps we have simply excluded architecture from the critical gaze because its practitioners do not immediately resemble all these other reformers and do-gooders; architecture, after all, at least looks like a natural science, and has always occupied a liminal zone between science and art. Sex, and law are rather as Durkheim instructed us the objects of social construction rather than of physical construction; it is as though architecture has slipped off these cognitive maps, becoming peripheral, like death, to our mainstream.

Yet all this seems impossible, for we know and readily acknowledge that alongside modernism as a radical literary form, the postmodern arrived semantically through architecture, as modernism itself was powered not only by image or form but by Bauhaus, where cleanness of line, simplicity and order prevail. Bauman saves Bauhaus from attack here; both, perhaps, set out as builders of alternative orders. Corbusier offers the more adequately erratic example of architectural modernism run amok. The architects of Bauhaus, like those of Critical Theory, identified modernism with radicalism of the left; their flight from Nazi Germany to America indicates some shared sympathy. Corbusier was happy to work with any tyrants, propagating modernism at any ideological price; for tyrants, too, were modernizing across this period. Plainly Corbusier lacked the destructive enthusiasm of a futurist like Marinetti. The spirit of function was more important, but some sympathy of spirit is apparent all the same; as though we, the urban reformers, could start all over. The Radiant City of the Future would mean the death of the past and all that went with it, including the street: streets for cars, boxes for persons (1998a: 42). All the paranoia of Corbusier was appropriate, for like Fourier, he spent too much of his life on paper, waiting for the financial blessings of rich patrons, and like Fourier, he was a romantic, as later enthusiasms for the organic in Ronchamp show. Others again, like Oscar Niemeyer, took on the futurist baton, and built Brasilia, capital of Brasil, a monumental error that makes other utopian Ikea capitals like Canberra or Washington DC look like cities. The utopian echoes are powerful; Brasilia, after all, is in the middle of nowhere, the perfect location to start from scratch, while São Paulo and Rio de Janeiro go on their own way, ramshackle and high modern at the same time (1998a: 43). Brasilia was built for those who cannot live outside *Brave New World*, that there should be no people in it. For ultimately the agora is not a place, but an expression of culture. You cannot build a space for politics and then expect something political to happen in it, like spontaneous combustion. Postmoderns would rather do politics somewhere else, like at home, or perhaps especially in the academy, where they anyway have little enough else to do.

Ah! The social engineers, aspirant or actual: they long for nothing better than to help other people be good. They cannot interpret without beginning to legislate in their own heads, and if at all possible in other people's lives, and all for the sake of their own ideals. Bauman here implicitly aligns Corbusier with Robert Moses, the redeveloper of New York City, for these are Faustians all, some more of word, some of deed. Against these cerebralists, victims of their own abstract commitment to rational planning, Bauman pits the views of recalcitrants such as Jane Jacobs and Richard Sennett, against the megalomaniacs who visit havoc upon 'the lives of real people for the sake of realizing some abstract plan of development or renewal' (1998a: 45). We are back, therefore, in terms of Bauman's own work not only with *Memories of Class* (1982) and *Legislators and Interpreters* (1987) but with the concerns of order and ethics. The good society, like the good city, cannot be prepackaged, for the punters to sort out later under the rule of the planners or the philosopher-kings. Neither politics nor ethics can be conferred upon the people, as a gift. If the idea of social harmony is to be aspired to, then the fact of conflict first has to be recognized and creatively learned, for the canons of modern civility teach us only to disagree politely, which is probably one reason for existing levels of violence; civility in the seminar room (more or less), punchups in the carpark. Utopia here stands as the refusal of ambivalence and uncertainty, born of difference and variety (1998a: 46–7). The problem, for Bauman, is a familiar one: uniformity breeds conformity; the enemy now lurks within the city walls, rather than outside as was originally the case.

The city air no longer makes us free, as was earlier thought to be the case as the victims of the closed frame of *Gemeinschaft* escaped to the new, open prisons of *Gesellschaft*. Nor is this radically altered by the communications revolutions which offer, yet again, to make us all free, or at least connected. This is yet another case of middle class, intellectual projection where our own enthusiasms for Internet or whatever are narcissistically expanded as though all global citizens could use them all the time, whereas most of them are preoccupied with more pedestrian tasks such as feeding their families. The immediate effects of globalization may well be more direct and negative than this techno-euphoria suggests. To undo the nation-state, practically or symbolically, is also directly to deconstruct those social democratic forms of solidarity developed especially after the Second World War. The attack on the nation-state is also an attack on the welfare state which, however capable of reproducing domination, also helped to alleviate some of its negative effects. To erode the welfare state in order to replace it with nothing more than rhetoric about market provision is a retrogressive step, not necessarily because we value the welfare state highly, any more than we still harbour roseate images of *Gemeinschaft*, but because to deprive people of its support is to force new life-strategies upon them without notice. All of this is more disturbing, in the late 1990s, because we have now had time enough to observe some of the effects of the new world disorder. Tourists and vagabonds loom large in Moscow as well as in Middletown. The new, postmodern principle of openness cuts both ways; just as we as individuals feel no responsibility towards the other, so does the sense of political responsibility for social problems weaken. Bauman agrees with Offe, his constant companion in the critique of the political economy of the welfare state, that the state's capacity to make collectively binding choices and to carry them out has become problematical (1998a: 68). Reminding us again of Michel Crozier's theorem in *The Bureaucratic Phenomenon*, that the politics of domination always seeks to maximize room for manoeuvre of the dominant and constraint for the subordinate, Bauman proceeds to explain political fragmentation and economic global-ization as symbiotic. Integration and parcelling out, globalization and territorialization are mutually complementary processes (1998a: 69). Globalization both opens the world, for some of us, and imprisons its others.

Just as violence is the other face of civilization, so is poverty the reverse side of prosperity. Bauman quotes Jeremy Seabrook:

> Poverty cannot be 'cured', for it is not a symptom of the disease of capitalism. Quite the reverse: it is evidence of its robust good health, its spur to even greater accumulation and effort. (Seabrook, in Bauman, 1998a: 79)

Just as freedom rests upon dependence, so is poverty a permanent sign, rather than a residual, of modernity's achievement. If postmodernity is a matter of modernity without the older illusions, then perhaps we have lost some of the more necessarily consoling illusions among them; illusions, for example, that poverty could be overcome. The new illusions of postmodern consumerism include the idea that we all inhabit the same universe of possibilities. If there are no longer class cultures or subcultures in the earlier sense highlighted by British cultural studies, then we all, rich and poor alike, participate in the same fantastic race after surplus material satisfaction. The difference, these days, is that if we longer pursue different goals, then that race is nevertheless stacked against the poor. Vagabonds and tourists, in other words, all seek the same satisfaction of the same longings (1998a: 96–7), and as with the old class system random change can occur so that this tourist can become a vagabond, or that vagabond might arrive as a tourist, without the structure of the dichotomy being at all destabilized. The difference, again, is that where, as Marx put it, the proletariat sought money for survival and the bourgeoisie sought capital for investment, the aspiration today is uniform: it is the shared utopia of endless consumption. A world without vagabonds becomes the utopia of tourists, but the utopia of the vagabonds is not one without tourists, but the fantasy of tourism for all, this in a world where clearly the illusions of the tourists are held up by the endless works of the vagabonds (1998a: 97).

In Search of Politics

Globalization: The Human Consequences (1998a) is not a particularly cheerful book. It closes with a discussion of criminalization and the new prison system, as close perhaps as we get to the Gulag or Auschwitz in California. The messages are necessarily mixed; whereas those genocidal institutions stood for two paths into early high modernity or modernism, the substitution of prisons for schools represents in budgetary and symbolic terms an early postmodern phase where mobility for some is bought at the expense of incarceration for others, a group of victims not racially or ethnically defined except by default. Just as it is Bauman's strategy to compel us to glimpse into the abyss, so does he step back, in order to remind us that this abyss is of our own making. So follows the next book, and the final in our survey of Bauman's work, a spin back into the feasibility of change, for as Castoriadis says, we have changed at least once before and may therefore change again.

In Search of Politics (1999b) is the call and return to the more distressing themes canvassed in *Globalization*. The text opens with an expression of political ambivalence about that which sociologists typically subsume to the 'structure/agency problem': how is it that we can be so obsessed with our own freedom, and yet feel so powerless in the face of change? Everywhere we are free and yet in chains, not least in the consumer democracies of the centres. In the terms of classical politics, the problem is that we have lost the agora, that space neither fully private nor entirely public, the space where private problems meet in a meaningful array. To leap millennia and therefore to change vocabularies, what we lack is some third space where we can develop what C. Wright Mills called the sociological imagination, that realm which creatively might connect the self and the other, private worries and social issues, individual identity and the public good (1999b: 13).

Today we suffer, according to Bauman, from a condition best called *Unsicherheit*, that German term which rendered into English would cover not only uncertainty and insecurity but also unsafety (1999b: 5). This generalized sense of heightened middle class anxiety is doubtless what Ulrich Beck cornered so successfully into his book on *Risk Society*, timed brilliantly to coincide with the fall of the Wall which itself so nicely captured that sublime sense of freedom and horror generated by ruptural change. Ours is indeed the age of anxiety, where the prospects of both potential threats and possible rewards seem clear, and high. Only if we are afraid and uncertain, then we are hardly free to act, or at least to act positively or openly. Only these are more than personal problems. On the wider horizon, political institutions seem hopeless because they reduce *Unsicherheit* to safety; they cannot or will not help us against insecurity. And 'safety', as Bauman argues in unfolding his book on *Globalization*, can as easily result in criminalization as anything else. More, politics becomes banal, for there is not only an absence of citizenship but a striking absence of agency. When politics ripples out through civil society, in response say to civil rights infringements, the environment or the drug problem, the messages somehow become lost, for parties and unions are unable or unwilling to mainstream them. The widely observed problem in political sociology, then, is not that politics does not happen but that it happens outside what we have grown accustomed to calling political institutions, so that one kind of politics fails to meet up with the other.

Such is the plot of *In Search of Politics* – the problem of where politics happens and how, how the existing agencies miss the boat, and how a new (or old) vision might be rearticulated for the project of an autonomous society. Though Bauman sits comfortably in his director's chair, it is as though the play rests on the idea that Mills meets Castoriadis, perhaps with Claus Offe as the third term. For while Bauman's own social theory works habitually and comfortably at the level of vision, he also wants to touch at least upon problems to do with policy. How might an autonomous society be achieved, if it cannot be engineered or gifted to others? So, once again, we are in the company of our old friend, utopia. At least one rendition of the postmodern also is postideological or posthistorical, and to this extent postutopian (1999b: 8). Yet to be postutopian is, absurdly, to be ahead of ourselves, and therefore despite ourselves to remain utopian. If Bauman after all these years is unable to escape from utopia, then perhaps utopia remains behind us as well as ahead; that, or else it is our carapace, as moderns, our shell against all historical possibilities either side of us. We can never be behind what is always ahead of us.

If political institutions or organizations fail us, however, then this is not the extent of the matter; for to argue in this direction with too much conviction would be to argue like a populist Trotsky, that the masses were like the steam waiting for our appropriate piston. The conduct of social politics, as contrasted to state politics, is no great cause for self-congratulation. As Bauman argues, moralizing tends often to substitute for politics, as in the victim/offender bashing which makes particular individual criminals into public celebrities as objects of hatred and stigma. Televisual lynch mob justice is what results from this, expressing fear rather than hope, or manifesting the sense of personal anxiety rather than the possibility of social hope. In short, there are for Bauman deep problems in politics which reflect fundamental problems in community. Communities, however, generate all kinds of results, some positive and enabling, others negative and stigmatizing. The larger problem is that increasing volumes of world-citizens are expelled from labour-markets, leading to the bizarre speculation that in the longer term only something like 20 per cent of the population will be required to keep each major national economy 'working'. The problem, however, is less one of counterintelligence than of running against the current:

> One can think (and many do) of the ways to reverse, arrest or at least slow down the trend – but the major issue today is no more *what is to be done*, but *who has the power and the resolve to do it.* (1999b: 20)

Glossy globalization brings with it the direct political imperative, that national sovereignty is no longer possible. Flux replaces certainty of any kind, including the idea that I might still have a job tomorrow, or that my job specification might be the same next week as it is this week. Just as Beck captured the mood of the moment by popularizing the slogan of 'risk society', so in a previous moment of emerging anxiety did Marshall Berman rediscover Marx's idea – itself borrowed from Carlyle and others – that our deceptively solid realities melted around us into air. Flux, flow, liquefaction, plasticity, flexibility, all the buzzwords of our epoch point to the image of the sublime, promising us titillation with the sense horror submerged, or occasionally celebrated, for there is a fine line between pleasure and pain, at least within this optic. Consequently postmodern love of mobility replaces the modernist curiosity about personal direction; the important thing is to keep moving, not to wonder why or where we might be headed (1999b: 20). These various themes anticipate Bauman's next, and 'final' study, *Liquid Modernity* (Bauman, 2000).

All of this is politically problematical, not least because a political culture rests among other things on some time for consideration, even contemplation. To do or even just to think politics takes time, rather than space, and time has become our enemy. The active society demands of us that we keep moving, keep consuming, experience everything, travel, work as good tourists more than act as good citizens, work, shop and die. To keep moving is the only way left in our cultural repertoire to push away death, or meaning, for we now live our lives (those of us who are lucky enough) according to two axioms – that the self is indeterminate, any self is possible; and that the process of self-creation is never finished (1999b: 22). Faust has become our God, but our realities are more tawdry: when we are told and shown that everything is up for grabs, then endemic human insecurity is the only non-perishable result (1999b: 23). The prospects, and forms of social solidarity available to us shrink before our eyes.

Bauman therefore agrees with various social liberals such as Titmuss and Beveridge that security is one precondition of the idea of the good life. His entire project, from *Between Class and Elite* (1972) through to this study 30 years later, however, is also informed by the marxian scepticism – it could also be weberian – concerning asymmetrical distribution of goods and of life-chances. When do we witness the positive-sum, win–win outcomes promised us by rational choice economists? Bauman adheres rather over the years to the fact of scarcity as a starting point in any talk of political economy. No matter how exponential the generative capacity of capital, itself also much applauded by Marx, there will never be enough to go around. One tourist's gain is another vagabond's loss, once we accept the general scenario in which inclusion, employment and citizenship all go together.

> Advocates and warriors of flexibility are not after freedom of movement for all, but after exhilarating lightness of being for some, rebounding as unbearable oppressiveness of fate for the rest; the right to avoid the consequences for some, the duty to bear the consequences for the others. (1999b: 26)

After all these years fighting those totalitarianisms delivered by the state, we are now faced by the effective totalitarianism of the Market. For we now face a discursive monopoly of claims to value, where only the market counts, and other kinds of value are for losers. Perhaps only the hope of romantic love survives as a life strategy against mortality, though it, too, has been colonized as ruthlessly by Hollywood as has thirst (or reality) by Coca-Cola. None of which is to say that humans have no place any longer in this world; the question, rather, is what kind of room for manoeuvre they, we, have, and whether this is really the only, best, possible way for us to live.

And so Bauman returns to the theme of mortality and our incapacity to look it in the face. We know that we are going to die; we know we know; we know that there is no escape from death. The fleeting prospect of eternity now becomes a frenzy, as though everincreasing levels of hyperactivity will drive this wolf away from the door. For the old, modern prostheses are no longer so readily available to us. They were, as Bauman summarizes here, nation and family, a perfect couple when it came to dealing with the prospect of modern mortality, the larger community and the smaller nesting within it. Nation-building, of course, was also a particular strategy of family-building; both conferred identity, local and larger together. But both are now porous, threatened with redundancy as intermediate circles or forms held between the individual and the globe. Our new globalized world offers to free us of these restrictions, so that there will only be the heroic individual (me, or you?) astride the cosmos (1999b: 35). Of course, nation-building and family building were also destructive processes, and in more ways than one; both units destroyed what went before, and both claimed lives as a cost of their consolidation. Yet they also conferred meanings of kinds which the new order can barely recognize, heteronomies as well as autonomies, all bound up. If this modern life strategy offered the possibility of immortality through nation or family, then the postmodern equivalent is miserable in comparison – the individual can either be everything, paranoiac, or nothing, obliterated (1999b: 38). God, contrary to Durkheim, is no longer the community or the social but the self, or the world-system. We no longer simply die alone; we are also compelled now to live alone. Solidarity (is gone) for ever.

This is a worst-possible scenario, the result of staring into the distance as far as we can. The bleakness of the picture rests on its sense of the absolute erosion of all alternative forms, and social alternatives. The blackness of the diagnosis is what also makes utopia possible, desirable and necessary. Bauman talks his way out of this picture in the company of John Carroll, as he is occasionally wont to do. Where Carroll's *Humanism* left little standing, his more recent work, *Ego and Soul* perhaps resonates more powerfully with Bauman's present predicament, as it balances the gravity of analysis with a more optimistic sense of ordinary human intelligence and perspicacity. Carroll reminds us that once killed, gods tend to be reborn as diseases; psychopathology is the modern form of illness. The self-absorption of ego today stands in for the soul (1999b: 42). Body, too, replaces soul as the machine we think we can perfect, pushing away death through the struggle of physical self-development:

> Doctors proclaim with pride that fewer people 'die of natural causes': at the horizon of the autonomous strategy looms the vision of such life as may come to the end only because of the self's neglect of duty, so that the self-contained and self-centred life-policy with the care of the body firmly placed at its centre could truly become an adequate and sufficient source of life-meaning. When there are so many means to attend to, who would waste time to examine the ends? (1999b: 43)

We are back again, with Ellul, or with Adorno: why bother worrying about which value to choose, when we already know that there is a multitudinous variety of smaller, closer things to be going on with? Why worry about the goal, when we already have the instruments? These days we seem to know how to fix our problems, even when we are uncertain what they are.

Today we inhabit a confessional culture. The 'public' in the meantime has been emptied of its own separate concerns; it has been left with no agenda of its own, it is now nothing more than an agglomeration of private troubles, worries and problems (1999b: 65). Instead of the agora, we have Oprah, or worse, the televised shame culture of Jerry Springer. The Enlightenment's promise, that there was nothing which the human species on its own could not accomplish, has been like so much else privatized. The hope of the freedom of mankind has been cashed in for the freedom of each of its individual members. The big banknote has been exchanged for a barrelful of pennies, so that all individuals may carry some coins in their pockets (1999b: 68). Deregulation does not end regulation, it merely shifts it away from political institutions and towards the hidden hand of the state. Only just as the market is both everywhere and nowhere, so is the prospect of politics dispersed in the process. Politics also becomes adiaphoric, that is, of no interest to the political authorities (1999b: 74). The idea that the sphere of freedom has expanded therefore misses the point, unless it ideologically interprets the decline of the welfare state as part of the attack on negative freedom. The point is that the individual has been transformed from prospective political citizen into would-be market consumer (1999b: 78). The political citizen knows both how to aspire to freedom and where to acknowledge that the value of freedom is impertinent, as in the conduct of routines of habit where the citizen also serves. The image of absolute freedom takes us back to another world, that of Faust; there is not enough space here for us mortals. The prospect of the autonomous society rather has to recognize and build upon uncertainty, yet its very possibility depends at the same time upon the critical reflection and therefore on the relative security of its enthusiasts (1999b: 85).

The theme of totalitarianism so central to *Modernity and the Holocaust* (1989a) resurfaces here, not least because Bauman's reconsideration of the question what makes up a good society returns him to Arendt, and more explicitly here to Castoriadis. Totalitarianism as we have known it is primarily an attack on the private sphere, on the very idea that there can be or ought to be anything outside the state or its ideology. Yet totalitarianism is also an attack of the most ruthless kind on the very idea of politics itself; for where there is a state claim to truth, backed up by the monopoly of violence, legal or illegal, there can be no politics. More, as Bauman reminds, the avant-gardism of the modernist movement was also a kind of totalitarianism, and not only because of its various passing infatuations with dictators like Mussolini. For the modernist vanguard was also Faustian, hungry for change of almost any kind, especially if it were at the expense of others (1999b: 92). Ultimately the avant-garde also suffered from that kind of projection so repeatedly characteristic of middle class intellectuals; they could not tell the difference between aesthetics and politics, and imagined that reorganizing urban forms on paper or the colours on their palettes was no more or less harmful than the prospect of frogmarching the great unwashed masses into a violent new world. The old world was stupid, cowardly, inert. The modernists sought powers mighty enough to match the size of their own ambitions; only the political extremes of communism or fascism seemed up to the challenge (1999b: 93). In the blackshirted nights of the 1930s, all liberals were made to look pathetically grey.

After Order

These were the self-appointed saviours that we have lost; now we have no leaders at all, for as Bauman explains it, there is nothing a politician now fears more than an outbreak of politics. The ideologies, however, still inhabit the agora, now speaking again the language of populism for which the aesthetic vanguard had nothing but contempt. For the avant-garde is both the proponent and the victim of modernism; the revolution devours its children, but also its artists, and we end up with the farce called 'socialist realism', populism reborn, the art of praising the rulers in terms they can understand (1999b: 95). The state colonizes the agora; this is how the romance of modern intellectuals with totalitarian power comes to an end. In the meantime, however, the problem shifts, towards the domination of the agora by the market. The agora is invaded again, this time by the market. The Greeks, too, knew about difference; contrary to the conceits of developmental sociology, it sometimes looks as though modernity becomes more simple, or identitarian in its logic. So market leaders, or owners, become political leaders by default; even the idea of the autonomy of politics today looks ridiculous. As Offe and others then explain, the practical problem emerges that there is no ground to sustain the institutions or agencies that might take formal responsibility for different social sites or spheres of our existence. The prospect of collective action shrinks as the identity of actors, parties, associations and unions is collapsed into principles of global economic growth. The agora is in effect closed to its previous inhabitants, while the real actors become invisible; there is no international agora. This is the down-side of the end of the modern project. Indeed, on this account modernity is the last utopia; globalization is not a project, but an ideology. The integration and reproduction of the new 'global order' takes on the guise of the hidden hand, presents itself as a spontaneous and self-propelling process. The great novelty of modernity, according to Bauman, was rather to present the creation, preservation and continuity of 'order' as a task. 'But order-making is not seen as a task anymore' (1999b: 99) – to the contrary, alternative, purposeful action becomes subversive of the global imperative.

This is potentially a shift of the same order as that indicated by the Enlightenment. What became, in the twentieth century, an obsession with making order, has now shifted (or is shifting) completely to a post-brave new world where everything is left to its own. This shift is more potentially powerful than anything we might associate with the idea of the postmodern, though the problem-complexes crossover. The postmodern, Bauman argued in *Legislators and Interpreters* (1987), represents not only the belated, sceptical turn in the self-understanding of the intellectuals; it also reflects the social ramifications of this change in the sociology of intellectuals. To have intellectuals step back from their Faustian illusions is a great and positive thing; only now the forces of world transformation take on a life of their own, exactly as in the Goethe story. The sorcerer's apprentice only starts the story, which outlives him (though Mickey Mouse seems immortal). Having stepped aside from this passion play, the intellectuals find themselves less now to be interpreters, than to be functionally useless in systemic terms. Having sought earlier to rule the world, they are now back to translating for friends and relatives. For now:

there is no need for knowledge classes to assume the role of the intellectuals – the spiritual guides intending to make people different from what they now are by teaching them things they would not learn themselves and teaching them first of all that learning such things is worth their while. There are no big tasks, and so there is no use for big ideas. (1999b: 100)

Perhaps we should all then cultivate our gardens, return to those incomplete novels in the bottom drawer, or learn to write biography. Bauman picks up a cue from Umberto Eco to suggest that the choices are stark – the choice is that between insiders and outsiders, intellectuals today can either be 'integrated' or 'apocalyptic'. The integrated carry on with the tasks of the day, business as usual; they may be privately critical of social trends or cultures, but it is beyond their remit to say so. The others, like Bauman, free of the immediate need to please their masters, can take more than the occasional snap at the hands that claim to feed them. In the meantime, however, the actual availability of such hands has much diminished; the postmodern outsider needs to sell enough copies of each instalment of apocalyptic critique in order to keep bread on the table, or vodka in the freezer. Given the modern restlessness, given our propensity to romanticism, our incapacity ever to fully embrace the world we inhabit, and given the presence of any decent, thriving café culture, a new, small economic cycle has been set up; some intellectuals can still make a living out of telling yuppie punters what they want to hear, that everyday life today is impossible, even if we never want really to go 'back'. Theory becomes less like education, more like therapy. Only the risk remains, that the apocalyptic intellectuals are bemoaning the departure of what is already long gone. There is little concern with the disappearance of politics in their texts, which perhaps are more like movies than books. We no longer believe in missionaries, but our universities have mission statements. Intellectual life becomes televisual. Public intellectuals are televisual intellectuals; they no longer get 15 minutes, only 15 second grabs, and must needs simplify; as well as purring appropriately to the camera. As Bauman argues, the pragmatics of television and of intellectual work differ sharply. Television is ruled by ratings, and speed; but mass audience and high velocity are enemies of thought, complexity, ambiguity, ambivalence (1999b: 105).

So perhaps there is some social space for ideologists, if not for intellectuals (or for intellectuals as ideologists). As Bauman indicates, the successful career of the idea of globalization already tells us that whatever else has expired, ideology is alive and well. Yet the idea of ideology also has a life of its own, as Bauman reminds, sketching out its path through the French Revolution, with Destutt de Tracy's positive definition of ideology, Marx and Engels' attack on that species of rationalism as idealist, and its final arrival in the twentieth century first as a nasty (fascism as an ideology) and finally as a non-entity (the 'end' of ideology) (1999b: 113) with a last marxist hiccup in the scientism of Louis Althusser (science good, ideology bad). This is a parallel path to that which Bauman essayed earlier in

Hermeneutics and Social Science (1978), where critical intellectuals figure as ideologues rather than as hermeneuts. Ideology, of course, becomes the object of critique inasmuch as it misrepresents the particular as the general; as Marx indicates, the bourgeoisie falsely universalizes its own interests, as though it represents all. Only Marx, too, in turn falls into the path of ideological thinking as he explicitly universalizes the proletariat as the people, and implicitly makes man stand for woman. What is striking about this universalistic fallacy, in Bauman's critical argument here, is that it also necessarily indicates the local orientation of the intellectuals who generated such ideologies. It is not only that nationalism, or national particularism, became one dominant modern ideology, where all 'humans' were made to look like Englishmen, French or Germans. More, the very content and context of ideology-making were locally grounded; so intellectuals were national intellectuals, even as they professed cosmopolitanism. The knowledge classes worked with, and sought to educate, particular national audiences. Now globalization reenters, for it is not only capital that is freed of local bonds. Capital and knowledge have both been emancipated from their local confinement (1999b: 122). Some intellectuals can enter the system, make themselves useful as managers or technicians; some few might still act as the ideologues or advertisers of glossy globalism. Some even find their way out of the periphery, into the centres on these newly established networks of influence. But others will have nothing left to sell, for the institutional matrices of their earlier existences have disappeared or been rebuilt without them. Cultural capital, at the end of the day, is still a metaphor; critical intellectuals have little left to sell in a consumer culture where fast food prevails. Utopia is a hamburger.

What an extraordinary outcome for the intellectuals, for the new middle class which constructed a project of its own between the original, historic classes, bourgeoisie and proletariat. As Bauman puts it, the intellectuals staked their claim to power, to reform, to educate, to plan and to engineer, on the fact of their self-production: it was the vocation of the middle class to be a 'class-producing-class' (1999b: 128). Self-production also meant self-promotion; and now, if the middle class missionaries have lost their constituencies, then they cannot face up to the task of representing themselves. What marks off most conspicuously the present-day thought of the knowledge classes is its self-referentiality, its acute preoccupation with the conditions of its own professional activity and an increasingly non-committal stance taken towards other sectors of society (1999b: 129).

Once again, however, Bauman recognizes that there is no point asking now for a return to the old order, which is disappearing before our eyes. Instead he mounts a case for the recovery of tradition, as opposed to habit. Habit is effectively areflexive, whereas traditions suggest choices between repertoires of thought and action. All traditions are invented; the idea of 'invented tradition' (Hobsbawm) is nothing new, it only refers to particular instances where the inventors were caught in the act. The idea of post-traditionalism (Giddens), similarly, exaggerates its own novelty; for all that it really identifies is the plurality or surplus of traditions from which we can now choose (1999b: 123). Our existential fate still a century later does not differ radically from that identified by Max Weber: we have to choose our own gods, knowing always that we have made the choice. Our choices need not be final, that is to say; we do not become traditionalists, mere followers, once we choose this tradition over that, for our practices are neither so rule-governed nor so final. Even if we seek to close on our images of the past, we cannot sign up as life-time members in advance for particular hopes of the future.

Conclusions: Crisis and Critique

Where does this leave us? In crisis, and so Bauman turns to the idea of crisis and its opportunities. He returns to Habermas, the great hope and sub-sequent disappointment of Critical Theory. Twenty years ago we read *Legitimation Crisis* with enthusiasm, before Habermas used it as filler upon which to build the monument of *Theory of Communicative Action*. Already in those distant days some detected the slippage to systems theory within *Legitimation Crisis*; all the same, that book had a sense of urgency, indeed, a mission, to connect up economic and cultural crisis and critique, to gaze into the present as though it were still open, for 'crisis' still then suggested choice, rather than the regime of permanent chaos which we now seem to think of as crisis. Contrary to Habermas, however, Bauman wants to suggest that the idea of crisis is first of all experiential, rather than systemic. The sense of the normal does not generate that of crisis; the idea of crisis rather makes us wonder about the norm. Inasmuch as crisis indicates transience or transition, crisis is in fact the norm in any case. Crisis means nothing more than living with ambivalence, an idea we have still not got used to, at least not in the streets or in our kitchens rather than in the study. Crisis is the ambivalence we have to learn to live with, which suggests in effect that the idea of crisis is redundant, which in turn makes sense because it is everywhere and nowhere.

We could, then, embrace crisis, or contingency, and make of it a virtue; for there is little enough sense otherwise of room to move. What visions might then be available to us? Bauman has no patience for neo-tribalism, and is ambivalent at best about the nation-state. The image of the agora, and the radical classicism of Castoriadis' work resurface here, as does the image of the republic as an antidote to the nation-state; Castoriadis' enthusiasm for the Greeks has always been open to the criticism that something else happened (by way of scale and complexity) on the way to modernity. Nationalism demands loyalty, my country right or wrong; the idea of republicanism, in contrast, puts critical inquiry at the heart of community membership. Globalization therefore undermines not only the fact of the nation-state, but also the possibility of the project of republican-ism. The project of republicanism, in turn, depends upon the forms of the welfare state. The result of globalization is less that there will be no nations than that there will be no (welfare) states. The precondition of any possible advance, for Bauman, however, is provision, for we need to have some kind of hold on the present before we can begin to take on the future. The present political economy of uncertainty returns us to habits of survival, not extension or revision (1999b: 173). Populations made 'redundant' are hardly likely to push themselves forward as willing candidates to remake the world. Poverty therefore emerges as the central issue today:

> Lifting the poor from their poverty is not just a matter of charity, conscience and ethical duty – but an indispensable (though only preliminary) condition of re-building the republic of free citizens out of the wasteland of the global market. (1999b: 177)

The poor are the local Other of the frightened consumers; the deprived are turned into the depraved, the internal, infernal enemy at the door. Yet even for those in work, work today is like a daily rehearsal for redundancy (1999b: 179). We need to help the poor, not only because they are there or because we may at any moment join them, but also because their presence makes the very idea of social progress a mockery. We all together need some kind of existential security if we are even to think again about making politics. This means, in the meantime, that we must revisit the policy idea which also did the rounds in the time of *Legitimation Crisis*, and of Offe's pioneering work in radical social policy: basic income, guaranteed adequate income, income decoupled from labour market participation.

Politics follows existence; provision will not generate citizenship of itself, but may well be its necessary condition. This, indeed, is exactly Bauman's concern here. It is ethical to care for the other, that is one issue; another, larger issue has less to do with the quality of life in common than with its political significance (1999b: 183). Basic income is not just good or just social policy, it is the chance to open ethical debate about human value, and potentially it offers the space for the revival of participation. The more immediate problem, itself political, involves the absence of an actor or will-to-power sufficient to introduce basic income. The old hands of radical social policy might in turn now deride the argument as old hat. Bauman's reply, through the haze of his pipe-smoke, is obvious; we need first of all to set out in search of politics. *In Search of Politics* opens the door; if it barely begins the journey, then this is to pass the puzzle on to others in all its contingency. At the least, we are back, with Bauman, with questions, and with big questions. Not the arrival, but the journey matters; and this is a journey that never ends. No critique without crisis; no crisis without critique – at this point, having tracked the human condition, he hands on the baton.

Epilogue: Mediations

What is it then, in conclusion, that Bauman hands on to us, to use and to extend? This is a good question, and it is difficult to begin to answer. Bauman is, among other things, a cultural messenger between us and his own peers, and between us and the classics of social theory. The larger field in which he operates is plainly that which we still today call critical theory, starting with Marx, out through the work of the Frankfurt School and into its French parallel paths, via Foucault. Inasmuch as critical theory in this ecumenical sense is primarily concerned with the critique of modernity, it therefore follows that Bauman's work, too, is necessarily a contribution to the critique of modernity. The specific inflection of Bauman's critique of modernity is as a critique of order; it is this which places *Modernity and the Holocaust* (1989a) and *Modernity and Ambivalence* (1991a) at the centre of his project. Structure is the hardest illusion; order is the harshest imperative, once added to modern forms of enforcement and implementation. Yet Bauman remains ambivalent, rather than unremittingly negative, about the world we thus generate. Ours is a dialectic of modernity. Modernity, or modernism crushes ambivalence, yet fosters it; the modernist urge to control is deeply superstitious, and in this sense modernity remains traditionalistic rather than innerly modern. Bauman's formal enthusiasm for the postmodern, in this context, responds to the in-principle possibility that the postmodern might expand the space available for ambivalence. It is not the case that modernity cannot abide difference, or ambivalence; rather, the problem is that high modernity combines the political will and the technological means to reinforce conformism, at least outwardly. Bauman's concern is that humans are, and ought to be ambivalent, at least sufficiently uncertain to remain open to the world, to both value differing traditions and to remain open to the possibility of change. Human ambivalence is the precondition of social change.

In all this we remain creatures of second nature, creatures of our own collective creation. Second nature, this idea posited by Hegel and developed by Marx, becomes via Critical Theory something more like history, or the social. Here we can see Bauman operating both as messenger and as mediator, or innovator. As Marx explained in scattered passages across his manuscripts, from the *German Ideology* to the *Grundrisse*, that new problem-complex which he calls capitalism (and we call modernity) naturalizes itself. Capitalist activity universalizes itself, reinventing history as the history of capitalism and individualism, leaving no public place for citizens to enquire into whence private property or commodification came. Capitalist modernism radically reduces the spaces within which we can think outside its imaginary. In the 1970s, marxists responded to this problem mainly in terms of ideology-critique. The problem with modernity, in this optic, was that capitalism reproduced itself through ideology; only ideology, in these forays, often looked like something fogged up on capital's spectacles, rather than part of our being, or nature. As Adorno wrote in *Negative Dialectics*, however, ideology is not superimposed as a detachable layer on the being of society; it is inherent in that being (Adorno, 1966: 354). The abstraction from difference is built into the value-form, as Marx showed in his masterwork, *Capital*. The natural growth of capitalist society is real, and at the same time is semblance. We are both authors of this world and its victims, for these illusions become as hard as steel. Having driven God out of the temple, we praise the commodity, instead, in the hallowed space of the shopping malls, for these are what we are left with, the cathedrals of capitalism.

But this is an anthropological problem, and not only one to do with commodification or even objectification. As Adorno and Horkheimer wrote in *Dialectic of Enlightenment*, civilization is the victory of society over nature which changes everything into pure nature (Adorno and Horkheimer, 1944: 186). This in turn becomes especially difficult, because all perception is based on projection. Modernity is the social regime of projection par excellence. Yet European civilization is simultaneously another story. Europe has two histories: a well-known, written history and an underground history (Adorno and Horkheimer, 1944: 231). Modernity moves by its dark side; this is why the experience and image of the Holocaust remain so central for us, generations on, even in far-flung places.

What a challenge it is, all the same, to remain both historically located and intellectually open. We are, indeed, creatures of our pasts, though sometimes our pasts, real or imagined, also become intellectual safe houses; we often feel the need to be who we think we came from, rather than to be what we are. As Alain Finkielkraut shows in his extraordinary book *The Imaginary Jew* (1994), yet another of Bauman's various stimulants, keeping the Holocaust alive after the fact both risks disservice to the event and potentially misplaces us, as actors in a world after that fact. Likely the living will never escape the nightmares of the past; the problem is how to seek out the balance, both to recognize and remember and to take on the present, even the future.

If the figure of Marx stalls and recedes in all this, what happens, then, to Heidegger? Bauman makes clear his distance from Heidegger, as from romanticism; modernity is deeply problematical, but the only possible way out is forward. In any case, notwithstanding the presence of some apparently Heideggerian motifs in Bauman's work, it seems to me rather to be the case that Bauman's Heidegger is mediated through the brilliant but often critical work of Heidegger's Jewish students, Jonas, Arendt, Levinas and Marcuse.

The difference indicated by this mediation is crucial; whatever else he was, critic of modernity as technology, theorist of framing, Heidegger was a

Gentile and a Nazi. The defining attributes of his followers were sharply distinct, both Jewish and in different ways, radical. We have observed various echoes and sympathies in Bauman's work with the projects of these thinkers. Bauman agrees with Jonas, in the spirit of this argument concerning second nature, that we become the objects of our own fabrications. Our means become ends, our prostheses become our culture; but innerly? some other chance remains, for second nature is second chance. Bauman's sympathies with Arendt are abundant, not least in that Arendt both maintains the classical dedication to politics and the republican enthusiasm for democratic forms of political participation. And then, of course, there is the debt which any book like *Modernity and the Holocaust* (1989a) must owe to Arendt's great study of *The Origins of Totalitarianism*. Bauman's connection to Levinas is obvious in the party of two that goes to make up much of *Postmodern Ethics* (1993a). The presence or influence of Marcuse is different, more opaque. While there are some well-observed parallels between Marcuse and Foucault, it is the latter whose critical work arrives at the significant moment in Bauman's journey, between *Memories of Class* (1982) and *Legislators and Interpreters* (1987). Yet there are ongoing sympathies of a looser kind between Marcuse and Bauman, as there is a kind of undeclared dialogue between Bauman and Adorno and, in a different register, between Bauman and the early Habermas – the Habermas of *Theory and Practice*, before the Durksonian turn.

The figure of Habermas remains enigmatic here, not because of this turn so much as due to the question of his unresolved relationship to Heidegger. Habermas' political rage against Heidegger's refusal to confront his Nazi past has served to leave the question of Habermas' debt or parallel path to Heidegger undisclosed. Reading the work of the later Habermas, it is difficult not to sense that his grand theory has a place for virtually every Western thinker apart from Heidegger. And yet the legacy of the Critical Theory of the Frankfurt School is nothing, if not the critique of technology.

Jonas, Arendt, Levinas, Marcuse . . . there is one figure missing from this list of influential mediators between Heidegger and Bauman: Karl Löwith. Löwith is a striking absence not least because, as I indicated above, Löwith's lasting contribution to Critical Theory was, following the clue in Lukács' 1923 *History and Class Consciousness*, to seek better to align Marx and Weber as philosophical critics of modernity in his 1932 essay, *Max Weber and Karl Marx*. Probably there is little in Heidegger for sociology that a sensitive reader could not find in Weber's work, in its Nietzschean pathos, not least in the emerging critique of technical rationality. Bauman's most brilliant engagement with Weber's *Protestant Ethic* is with its own component of projection; sociologists are suckered by the image of the Puritan, the upright, disciplined, hard-working citizen . . . sounds just like us. Bauman passes on the opportunity to engage more directly with those last several pages of *The Protestant Ethic*, where Weber outlines his anxieties about the future, the infamous problem of the 'iron cage'. Yet at the same time, much of Bauman's work reads something like a dialogue with the ghost of Weber. In Simmel he has little to disagree with. Weber's presence, I think, remains more discernible in the margins.

For the closing passages of *The Protestant Ethic* also rehearse an argument concerning something like second nature, and its vicissitudes. There Weber discusses the 'light cloak' which we moderns fabricate for ourselves, and speculates about the way in which it becomes a casing as hard as steel, the '*stahlhartes Gehäuse*' which the young Talcott Parsons mischievously translated as the 'iron cage'. Weber contrived this image of society as the casing as hard as steel in 1904/5, some years before Kafka published *Metamorphosis*, though they seem in some way possessing of affinity. Weber's housing is a carapace, a house like a rod that we make for our backs but which we possibly can bear, as the snail or crustacean makes its way carrying its habitus. It protects, even as it insularizes, this self-constructed house or prison, constructed by our predecessors, taken on by us as natural, as second nature. Perhaps, then, the horror image of Kafka, like the prison-image of society taken out of Foucault, is more provocative than persuasive as an intellectual device; no house, no home. Second nature hardens, and limits us, but it also serves to mediate between us and the world. If there is anything in this way of thinking, then it would follow that our challenge is less to escape from this box than to be vigilant against the perils of conformism which habit prescribes, and tyrants encourage upon us. On this view, there is no life we can know or imagine outside of our institutions; what we forget, rather, is that instituting is an activity, not only a result, and that organizations do nothing; actors do. This is the message which Bauman passes on to us, to interpret sufficiently well to know how and what in our surroundings to value; to criticize what in them is destructive, and to remember that ordinary intelligence and intuition can enable us to live decent lives within second nature, for there is nothing else beyond modernity than this basic challenge of the human condition.

References

Note: The most comprehensive bibliography of Bauman's work, to 1995, is available in Kilminster and Varcoe (1996: 248–60). Entries marked with an asterisk (*) below are included or excerpted in Beilharz (2000).

Arnason, J.P. (1993) *The Experiment that Failed*, London: Routledge.
Adorno, T. (1966) *Negative Dialectics*, London: Verso, 1979 edn.
Adorno, T. and Horkheimer, M. (1944) *Dialectic of Enlightenment*, New York, Continuum, 1973 edn.
Adorno, T., with Frankel-Brunswick, E., Levinson, D.J. and Nevitt Sanford, R. (1969) *The Authoritarian Personality*, New York: Norton.
Bauman, J. (1986) *Winter in the Morning*, London: Virago.
Bauman, J. (1988) *A Dream of Belonging*, London: Virago.
Bauman, J. (1998) 'Demons of Other People's Fear: The Plight of the Gypsies', *Thesis Eleven*, 54.
Bauman, Z. (1968a) 'Modern Times, Modern Marxism', *Social Research*, 34.*
Bauman, Z. (1968b) 'Marx and the Contemporary Theory of Culture', *Social Science Information*, 7, 3.
Bauman, Z. (1972) *Between Class and Elite*, Manchester: Manchester University Press.
Bauman, Z. (1973a) *Culture as Praxis*, London: Routledge.
Bauman, Z. (1973b) 'The Structuralist Promise', *British Journal of Sociology*, 24, 1.
Bauman, Z. (1976a) *Socialism: The Active Utopia*, London: Allen and Unwin.*
Bauman, Z. (1976b) *Towards a Critical Sociology*, London: Routledge.
Bauman, Z. (1978) *Hermeneutics and Social Science: Approaches to Understanding*, London: Hutchinson.*
Bauman, Z. (1982) *Memories of Class: The Prehistory and After-Life of Class*, London: Routledge.*
Bauman, Z. (1984) 'Dictatorship Over Needs', *Telos*, 60.*
Bauman, Z. (1987) *Legislators and Interpreters: On Modernity, Post-Modernity and Intellectuals*, Oxford: Polity.*
Bauman, Z. (1988) *Freedom*, Milton Keynes: Open University Press.
Bauman, Z. (1989a) *Modernity and the Holocaust*, Oxford: Polity.*
Bauman, Z. (1989b) 'Hermeneutics and Modern Social Theory', in D. Held and J. Thompson (eds) *Social Theory of Modern Societies: Giddens and his Critics*, Cambridge: Cambridge University Press.
Bauman, Z. (1990) *Thinking Sociologically*, Oxford: Blackwell.
Bauman, Z. (1991a) *Modernity and Ambivalence*, Oxford: Polity.*
Bauman, Z. (1991b) *Mortality, Immortality and Other Life Strategies*, Oxford: Polity.
Bauman, Z. (1992) *Intimations of Postmodernity*, London: Routledge.*
Bauman, Z. (1993a) *Postmodern Ethics*, Oxford: Polity.*
Bauman, Z. (1993b) 'The Sweet Scent of Decomposition', in C. Rojek and B. Turner (eds) *Forget Baudrillard?*, London: Routledge.
Bauman, Z. (1994) 'Narrating Modernity', in J. Burnheim (ed.) *The Social Philosophy of Agnes Heller*, Amsterdam, Rodopi.

Bauman, Z. (1995) *Life in Fragments: Essays in Postmodern Morality*, Oxford: Polity.*

Bauman, Z. (1997a) *Postmodernity and its Discontents*, Oxford: Polity.*

Bauman, Z. (1997b) 'Giddens In Defence of Sociology', *Thesis Eleven*, 51.

Bauman, Z. (1998a) *Globalization: The Human Consequences*, Cambridge: Polity.*

Bauman, Z. (1998b) *Work, Consumerism and the New Poor*, London: Open University.*

Bauman, Z. (1999a) *Culture as Praxis*, London: Sage (2nd edn).

Bauman, Z. (1999b) *In Search of Politics*, Oxford: Polity.

Bauman, Z. (2000) *Liquid Modernity*, Oxford: Polity.

Beilharz, P. (1987) *Trotsky, Trotskyism and the Transition to Socialism*, London: Croom Helm.

Beilharz, P. (1992) *Labour's Utopias: Bolshevism, Fabianism, Social Democracy*, London: Routledge.

Beilharz, P. (1994a) *Transforming Labor*, Cambridge: Cambridge University Press.

Beilharz, P. (1994b) *Postmodern Socialism: Romanticism, City and State*, Melbourne: Melbourne University Press.

Beilharz, P. (1997) *Imagining the Antipodes*, Cambridge: Cambridge University Press.

Beilharz, P. (1999) 'McFascism? Reading Ritzer, Bauman and the Holocaust', in B. Smart (ed.) *Resisting McDonaldization*, London: Sage.

Beilharz, P. (ed.) (2000) *The Bauman Reader*, Oxford: Blackwell.

Beilharz, P., Considine, M. and Watts, R. (1992) *Arguing About the Welfare State*, Sydney: Allen and Unwin.

Berman, M. (1984) *All That is Solid Melts Into Air*, Harmondsworth: Penguin.

Calhoun, C. (1982) *The Question of Class Struggle*, Oxford: Blackwell.

Castoriadis, C. (1981) *Devant la Guerre*, Paris: Fayard.

Castoriadis, C. (1987) *The Imaginary Institution of Society*, Oxford: Polity.

Davidson, A . (1977) *Antonio Gramsci: Towards an Intellectual Biography*, London: Merlin.

Durkheim, E. (1959) *Socialism*, London: Routledge (first published 1894/5).

Fehér, F., Heller, A. and Markus, G. (1983) *Dictatorship over Needs*, Oxford: Blackwell.

Finkielkraut, A. (1994) *The Imaginary Jew*, Lincoln: Nebraska University Press.

Goldhagen, D. (1996) *Hitler's Willing Executioners*, London: Little Brown.

Gouldner, A. (1975) *The Two Marxisms*, New York: Seabury.

Habermas, J. (1962) *The Structural Transformation of the Public Sphere*, Boston: MIT, 1989 edn.

Herf, J. (1984) *Reactionary Modernism*, New York: Cambridge University Press.

Kilminster, R. and Varcoe, I. (eds) (1996) *Culture, Modernity and Revolution: Essays in Honour of Zygmunt Bauman*, London: Routledge.

Löwith, K. (1982) *Max Weber and Karl Marx*, London: Allen and Unwin (first published 1932).

Lubasz, H. (1976) 'Marx's Initial Problematic', *Political Studies*, 24, 1.

Lukács, G. (1971[1923]) *History and Class Consciousness*, London: Merlin.

Marshall, T.H. (1950) *Citizenship and Social Class*, Cambridge: Cambridge University Press.

Moore, B., Jr (1978) *Injustice: The Social Bases of Obedience and Revolt*, London: Macmillan.

Moscovici, S. (1996) *The Invention of Society*, Cambridge: Polity.

Musil, R. (1995) *The Man Without Qualities*, New York: Knopf.

Patterson, O. (1991) *Freedom*, New York: Basic.

Prawer, S.S. (1978) *Karl Marx and World Literature*, Oxford: Oxford University Press.

Rundell, J. (1994) 'Gadamer and the Circles of Hermeneutics', in D. Roberts (ed.) *Reconstructing Theory*, Melbourne: Melbourne University Press.

Seabrook, J. (1985) *Landscapes of Poverty*, Oxford: Blackwell.

Sebald, G. (1998) *The Rings of Saturn*, London: Harvill.

Smith, B. (1996) 'Two Meanings of Art', *Thesis Eleven*, 44.

Smith, B. (1998) *Modernism's History: A Study in Twentieth-Century Art and Ideas*, New Haven, CT: Yale University Press.

Smith, T. (1993) *Making the Modern*, Chicago: University of Chicago Press.

Spengler, O. (1918, 1922) *The Decline of the West*, London: Allen and Unwin 1926, 1928.

Theory, Culture and Society (1998) 15, 1.

Touraine, A. (1987) *The Workers' Movement*, Cambridge: Cambridge University Press.

Touraine, A. (1992) 'Is Sociology Still the Study of Society?' in P. Beilharz, G. Robinson and J. Rundell (eds) *Between Totalitarianism and Postmodernity*. Cambridge, MA: MIT Press.

Triado, J. (1984) 'Corporation, Democracy and Modernity', *Thesis Eleven*, 9.

Index